From Affluence to Praxis

FROM AFFLUENCE TO PRAXIS

Philosophy and Social Criticism

Mihailo Marković

Ann Arbor Paperbacks
THE UNIVERSITY OF MICHIGAN PRESS

First edition as an Ann Arbor Paperback 1974

ISBN 0-472-64000-3 (clothbound)
ISBN 0-472-06191-7 (paperbound)
Library of Congress Catalog Card No. 72-94763
Published in the United States of America by
The University of Michigan Press and simultaneously
in Rexdale, Canada, by John Wiley & Sons Canada, Limited
Manufactured in the United States of America

1983 1982 5 4 3

Acknowledgments are made to the following publishers for permission to quote from copyrighted materials:

To Doubleday & Company, Inc., for excerpts from *Writings of the Young Marx on Philosophy and Society*, translated and edited by Loyd D. Easton and Kurt H. Guddat. Copyright © 1967 by Loyd D. Easton and Kurt H. Guddat. Reprinted by permission of Doubleday & Company, Inc.

To International Publishers, for excerpts from Marx and Engels, *Selected Works*. Reprinted by permission of International Publishers Co., Inc. Copyright © 1968.

Foreword

Contemporary Yugoslavia, little known before 1940 except as part of the troublesome Balkans, has become one of the most interesting and admired countries in the world — at least to many of those who do not judge a country by the number of its automobiles and of the neon lights in its shopping streets.

The reasons for this admiration lie in three extraordinary achievements. The Yugoslavs have fought both Hitler and Stalin. They fought and defeated the Nazis, not as a regular, traditionally trained army, but as partisans. However, these partisans grew into an army which eventually was victorious over the German occupying troops. They were not 'liberated' by anyone and particularly not by the Russian armies as Stalin claimed when the war was over.

Their fight against Stalin was of a different nature. It was born out of a fierce sense of independence, courage and executed with a remarkable amount of political realism and skill. They did not have to fight militarily this time because their attitude thwarted Stalin's idea of an easy occupation. Freedom spoke to power — and won.

The second remarkable achievement is the construction of an entirely new and original type of socialist society.

Instead of the ownership of all means of production by a powerful centralized state, the Yugoslavs, after their break with Stalinist Russia and its ideology, conceived of an entirely new and original idea. Not the state but those who work in an enterprise own and manage it. This system culminated in the by now famous concept of self-management of the workers. Instead of state ownership there was social owership, instead of centralization, decentralization, instead of the worker being the object of an all-powerful bureaucracy, he was the active participant in his own enterprise. The perversion of Marx's concept of socialism, the control of the masses by a powerful bureaucracy, was challenged in practice, as Rosa Luxembourg and others, years before had challenged it in theory. The praxis was formulated in the laws of the land and its new social organization.

The return to the real Marx as against the Marx equally distorted by right wing social democrats and Stalinists, was the goal of the Yugoslav school of Marxist philosophy. This school is a third achievement of post-war Yugoslavia. There had, of course been, and are, humanist Marxists in Poland, Czechoslovakia and Hungary (the most outstanding of Marxists, the Hungarian George Lukács, who passed away recently) but what characterizes the Yugoslav development is the fact that there were not only individual philosophers concerned with the restoration and development of genuine Marxism, but that this was a concern and the life work of a relatively large group of people teaching in various universities in Yugoslavia.

The significance of this achievement may not mean much to those who naively assume that Soviet philosophy was the true guardian of the Marxist philosophical heritage; however, quite to the contrary, Stalinist Marxism had essentially only an apologetic function; it had to make Marx fit the practice of Soviet society and like all apologetic science it had to become dogmatic and dull. This vulgarized version of Marxism made it appear as if socialism for Marx was identical with socialization or nationalization of the means of production and did not include the vision of an entirely new form of society in its human and economic aspects. The Yugoslav school of Marxism restored Marx's ideas to their true meaning with the insight and knowledge of philosophers who were well aware of the philosophical movements in the last hundred years. But this awareness did not turn them into "existentialists" or "phenomenologists." They also did not speak of "socialism with a human face," since they knew that socialism has not only a human face but also a human body. They were concerned with a theory for which the root is man, and the goal is a socialist society as the basis for a harmoniously developed, independent, self-reliant individual.

The concentration on Marx's theory was part and parcel of the new Yugoslav social structure. The philosophers were greatly encouraged in their effort by the new and imaginative institutions which Yugoslavian law and social practice developed and these new institutions in turn were greatly supported by philosophical thought which could demonstrate that the theory of Marx was the soil in which they were rooted.

I do not mean to idealize the Yugoslav achievement. Due to many obvious factors, the new social economic system could not be as successful as many friends of Yugoslavia had hoped. A small and relatively poor country in the midst of highly developed industrial countries with whom it needs to have economic relations, is subject to many economic and ideological influences which affect its development. Difference in language, tradition, and especially in economic development make unification of the various parts of Yugoslavia difficult and feed dissent and nationalism. The Yugoslav philosophers have understood the reasons for these difficulties very well. They have faith in socialism and in the Yugoslav way of socialism. Because of this, they have not assumed the function of being apologists for errors and defects in the Yugoslav system but have retained the attitude which is basic for any Marxist philosopher — that of being critical. They have followed their own path of thinking with great courage, dignity, and wisdom and thereby not avoided being often criticized in their own country. But it speaks for the spirit of the Yugoslavian system that in spite of some frictions and conflicts, they function productively, not only in their writings, but also as university teachers and by continuing to organize the summer school in Korčula, which for years has attracted outstanding Yugoslav, European, and American Marxist philosophers for discussions of significant problems of Marxism and socialism. Furthermore, *Praxis,* an international journal which contains English, French, and German translations of papers published in the Yugoslav edition of *Praxis,* is well known in the world and gives a picture of the aliveness of the Yugoslav school of Marxist philosophy.

The author of this book is one of the leading members of this school. It is an expression of their own adherence to the connection between theory and practice that this school has no stars and that no member of it has tried to make himself the leader. It would be quite in contrast with this tradition if I were to try to single out the author and to emphasize his differences from others. That does not mean that there are no differences and that the various members of the school are not very marked individuals both personally and philosophically, but I am sure the author as well as the other members of the school prefer to be praised as members of a collective, rather than to get special credit.

Foreword

This work, like those of other Yugoslav philosophers, is not facile, and “food” for those who like simplified arguments. It is thorough and honest, and I hope it will interest many people who are fed up with “revolutionary” phrase-making presented as brilliant “reinterpretations” of Marx.

ERICH FROMM

Preface

This book is intended to contribute to building up a modern critical social philosophy, continuing the tradition of Marx, the early work of Lukács, the thought of Gramshi, and of the Frankfurt School. I have attempted to focus on crucial social issues, to show the profound crisis of existing forms of contemporary industrial society, and also to examine the philosophical foundations of critical social theory in order to explore the possible ways out of the present day impasse. The dialectic method applied orients one to seek the solutions of problems by discovering the basic limitations of existing social forms and by indicating alternative, more rational, and human historical possibilities of social organization.

My own background includes active participation in the struggle for national and social liberation of Yugoslavia during the Second World War, then a few years of hot debate against Stalinist dogmatism (1948–53). This was followed by ten years of study and writing in the field of philosophy of science and logic, including two years study in London under A. J. Ayer. At that time I felt scientific and logical objectivity to be the best weapon against any ideological mystification. That was partly true. By 1960, philosophical dogmatism was practically dead, at least in Yugoslavia. But in all those years of extensive traveling and upon closer scrutiny of our own society, it became increasingly clear to me that Stalinism could not be the only target, but that the sickness is much more general and widespread, and that the intellectual tools of analytical philosophy, no matter how sharp, do not suffice even to pinpoint the diagnosis, let alone the therapy.

In 1962, during the Cuban crisis, the world was on the brink of catastrophe. It is true that both leading countries of the two great political camps were undergoing changes, but there was scarcely any doubt that powerful social forces everywhere blocked any structural transformation, and that the enormous possibilities opened by modern technology were being wasted. Some of the hopes inspired by the successes of Yugoslav socialism began to evaporate. While the period 1952–61 was characterized by a spectacular process of economic and social democratization and one of the highest growth rates in the world, during 1962, several serious difficulties came to light.

By that time a whole generation of young philosophers and sociologists, ready to tackle the concrete theoretical issues of socialist society, appeared on the scene. The "Korčula Summer School," a free, unofficial institution organizing international philosophical conferences each August, and the journal *Praxis* emerged in 1963 and 1964. Erich Fromm, who attended a conference on "Man Today" and the first international session at Korčula in 1963, gave his full support to the group in this important first moment. He invited six Yugoslav authors to contribute essays to the collection *Socialist Humanism,* edited by him and published in 1965 by Doubleday. My essay "Humanism and Dialectic" became the focal point for a series of other texts of mine, written prior to 1967: these deal with methodological problems, various dimensions of contemporary humanism, and some crucial issues of socialist society, especially self-management and social planning. A collection of these essays is being published in book-form in English under the title *Marxist Humanism and Dialectic* by the University of Illinois Press.

This present book continues along the same line. It includes some papers written in 1968 and 1969, but most of it is based on my lectures given at the University of Michigan in Ann Arbor during the fall, 1969, and spring, 1970. The principle of composition is again the development from the abstract to the concrete, from the basic assumptions to the projection of a possible future, from the pure theory toward praxis.

If my point of view should be classified, it might fall under the category of "Marxism," provided that we accept any classification *cum grano sali.* It makes perfect sense to acknowledge our indebtedness to those great thinkers of the past who posed the questions which are still alive and unanswered at the present, who expressed the ideals which are still living and relevant to our lives, and who described spiritual horizons within which we are still moving. Marx is such a thinker. Sartre was right in saying in his *Critique of the Dialectical Reason,* that "far from being exhausted, Marxism is still very young, almost in its infancy; it has scarcely begun to develop." That is why I do not mind being called his follower. And that is why in this book I have so often commented on him and quoted so much material from his writings.

But Sartre was also more or less right in criticizing "lazy," superficial, reductive Marxism. I find myself in profound disagreement with most of the people who describe themselves as Marxists. The reason is that faced with Marx's complex, ambiguous work, which contains several levels of meaning, they invariably pick up the surface level, and, for pragmatic reasons, insist on the least significant or even obsolete elements of his doctrines. They completely overlook his profound philosophical insights which still retain their full validity. In addition, they betray an almost theological attitude toward the authority of Marx when the essential thing is not whether Marx, or any creator of a great tradition, was unconditionally right, but whether he can help us to solve our present problems.

Belgrade, Yugoslavia. MIHAILO MARKOVIĆ

Acknowledgments

I wish to express my gratitude to all those students in the University of Belgrade and the University of Michigan at Ann Arbor, who inspired me to think about the present society in terms of the world in which they will have to spend their lives. Without their questions this book would be short of many of its ideas.

I wish also to thank my colleagues and friends from the editorial boards of the Yugoslav journals *Praxis* and *Filosofija.* Without a continuing ferment, dialogue, and mutual support, a work of this type would hardly have been born.

I am grateful to: Abraham Edel, Kurt Wolff, Corliss Lamont and William McBride who read the manuscript and sent me valuable critical remarks.

I should also like to thank Helen Parsons for her numerous valuable editorial suggestions.

Contents

INTRODUCTION

Principles of a Critical Social Philosophy

What Is Philosophy?

Philosophy has always been much more than a simple clarification of concepts. Most great philosophers in the past have attempted to say something about the most general, fundamental structure of reality, the basic principles of cognition, the nature of man, and the kind of society we should seek to build. Even some of those philosophers who reduce philosophy to conceptual analysis admit that the importance of these problems entitles them to an exemption from their narrow criterion of philosophical meaningfulness.

It should be pointed out that the totality which characterizes philosophy is not the totality of the universe in itself. It has always been the ambition of most system builders to express truths about the essence of reality, or in the case of social philosophers, about the universal laws of nature, society, and the human mind. In all theories of this type: Plato's ideas, Aristotle's identification of categories with attributes of being, Hegel's absolute spirit, or Engels's dialectical laws of nature, one finds a typical fallacy of objectification, in which a temporally, linguistically, and conceptually limited view of the world is projected into the external world and declared eternally true. No doubt some of them contain components that are probably similar to certain properties and relations of objective reality.

On the other hand, in all our theories there are subjective human features, products of our imagination, of our needs for order, for security, for a certain ideal — it is we who select, interpret, clarify and build up systems. When we establish what is objective and what is subjective we attempt to eliminate subjective elements and supersede the old theory. However in the new theory we still do not know which of its elements are purely subjective and without any counterpart in reality. Therefore the totality which is the subject matter of philosophy should not be identified with the universe in itself. No matter how objective, philosophy is essentially human, it is a product of human practice and a phenomenon of human history.

In what sense is philosophy *rational?* In the sense of harmonizing human desires, visions, dreams, and aspirations with a global awareness of what is. It is a theoretical activity in which reason, both in the sense of *Verstand* ("understanding") and *Vernunft* ("reason, in the sense of synthetic critical activity"), plays a decisive role. The subject matter of philosophy can be also the irrational, the emotive, the instinctive. Nevertheless, philosophy deals with such subject matter in a rational, conceptual way. Philosophy can strongly involve emotions, and it can even contain an element of poetry. But even the most poetic philosophy will differ from the philosophical poetry insofar as it will not be primarily the *expression* of a personal, subjective vision which is valuable to the extent to which it moves us; on the contrary, it will be, in the first place, a statement about man and the world, a statement which is valuable to the extent to which it is true. This search for truth definitely characterizes philosophy as a kind of *knowledge.* In contrast to the partial knowledge provided by the various branches of science, philosophy tends to be a *synthesis* of knowledge. The time of individual encyclopedists — men like Aristotle, Descartes, Leibniz, and Hegel — is over. Philosophy today is a synthesis of knowledge only in the sense of being a collective product which embraces the generalization of special scientific inquiries.

There are philosophers (Dilthey and his philosophy of life, Bergson and his intuitionism, phenomenologists and existentialists) who reject any scientific element in the conception of philosophy and who consider knowledge as basically a conservative force. The only justification for such a negative attitude toward science and scientific knowledge is constituted by the fact that the achievements of scientific inquiry are being misused by the ruling elites of most advanced societies on a large scale and in a way which is threatening the very survival of mankind. In addition, the most scientific contemporary philosophy, positivism, makes this misuse and abuse more feasible by deliberately restraining from any criticism, by reducing philosophy to a neutral, value free, uncritical theoretical activity, which either avoids all vital human issues or, even worse, becomes a servant of an existing ideology.[1]

It should be remembered, however, that even pure, positive value-free knowledge can be used both for evil and for good. It does not simply provide a description and explanation of what is. It could also be, remaining strictly scientific, an extensive exploration of real possibilities. There need not be anything arbitrary or utopian about this. In contrast to an entirely free, intuitive projection of possibilities in which imagination and emotional needs play a dominant role, scientific prediction is constituted by certain operations of extrapolation and interpolation which are based on empirically established tendencies of behavior. It is crucial to understand that these tendencies need not necessarily support the existing structure. Some of them are tendencies which lead to radical change of the whole system. They open up new, revolutionary possibilities. Thus, knowledge may play both a conservative and a revolutionary role. Instead of confronting revolutionary utopian and conformist scientific thought, critical social philosophers might do well to support their radical projects with a reliable knowledge of social tendencies and thereby open up an entirely new space of historical possibilities.

Nevertheless, philosophy can by no means be reduced to a knowledge of what is and what might be. There are several or even many possibilities in a given situation, and to make a rational, enlightened choice, a criterion is needed. This criterion may vary from one special field to another; what gives a certain unity, coherence, and sense of direction is the general philosophical project to create what ought to be. Man differs from all other animals insofar as he not only acts in a universal way and profoundly changes his surroundings, but also insofar as he establishes certain goals and shapes his own decisions in such a way that he creates himself and his nature anew. Philosophy is a theoretical expression of a global human ideal of a whole historical epoch.[2] The awareness of an ideal gives the profound sense to each particular event and deed. Philosophy is, therefore, an effort to give meaning to human life as a whole.

The awareness of an ideal is in the same time awareness of the limitation of the present mode of existence. Man cannot indefinitely bear the relative limitation and narrowness of any given mode of his being. This is why he rebels against compulsion, against alien institutions, and even his own patterns of behavior in the past. This is also the reason why he tends to change and to improve his social and natural surroundings, and his own style of life, in order to overcome those features of his life condition which he evaluates as limited and negative. However, man cannot evaluate anything as a limitation, nor distinguish consistently between good and evil, between positive and negative, if he does not have any ideal, any consciousness of what ought to be in the future. In fact, a developed consciousness about the future directs man in his critique of the present. In this sense philosophy is always a *critical consciousness* with respect to any existing human situation.

Here, the question arises: What kind of critique can be provided by philosophy taken in traditional sense as pure abstract thought, as a particular, isolated, exclusively theoretical sphere of social consciousness which is the subject matter studied by a group of intellectuals who not only have no social power to change things, but in most cases do not take any part in social practice? Solutions of such a purely theoretical, abstract, isolated philosophy would be pseudosolutions because they would not be applicable anywhere; the criticism generated by such a philosophy would be pseudocriticism because it would lead to the resolution of existing conflicts and discrepancies only in the head of the philosopher — not in real life.

This approach to philosophy led Marx to state his well-known eleventh thesis on Feuerbach: "Philosophers have only *interpreted* the world in various ways, the point however is to *change* it."[3] Marx is not denying that in the past there have been some philosophers who have attempted to unite theory with praxis or that some have been successful in applying their philosophical ideas in science, arts or politics. It does not follow that a certain distance between abstract theoretical solution and concrete praxis can ever be fully overcome. What Marx meant is that a philosopher should always attempt to supersede the abstractness, isolation, passivity, and powerlessness of his thought. In science, arts, politics, and other particular spheres of social activity, philosophy might find not only a rich source of new experiences and new questions, but also a vast field for application of its solutions. This is obviously an indirect form of unification of theory and practice. In addition, a philosopher should live *his* philosophy, engage actively for the realization of his ideas. His task is not only to derive philosophical principles from human life, but also to try and raise human life to the level of philosophical principles. Only in that way can he overcome the alienation of pure theory and become a total theoretico-practical being.[4]

What Is the Specific Nature of Social *Philosophy?*

In a broader sense every philosophy is social: it is the product of a social being and it deals with problems in a more or less social perspective.

No matter how individualistic and how isolated he is from the social problems of his time, a philosopher can hardly escape acting as a social being: he starts with experiences acquired in a community, he inevitably inherits from the preceding generations certain general beliefs and continues a certain tradition, often without even being aware of all his assumptions. After all, he expresses his thoughts in a symbolic medium, language, which is the final product of a long social evolution and which already contains in itself a whole *Weltanschauung.*

On the other hand, all philosophical problems, no matter whether those of logic or of metaphysics or of philosophy of nature, bear directly or indirectly the mark of a definite social situation, of a cultural climate, of certain socially conditioned human needs and aspirations. That ancient logic is purely deductive, static, and not relational, can be explained by the fact that it was founded by people who were free from work and who were more interested in analyzing general notions than in discovering new empirical truths. The ancient Greeks did not and could not see any perspective of progressive change in their society, and their whole way of thinking remained essentially static and ahistorical. The history of metaphysics and natural philosophy also reveal the strong influence of social perspectives, as is obvious in the controversies associated with Copernicus, Galileo, and Darwin. Certain social issues were reflected even in such apparently remote fields of contemporary physical science as the theory of relativity and quantum mechanics.[5] Consequently, nature and society, natural and social science, cannot be construed as two sharply separated spheres of being, which need two essentially different methods of study: a method of scientific explanation (*Erklärung*) in the case of natural phenomena, a method of intuitive understanding (*Verstehen*) in case of social phenomena. The difference between natural and social sciences is by no means as sharp as it was assumed by the Baden school (Windelband and Rickert) which introduced a division of all sciences into *nomothetic* ones, those which establish laws of nature, and *ideographic* ones, those which describe cultural phenomena.

The main point of all those thinkers who insisted on a sharp distinction between the study of social and natural phenomena (and these thinkers also include some contemporary Marxists, such as Lukács in his early work *History and Class Consciousness,* the late Lucien Goldman in his *Humanist Sciences and Philosophy,* and some Yugoslav philosophers connected with the journal *Praxis*) is (*a*) that the agents in the former case are conscious, value-oriented beings, who tend to realize some goals and may change their behavior in the most unpredictable way; (*b*) that a complete objectivity in a process of study of a social phenomenon is hardly possible because this phenomenon is a part of our own history, and the values of its agents may be the same or incompatible with those which motivate our own behavior.

The consequence of (*a*) is that social events have a definite meaning for all those who participated in them, and it is their meaning rather than their structure which has to be investigated. Another consequence is that social processes are much more variable than the natural ones because conscious agents may freely decide to give up their habits or to change the accustomed patterns of behavior, which leads to certain difficulties in the application of the concept of scientific law to the field of human history.

The consequence of (*b*) is the recognition that our choice of problems to be studied, our selection and interpretation of data, our projection of meaning, is inevitably subjective and strongly influenced by our own scale of values. The main merit of this view is that it opens up certain methodological problems and draws attention to certain important distinctions which have been completely overlooked by the current positivist philosophy of science. Social facts are not things and cannot be examined as things (in the sense of Emile Durkheim).

But when this distinction is granted the question arises whether it is so simple and sharp as it has been construed by the Baden School and its followers. Human individuals do not often behave as free agents against the overwhelming pressure of natural or alienated social forces; too often they are manipulated and compelled to accept definite goals and value-orientations. Even when they act as autonomous individual beings the interaction of opposite free actions might result in entirely unexpected and subjectively undesired outcomes. Under these conditions human behavior assumes thinglike characteristics, it discloses certain regularities which may be interpreted as (economic, social, historical) laws, and thus allows the possibility of relatively fruitful application of the statistical method. Instead of simply declaring that social actions *are* free, the real problem is: *Under what conditions* are they free and creative? When these conditions are not fulfilled the differences between natural and social phenomena are methodologically irrelevant.

As to (*b*) although natural events do not have any intrinsic meaning "in themselves," they become more or less meaningful "for us," that is, with respect to our needs, projects, and *a priori* conceptions.

If all philosophy is social in a broader sense, what are the *specific features and tasks* of that branch of philosophy which deals with social processes as its subject matter?

Like philosophy in general, social philosophy has its ontological, epistemological, and axiological component. In other words, it attempts to answer three types of questions: (1) what *there is*; (2) how do we *know* what there is; and (3) what there *ought* to be.

Ontological Assumptions of a Critical Social Philosophy

The main ontological difference between natural and social processes consists in the fact that while social institutions and historical processes may be studied as objective entities which exhibit structural simplicity, immobility, and continuity, they are composed of and created by conscious agents, and are thus potentially free and not fully predictable historical subjects. Time and again social scientists tend to forget this simple truth. There has always been a tendency to regard social institutions as objects, comparable to those in nature, and to forget that behind them is the vast complex of human experience and human decisions. In the legitimate effort to establish certain social laws there has always been a tendency to reify these laws, to construe them as if they are independent from human action, and to forget that they are only the expression of certain regularities of human behavior.[6] Specific potential characteristics of that behavior are *freedom* and *universality*. Man can gradually remove various limitations imposed by nature and by his own past; he can change the conditions under which the laws operate and extend the framework of possibilities among which to choose. He is able to learn and to do whatever other beings can do, and whatever men of other nations and civilizations have accomplished. Social philosophy must never reduce man to his momentary, actual mode of existence. It follows that *time* in human history has quite a different meaning and different structure than it does in the history of nature. Natural events simply repeat over long periods of time. Even when there is motion and change, it takes place in fixed patterns. Lukács was right in adding a qualification to Heraclitus's principle of universal natural change: it is true that everything flows and that we cannot enter two times into the same river. But rivers always flow in the same direction. They cannot change that by themselves.[7]

In natural history the only criterion of the passage of time is the presence of certain irreversible processes such as the distintegration of certain stars and galaxies, the disappearance of temperature differences between parts of a system, radioactivity, and biological evolution. What really exists is only the present: the past has disappeared and the future has not yet come.

In social history it is a very different matter. Both past and future are *living in the present*. Whatever human beings do in the present is decisively influenced by the past and the future. The accumulated experience of preceding generations, transmitted to the individual in the course of education and learning, constitutes a very important part of the background against which everything that happens will be interpreted and evaluated. Only man is able to feel tired and bored by the repetition of the same occurrences, only man is able to rebel and consciously seek something new. On the other hand the future is not something which will come later, independently of our will. There are *several possible futures* and one of them *has to be made.* Thus a selected project of future is contained in the present, it strongly influences the whole perspective in which we see things, it influences our choices, preferences, and our decision-making.

In this sense the study of social, historical time is a very important objective of social philosophy. Historical time does not coincide with physical time. There are long periods of stagnation, for example, China in the middle ages and modern times until the creation of Sun Yat-Sen's "Kuomintang" and later the rise of Mao's revolutionary movement. On the other hand, there are periods in the history of some nations when time runs extremely fast and radical changes with far-reaching consequences follow one another. It was obviously bad and nationalistic terminology when Hegel, and later, Engels, distinguished between historical and antihistorical nations. They thought German nations were historical, whereas Slavic and especially Asiatic nations were not. However, there is a real distinction (to which social philosophy must pay close attention) between historical modes of behavior and antihistorical, reified, alienated modes of behavior of classes and nations which are below the level of historical possibilities of a given society at a given time.[8] Social laws are flexible and open because man is *able* to learn, to introduce novelty into his behavior, and change the very conditions under which certain laws hold. The activity of historical agents, men, unlike the behavior of things and nonhuman living organisms, *can,* under certain conditions be free and universal. Time in human history does not coincide with physical time because man has the unique *faculty* of transcending the past and projecting the future according to his needs, instead of letting it be.

It is of essential importance to make a distinction between what man *appears* to be and what he is *able* to be, between the *actuality* and *potentiality* of the human being.[9] A social philosophy which fails to make this distinction, which assumes that man *is what prevails in his actual existence* is condemned to end as an ultimate ideological justification of the existing social order.

For example, man appears to be acquisitive, possessive, greedy, egotistic, power-hungry under certain historical conditions characterized by private ownership of the means of production, commodity production, market competition and professional politics. For an uncritical, positivist, social philosophy this historically conditional picture of human actuality is the picture of human nature itself.

One gets an entirely different ontology of man and a different social philosophy by taking also into account a whole range of universal human capacities. These are in each normal human individual in the form of *latent predispositions.* Under certain unfavorable technological, economic, political, and cultural conditions they remain blocked, arrested, and thwarted. They reappear and are actualized at a mass scale as soon as conditions improve.[10] They flourish in the life of individuals under favorable conditions of relative abundance, security, freedom and social solidarity.

The following human capacities, among others, may be considered fundamental:

1. *Unlimited Development of the Senses.* Man can have an increasingly rich and manifold experience of the world. Our sensory powers may be magnified by the creation of suitable instruments. On the other hand, they can be refined by progressive cultivation and they can be liberated to the extent to which our surroundings become dereified.[11] There is hardly any limit to the increase of our ability to see, to select, to interpret, to concentrate on one interesting dimension of our perceptive field, and to associate what we immediately perceive with a whole world of former experiences and thoughts.[12]

2. *Reason.* Descartes believed that there is nothing else in the world which is so well distributed among human individuals as reason. Even if it is granted that there are considerable differences in intellectual capacities of various persons, the fact remains that every sane human individual is able to analyze objects and situations, to grasp regularities, to discover order in constant change, to derive conclusions, and to solve problems. Unfortunately, in modern production, modern political life, and mass culture, man does not have sufficient motivation to develop this faculty.

3. *Imagination.* The given world is always a small, narrow world for man. In the most primitive communities, in the earliest phases of individual development, there is already manifest a capacity to transcend in thought the limits of the given, an ability to project idealized objects, human beings and situations.[13] In modern production and public life this capacity is redundant and is being wasted.

4. *A Capacity for Communication,* not only in the sense of learning a language, but also in the sense of an increasing ability to understand the thoughts, feelings, desires, and motives of other persons who belong to other nations, classes, races, and cultures.[14] Under favorable social conditions all forms of narrow-mindedness may be

transcended and the level of a universal social consciousness may be reached.

5. *A Capacity for Creative Activity,* one which does not invariably repeat the same form but introduces novelties.[15] Modern industrial society is inconceivable without this faculty; however, it favors its one-sided actualization toward increasing efficiency and success at the market. In modern industrial production of commodities, the producers are condemned to a complete uniformity and a renunciation of all creative impulses.

6. *The Ability to Harmonize Interests, Drives, and Aspirations* with those of other individuals. Without it men would not be able to live in a social community. Nevertheless, this faculty is very much blocked in social conditions favoring competition and struggle, and the survival of the fittest.

7. *Discrimination, Assessment, and Choice among Alternative Possibilities.* This faculty is the ground of human freedom. It can be actualized in a distorted way if an external authority (church, state, party) succeeds in imposing upon human individuals its own criteria of evaluation, its own conception of who they are and what they can be. That is why genuine human freedom coincides with the actualization of the capacity of *Self-Identification* and *Self-Consciousness.*

8. *Man's Ability to Develop a Clear Critical Consciousness about Himself.* This is the ability to distinguish between what he actually is and what he potentially could be. Owing to this capacity, man can decide to change his style, his social role, his relationship toward other human beings. This faculty accounts for sudden, discontinuous, consciously directed changes in human behavior which make human history so much more open and unpredictable a process than the history of physical nature.

Since the above qualities of man are the ultimate criteria of all critical evaluation, the question arises: Is there any way to support this list of fundamental human capacities? Is it not arbitrary, untestable, incomplete?

It is "arbitrary" to some extent if we take this term to embrace whatever is not demonstrated or even demonstrable. Principles in general, and ontological assumptions in particular, are postulates and cannot be derived from any higher-level statements. Nevertheless, the given list of assertions about basic human capacities is not fully arbitrary: human society as it has evolved in the past and as it is in the present, would not have been possible without such latent human dispositions.

This series is not testable in the sense in which special scientific hypotheses can be checked by well controlled observation and experiment. On the other hand, it is not without any empirical justification. All of the human capacities mentioned may be manifested and become observable if we create the necessary social conditions. This is precisely what happens at the mass scale during the periods of great revolutionary change. Study of the behavior of individuals and limited groups in changing social conditions provides quite relevant empirical evidence. It is true that the statements about basic potential human capacities are sweeping generalizations and, like any other philosophical statements, are inevitably vague. But they are less metaphysical than many other philosophical statements: it is possible to specify conditions under which some relevant experience may be acquired.

The most interesting way to challenge the given assumptions is to say that their listing is incomplete, that they do not include, for example, the human capacity to struggle for power and recognition, the capacity to inflict pain, to torture and kill, to find pleasure in suffering, and the capacity to accumulate goods even far beyond any observable utilitarian purpose. Even if we were to grant that these faculties are equally widespread, recurrent, and indeed universal, this is still no reason to take them as fundamental. What is fundamental depends on the nature of the problem. The main philosophical problem, which is at the root of all philosophy and which I intend to elaborate is: *How Can Man Realize Himself and Create Himself in a World Which He Accepts as His Own?*

Power can be the strength of a creative man who cultivates his senses, who fully uses his reason, imagination, and his talent for communication, who finds a way to harmonize his aspirations with those of other individuals, or it can be the sheer naked, external force which leads to loss of oneself and to alienation from the world. Recognition is either a byproduct of creativity and freedom, or is based on fear and hostility. In the same way, one wastes his chance of realizing himself and of remaining in harmony with other human beings and nature if he permanently engages in inflicting pain on others and himself, and in amassing useless objects amidst general shortage and deprivation. *The Standpoint of All Philosophical Criticism Is Man's Self-Realization in History and the Transformation of an Alien, Reified World into a Humane One.*

Epistemological Assumptions of a Critical Social Philosophy

The methods of inquiry employed in the natural sciences must be taken with necessary reservations when applied to social processes. They must be supplemented by some additional methods which allow us to grasp the dimension of human subjectivity in social processes. As I have already mentioned, this legitimate consideration sometimes takes the extreme form of a resolute rejection of all objective, behaviorist methods, and a very one-sided demand to give up the study of external, observable patterns of social behavior. According to some extreme representatives of the historical school, the quest for objectivity should be completely replaced by a study of the *meaning* of historical phenomena; the social theorist should try to penetrate into the minds and feelings of people, to describe and to try to *understand* their motives, their goals, their cultural assumptions and prejudices, their passions, the nature of the symbolic forms used in communication, in building up their myths, their religious, philosophical, and ideological creeds.

This approach is one-sided. In the first place, overt behavior is one of the most important clues for understanding human beliefs, drives, needs, and aspirations. Human subjective nature comes to expression in external, objective, material forms. What we really think can be established only by studying the sequences of visible or audible signs. We ourselves can be aware of our own process of thinking only insofar as we use the representations of signs. When we think that we think, but are unable to express our thought in any kind of signs, then we, in all probability deceive ourselves.

Furthermore, we unintentionally tend to deceive ourselves and others whenever we conceptualize about ourselves. Our self-consciousness under the pressure of previous experiences and accepted norms, tends to idealize or debase and underestimate ourselves. That is why there is considerable truth in the well-known phrase that man is not what he thinks he is, rather, he is what he does.[16]

The fact is that human beings often behave as things: immovable, conservative, afraid of any change, eager like children to listen time and again to the same stories or to take part in the same social plays. All too often human beings allow others to treat them as objects: as living tools and parts of the machinery in the process of production, as means to reach some private or public ends, as objects of pleasure. Because we have a body and this body can do various important things, we cannot help being objects, and being regarded by others as objects. What really degrades us is when we are treated solely as objects, when what we think, feel, suffer, or enjoy becomes entirely irrelevant.

There is another important mode of reification which can be used in support of a behaviorist approach to social processes. In the clash of various intentions and projects of isolated individuals, it usually happens that events occur which nobody wanted or planned, and that social processes take a form which deviates from all individual projections. Lack of coordination, unpredictable conflicts, and interactions tend to reduce people to things, no matter how conscious they are of their goals and how hard they try to realize them. Interactions here acquire the character of chance events and the apparently blind forces which prevail over individual human wills are nothing else but the central statistical tendencies of these large classes of chance events.

Even granting these justifications for the behavioral approach, the fact remains that human subjectivity cannot be *reduced* to the structures of overt behavior, social knowledge cannot be reduced to the description and explanation of these structures, nor can explanation be reduced to causal and functional explanation. Teleological explanation plays a very important role in history: the determining condition of many events is not simply an antecedent overt action but the awareness of a certain goal and an intention to realize that goal. However, explanation in the technical sense of that term is not the only way to answer the question *why* something happened. Explanation presupposes knowledge of at least one law which covers the case in question (which in this special case would have the following form, "Having the goal *G*, under the conditions *C* invariably leads to the effect *E*"). However, we sometimes do not have sufficient reason to believe that any association of a certain type of goals with a certain type of human actions holds invariably. Or we might have good reasons to think that in a given case existence of a certain goal in human minds gives rise to a quite unusual, exceptional kind of behavior and leads to rather specific results. After all, even if we reach an extraordinarily high level of concreteness in answering the question *why* something happened, it does not follow that we *understand the full meaning* of the phenomenon in question. To this purpose it does not suffice just to exterpate *one single relation* out of an extremely rich context and to embrace that complex whole by a simple abstract phrase: "under conditions *C*."

If we want to understand why ordinary Russians admired and many adored Stalin in spite of all his monstrous crimes, if we want to understand how it was possible that even persons who suffered unjustly in concentration camps for years were later again ready to die with Stalin's name on their lips, a behaviorist will not be able to help much. As has sometimes been said, "We must understand the Russian soul." The word "soul" here is essential. The Russians often complain that Western people do not understand their "soul." What this means is that Western people do not know their history, the great myths in their past (for instance, the tenth-century myth about Moscow as the third Rome), their inherited habits of political behavior under great tsars, or their lack of any democratic traditions. The Russian "soul" embraces a need for warm, personal, sentimental relationships; a very strong nationalist feeling;

a romantic attachment for a large glorious whole symbolized by the term "Mother Russia," therefore, an unusually strong inclination to idealize the leader.

Thus, critics of behaviorism have their point. One should live in a country, in a community, one should know its history and learn how people feel about their future, one should have direct, personal, intimate contacts with many individuals who live in that community, in order to grasp the *full meaning* of what is going on, and especially to feel the necessity of change, to forecast the direction which it will take. Behaviorism and positivism tend to assume the principle of uniformity, which is especially of great use in natural sciences. However, in social inquiry it is quite misleading without its counterpart — a principle of diversification. The principle of uniformity alone would not be able to predict or even account for social revolution. A revolution usually takes the form of a sudden eruption following overt events which were rather insignificant in themselves, such as strikes, demonstrations, and protest meetings. I do not underestimate the importance of these overt actions as clues of what is coming, but they may mislead us either to underestimate or to overestimate the strength of movement behind it. In the spring of 1967 I saw a huge demonstration for peace in New York and also, one year later, a small student demonstration in Paris. Several hundreds of thousands took part in the former, several hundred in the latter. Nothing spectacular happened after the former, whereas two weeks after the latter ten million French workers were on strike and the whole social system was on the verge of total collapse.

The conclusion should be that social philosophy must synthesize *erklären* and *verstehen* in its methodology instead of rejecting one in the name of the other. The former provides abstract analytical information about the facts and external, objective, structural characteristics of certain isolated social phenomena. The later supplements these informations by a concrete, qualitative, historical understanding of the subjective dimensions of a social whole.

There is no better name to designate such a complex method which synthesizes the essential features of behaviorism and phenomenology, of structuralism and historicism than "dialectic."

It is true that this term has been heavily compromised. Dogmatically minded followers of Marx have interpreted dialectic as primarily a universal ontological theory which expresses permanent patterns of change in the world, quite independently of man and human practice.

Two fundamental weaknesses of such a conception are:

1. The statements which tend to express the dialectical "laws" have been considered demonstrated by scientific facts, and absolutely true. The number of laws has been fixed. This position has led to paradoxical consequences: the theory of universal change becomes unchangeable, the method of approaching the whole world as a complex of processes becomes a steady thing. The only tolerable line of innovation is the introduction of new examples and illustrations from the history of science or the history of the labor movement. A double dogmatism is inherent in such an approach to dialectic: on the one hand, to legislate the totality of being "in itself," to forget that whatever we know and say about the world has been mediated by our experience and contains an element of subjectivity — amounts to ignoring the whole evolution of philosophy after Kant and returning to prekantian metaphysics. On the other hand, the treatment of dialectical laws as a closed system of *a priori*, given, sacrosanct schemes discloses a clearly antiscientific, theological attitude.

2. If dialectic is reduced to the general structure of the existing world and the method of knowing what already is, all activism of Marx's philosophical thought is ignored. A philosopher who intends to change the world, not merely to interpret it, does not stop at reaching reliable knowledge of what is. He also examines the realistic possibilities of what might be and engages in the practical realization of those possibilities which best correspond to certain objective human needs. A revolutionary social philosophy is, therefore, both knowledge and evaluation, discovery of general truths, and a radical social criticism. Dialectic is, then, not only a general theory and method of acquiring positive knowledge, but also a theory and method of revolutionary negation and supersession of the existing reality. When the latter is forgotten, dialectic is in danger of becoming a tool of rational justification of the given historical form of human existence, that is, an instrument of ideology.

Opposition to the dogmatism and conformism of simplified Marxist dialectic has resulted in a strong mistrust toward dialectic in general and, sometimes, toward any kind of general methodology in the social sciences. This attitude is especially widespread among empirical scientists. When they protest against the use of unclear and ambiguous concepts, carelessness in analysis and argumentation, simplification and ignorance in the presentation of scientific results which are intended to "prove" dialectical laws, when they refuse to be bound by philosophical considerations which are inadequate, imprecise, or outdated — one cannot but be in sympathy with them. But it is impossible to follow them when they declare that no social scientist has ever profited from dialectic, that no discovery has ever been made by the help of any general methodology and that therefore, there is no need for such a thing. This is very much like arguing that no people have ever created their language with the help of linguistics, no writer has written his novels thanks to the theory of literature, and no child has ever been born owing to sexology. These statements may be true, but they are irrelevant when the merits of these theories are considered.

For every practical activity a theory can be formulated which lays down general structural features of this activity and invariant standards of its evolution. The theory helps to bring to consciousness what one is in the habit of doing unconsciously. If the theory is valid it increases our knowledge about ourselves and our doing, it enables us to control our own powers, to reflect about them critically and rationally, and to improve our future ways of acting. If it is true that we follow certain rules whenever our activity is well organized and directed toward some goal, then ignorance of these rules is a specific form of *alienation.*

Scepticism toward general methodology is rooted in the prejudice that what matters in human activity is only that things are being done well, not that we know how to have them done well. This is an apology for blindness and irrationality. An increase of human self-consciousness in any field of thinking and practice has always been followed by considerable progress in that field, for example, psychology and psychotherapy after Freud, sociology and social welfare after Marx, economy after Keynes.

Dialectic is a general philosophical method and, while its application cannot be limited to social theory, the consequences of neglecting it in social theory are serious. Social phenomena are not simply given, they are produced by men as a result of conscious choice from among various possibilities. Perception is not simply contemplation and passive reflection of phenomena, but their selection and interpretation from one or another practical point of view. The question is always present as to whether social phenomena should be allowed to continue in the same line of development or whether they should be radically changed by the abolition of some essential components of their structure. Furthermore, social phenomena are so intimately connected with each other and so mutually dependent that any change which we introduce might have unforeseeable consequences; therefore we must regard them only as parts or moments of complex totalities, never as isolated items.

The unique feature of dialectic as a method of social philosophy is a tendency (*a*) to discover in each system its essential *limit*, that is, those structural features which prevent the evolution of the system toward a more valuable state and (*b*) to show the concrete possibilities and ways of *superseding such a limit.* This is the so-called principle of the *negation of negation,* the principle which Stalin completely excluded from his presentation of dialectic.

In Marx, and in a sense already in Hegel, dialectic is essentially a method of critical thought. In his *Economic and Philosophical Manuscripts* Marx noted that Hegel's dialectic, as expounded in *Phenomenology of Mind* is essentially a criticism of society, albeit "concealed, unclear and mystifying criticism."[17] The mystification lies in the very concept of human alienation. All its various forms: religion, wealth, state power, politics, law, and civil life are taken as forms of alienation from pure abstract thought, which implies that the supersession of alienation is only a supersession in thought. This is the negative moment of Hegel's dialectic. The positive moment is "the insight expressed within alienation, into the *appropriation* of the objective being through the supersession of its alienation." And Marx adds: "It is the alienated insight into the *real objectification* of man, into the real appropriation of his objective being by the destruction of the *alienated* character of the objective world, by the annulment of its alienated mode of existence. In the same way atheism as the annulment of God is the emergence of *theoretical* humanism, and communism as the annulment of private property is the vindication of real human life as man's property — the emergence of *practical* humanism."

However both are still mediated: theism by religion, communism by private property. "Only by the supersession of mediation (which however is a necessary assumption), a *positive* humanism arises."[18] What Marx discovered in Hegel's *Phenomenology of Mind* remained the essential feature of his method. Dialectic is primarily a method of criticism; not a criticism of concepts, but a criticism of real social relationships, "not a fictitious and mystifying but a real and truly revolutionary criticism."

Marx's main critique of previous forms of materialism was their lack of dialectic and of an initial humanist position. According to Marx's "Theses on Feuerbach," materialism has considered reality an object of contemplation and has thus neglected the importance of "revolutionary practical and critical activity" (First Thesis). By such activity man proves the truth of the results of his thinking (Second Thesis) and changes the circumstances whose product he is (Third Thesis). The essence of this change is that man is able to grasp the world in all its contradictions, to criticize it theoretically, and to supersede it practically by removing its essential contradictions (Fourth Thesis). Philosophical criticism should not take as its object the human essence conceived as an abstract property of each individual. In order to be concrete, it must aim at the real human essence — which is the totality of social relationships (Sixth Thesis).

This is a pregnant sketch of both a method and a humanist program. *Das Kapital* is the realization of both. In the well-known postscript to the second edition of that work Marx stated explicitly what he considered dialectic to be:

> In its mystifying form dialectic has become German fashion because it appears to be able to glorify reality. In its rational form it provokes the anger and horror of the bourgeoisie and its doctrinaire representatives because it is not satisfied with the positive understanding of the existing state of affairs; it also introduces an understanding of its negation, its necessary destruction, because it conceives every form in its movement and therefore in its transition, because it cannot bear to have anybody as a tutor, and because it is essentially critical and revolutionary.[19]

After Marx, dialectic was interpreted mainly as an abstract formulation of a method, a set of ready-made formulae, which could be illustrated by an ever-increasing number of scientific results and which were a sacrosanct and invariable part of ideology. Thus, Marxist dialectic started its alienated, ideological life. This was inevitable. Once the labor movement became a vast organization, it had to secure a certain minimum of ideological unity; it had to fix a Weltanschauung (which, under given conditions, might have been solely that of Marx); it had to give to Marx's theoretical and methodological principles a complete and rigid form to which Marx himself would certainly not have subscribed.

Besides the transformation of dialectic into mere methodology, which was conditioned both politically and scientifically, it was reasonable to expect the further development of dialectic as a concrete, vital method of looking critically at human reality. Such an expectation would have been in accordance with Marx's original conception; on the other hand, both reality and our knowledge of it have changed during the century since Marx's main work appeared. Marx knew well that a method and a theory of a subject to which it is applicable are mutually dependent; therefore, the application of a method is its self-development.

This further development of dialectic has not been realized for several reasons:

1. Dialectic has always been a favorite target for the attacks of defenders of bourgeois ideologies who have called it unscientific, speculative, or mystifying. In *Anti-Dühring* Engels addressed the central problem of whether scientific facts verify or falsify the laws of the universal dialectical process which were discovered by Hegel and "interpreted by Marx in a materialistic way." Thus, the question of the character of dialectic was posed one-sidedly, from the point of view of its defense and not of its self-development.

2. Right-wing social democrats headed by Bernstein rejected "the dialectical scaffolding" of Marx's theory for the same reasons that they dismissed his theory of revolution and the ultimate goals of socialism: they regarded it as a "residue of utopianism." An opportunistic attitude toward capitalist reality was irreconcilable with a method directed toward a radical transformation of that reality. The opportunists also found a way to make use of science — not, however, in order to defend dialectic, but to refute it. The theory of evolution was used to prove that there are no jumps in history, that the concept of revolution is unscientific, and that progress in society comes only from small modifications and legislative reform. How did the orthodox Marxists react to this? Instead of developing Marxist theory and method in new specific conditions, they called for loyalty to Marx.

3. The first successful socialist revolutions were ac-

complished in relatively backward countries. Instead of bringing the question of human relationships into focus, these revolutions had to emphasize technology and rapid industrialization. Problems of coal and steel pushed back problems of man. Communism was conceived of more as a wealthy, affluent society, and less as a humane and democratic one in which "free development of each is the condition for the free development of all." *(Manifesto of the Communist Party.)*

4. For Marx and Engels, capturing political power was only "the first step in the worker's revolution," leading to democracy, to the disappearance of class distinctions and of political power. Stalinism reduced the concept of revolution to the overthrow of the bourgeoisie and the creation of a socialist state. What should follow is the *building* of a new society. What role would a method "which introduces into the understanding of the existing state of affairs an understanding of its negation, of its necessary destruction" play in a purely positive, constructive building-up process?

If revolution is the whole social epoch in which not only the institutions of the old society, but also the provisional forms of the newborn social order (for example, the class rule of the proletariat, the state, the party) would be successively superseded, then such a concrete and critical method is indispensable for constantly directing revolutionary thought toward identification of the essential shortcomings of a given society. But in a society in which public criticism was not tolerated, a philosophical method implying such criticism could not have been tolerated either. In a society in which there are sacrosanct authorities, a method "which does not bear anybody's tutorship" could not possibly survive. Bureaucracy needs apology, not criticism. It requires its philosophers to direct all their critical and revolutionary zeal toward the external, capitalist enemy.

In socialism it was desirable to see growth in all its aspects: growth of material goods, of culture, of education, growth of the unity of all social strata. But when everything negative is construed as only "a remnant of bourgeois and petty-bourgeois consciousness" in the heads of people, it was impossible for any *new* contradictions to arise in the process of socialist development. To be sure, it has been customary to talk of dialectic as a guide to action. But this has meant little more than a *subsequent rationalization* of various *past* political conceptions and decisions. This is why Stalinism did not reject dialectic as a whole in the way it rejected its key principle — the negation of negation. The use of dialectical phraseology created an illusion of continuity in method. Furthermore, such a formalized and degenerate dialectic was needed to prove that whatever existed in socialism was necessarily such as it was — that it was rational.

The revolt against Stalinism in present-day social philosophy often takes the form of a simple, one-sided denial. Thus, a rejection of that vulgar, dogmatic, formalized version of dialectic which was used by Stalin and Stalinists often leads to the complete lack of interest in dialectical method in general and to a reluctance to use any dialectical forms of thought. Contrary to those East European philosophers who tried to replace formal logic with "dialectical logic" and to substitute the dialectical principle of contradiction for the classical principles of identity and noncontradiction, some Marxists go to the other extreme and too lightly concede that dialectic has nothing to do with logic. But surely, if dialectic has nothing to do with logic, and dialectic is taken as a general philosophical method, then there must be something wrong either with the one or with the other. And if logic is taken as it is, as a science which examines the patterns of noncontradictory thought then dialectic, with its emphasis on discovery of contradiction as an essential means to reach the truth, would have to be rejected as a general philosophical method. The difficulty here consists in mixing up contexts. Formal logic examines pure abstract forms of thought. It, therefore, studies either *possible* symbolic forms or forms of already given theories, of already existing habits of thinking. In both cases thought is taken in its fixed, given, frozen, synchronic mode of being. The result of this study is the establishment of the conditions of consistency, of formal correctness of thought, which is by all means an essential condition of truth.

What Hegel and Marx had in mind when they spoke of dialectical method were forms (regulative principles) of a concrete, living, evolving thought, taken not only in its synchronic but also its diachronic dimension. This distinction can be expressed by saying that the formal logical principle of noncontradiction is a *demonstrative* principle which regulates our thought when we ask such questions as what is being implied by a set of statements, or how to prove a statement or a theory; whereas the principle of contradiction is a *heuristic* principle which regulates our thought when we ask how to develop new knowledge, new not only in a quantitative sense of a growth of empirical data, but also new in a qualitative sense of transcending the present state of our knowledge and building up new theories, new systems, new general frameworks for our perceptions.

With this critical approach, with this concern for novelty, for development, the essential problem arises: What semantically and syntactically are the basic contradictions in our present knowledge? Do our theories fit new empirical data? Are they fully coherent, do we accept all the consequences of our assumptions? Do the expectations based on our theories correspond to the results of their practical application? Thus, a formal logical contradiction is only a special case of a contradiction in a much more general sense — taking into account not only the formal structure of a system, but also its empirical interpretation and practical application on the one hand, and its philosophical assumptions on the other. From this point of view, to discover a contradiction (of the form "*A* is both *B* and non-*B*") does not necessarily involve a mistake (because allegedly either *B* or non-*B* must definitely be wrong: *tertium non-datur).* The contradictions are important for the further development of our knowledge precisely because we might have good reasons to hold that both *B* and non-*B* are true.

B might be analytically true on the basis of some given definitions of its key terms ("Socialism is a higher level society in relation to capitalism"). Non-*B* might be synthetically true on the basis of actual usage of its key terms. A society called socialist (Albania) need not be a higher level society in almost any important respect in relation to another society called capitalist (Sweden).

B might be an inferred consequence of a theory or of a law of nature (expected result of Michelson's experiment). Non-*B* might be an observation statement.

B might be an accepted philosophical principle (responsibility of human beings for their actions). Non-*B* might be an empirical generalization. (Human beings are biologically and socially conditioned. According to genetics, five million genes determine our character. According to dynamic psychology, experiences in the first seven years of our life strongly condition our subsequent behavior.)

To construe the principle of dialectical contradiction as a principle simply favoring the assertion of mutually compatible statements is utterly misleading for at least two reasons:

1. Far from inducing us to assert contradictions, and to consider each contradictory statement as true *ipso facto,* the dialectical principle of contradiction directs us to discover hidden, concealed contradictions which exist in the totality of our theoretical and empirical knowledge. Especially important are those contradictions where both sides of the contradiction look true, are accepted as true for different reasons; they usually constitute the essential internal limit of the theory.

For both Hegel and Marx, consistency of thought was extremely important. But because they were interested in developing thought, in overcoming a present state of theory, they tended to take any given state as imperfect (as "incomplete truth" in Hegel's words) and to discover implicit contradictions in that state.

This is a much more general approach than the one customary in formal logic and the methodology of demonstration. The essential characteristic of this approach is the tendency to open up *new problems.* Any discovery of an important hidden contradiction is the opening of a problem and the starting point of further inquiry.

2. To think that the main idea of dialectic is to assert contradictions and to stop there, to take perhaps the presence of contradiction as a criterion of truth, amounts to missing the point entirely. The main idea of dialectic is to discover hidden contradictions *in order to resolve them,* in order to *supersede critically the present state of the theory* (and of the given social reality). Precisely in this sense the principle of contradiction is a dynamic principle of thinking. To supersede a given state of a theory by dissolving a contradiction means (*a*) to reject fully one side of the contradiction reaffirming the other side or (*b*) to modify both sides in such a way that the former incompatibility disappears.

In this way, by carefully qualifying the dialectical principle of contradiction and by establishing the conditions under which the formal principle of noncontradiction is to be applied, we come to the conclusion that these are not at all incompatible, that the former treats the problem of discovery and elimination of contradictions in the most general way, whereas the latter is its special case with respect to closed, static formal systems.

Axiological Assumptions of Critical Social Philosophy

It is obvious that dialectic, and indeed any conceivable method of a critical social philosophy, presupposes some value considerations. Also, the epistemology of such a philosophy necessarily involves certain axiological assumptions. In our case:

1. According to dialectic, studying isolated phenomena allows us to obtain only incomplete, abstract, and partial knowledge. Phenomena must be considered in their structural and historical contexts; we should study concrete, meaningful wholes. A concrete meaningful whole is not any arbitrary collection of objects, it is a historically conceived totality which is practically relevant to some of our goals and which meets some of our important needs. Thus, there are three important elements in the notion of a meaningful whole: (*a*) a structure of the set of some known phenomena, (*b*) the history of the set, and (*c*) our values (needs, aspirations, goals) which constitute the criterion of evaluation of the whole set and its component parts.

2. According to the dialectical point of view, we approach all objects as processes, as something which undergoes change. The problem arises whether this change has a fixed pattern within a closed system with eternal repetition or whether it is an open process of progressive or regressive character. In this latter case it is obvious that a process can

have a definite direction only if a certain ideal limit is assumed. And such an ideal limit presupposes a system of values.

3. According to dialectic, as a result of the accumulation of hardly perceptible, qualitative changes (which seem to constitute a continuum) discontinuous disruptions occur occasionally and new qualities emerge. In that sense, study of the conditions, possibilities, and ways of a *radical* change is characteristic of a dialectical approach to social processes.

4. The dynamic character of each system is primarily the result of the internal conflict of opposite forces. This does not mean that external influences, pressures, tensions, and conflicts should or could be overlooked. The idea is that these constitute an external framework within which the most important events take place, and that there is a transfer of external into internal forces so that it is these latter which really count.

Up to this point, critical analysis has a purely descriptive character. Now insofar as dialectic orients one who wants to apply it, not only to study change as such, but also the possibilities of progressive change, he has to evaluate the character of the forces in conflict and to establish which ones are positive, progressive, and which are negative, conservative, and regressive.

5. From the dialectical point of view neither rigid classical determinism nor indeterminism is acceptable. The former completely reduces human beings to things and overlooks sudden eruptive, qualitative changes of human habits, aspirations, patterns of behavior, which come about as a consequence of certain states of consciousness, such as satiety, boredom, frustration, revolt, and despair. The latter, indeterminism, assumes that all possibilities are open and that we are absolutely free to choose among them. All pos-

sibilities are certainly open in logic and mathematics, but not in history. The past lives in the present and sets the limits for the future. Past human praxis has been objectified in vast transformations of our natural surroundings, in technology, in existing social institutions, and in patterns of collective human behavior. Our contemporary habits, needs, potential powers, and aspirations are historical products. Human nature is not an abstract fixed, trancendental entity, nor is it something which can be created *anew* by an arbitrary decision of a free individual. In each historical epoch there is a general structure which is a crystalization of the whole past history of human praxis. This structure is a concrete dynamic totality which underlies all more specific determinants — those of class, race, nation, religion, profession, and individual character. It is constituted by the opposite general features and tendencies of human behavior and therefore is dynamic and open for further change. We have to move within these natural, social and cultural limits. But within these limits a process of *self-determination* takes place. We choose among possibilities, we create new possibilities. As there is more than one possibility, self-determination could obviously take place in various directions. The problem, therefore, arises: Which is the *optimal* historical possibility in the given historical conditions? Obviously the term *"optimal"* involves value concepts.

6. Value concepts are also inherent in the *principle of the negation of negation.* The first negation is an internal limit, an essential negative component of a system in the sense that it constitutes the main impediment to the realization of the optimal possibility of the system. This involves an act of critical evaluation. The second negation is the act of overcoming the internal limit. But this is by no means a simple act of destruction. It is transcendence in the sense

of the German notion of *aufheben.* To deny *dialectically* means (a) to abolish those elements of a system (those institutions of a society) which constitute a real obstacle to progressive, radical change and (b) to preserve and further develop all these dialectic elements of the system which are positive, that is, functionally compatible with the new form of the system. Thus, this second dialectical negation again involves an act of evaluation.

Values are always present in all our inquiry. This is one of the distinguishing characteristics of human inquiry. In contrast to "thinking machines," man is an emotive being. He has all kinds of interests and objectives — individual goals, the goals of various particular groups to which he belongs (family, nation, class, etc.), and those of mankind as a whole. In this context, tendency toward maximum objectivity means:

a) We do not want to mix up various interests: the more an interest is selfish and of particular importance only to certain individuals and groups, the more we wish to neglect and eliminate it in a theoretical inquiry. Thus, a tendency toward objectivity from this point of view is a tendency toward universality.

b) We do.not want to confuse factual and value statements. Before we wish to take a critical standpoint we want to know what the situation is. This is, however, a very difficult thing to do. We evaluate phenomena in the very process of perception by selecting some of their features and overlooking others, by interpreting them, by giving them names, and by classifying them under certain general conceptual schemes. Still a good part of our inquiry is constituted by an effort to establish an objective state of affairs.

Values are present in social theory in two different senses:

1. As goals in those particular forms of human behavior which are the subject matter of our inquiry
2. As our own assumptions

In both uses there is a clear difference between social philosophy and the philosophy of nature.

As to (1): Natural objects, including living organisms other than men, do not ever have goals, purposes, or motives. Causal analysis here usually takes the form of an examination of those antecedent *material* phenomena which are necessary and sufficient for the occurrence of the given natural event. Causes and effects are *mediated* solely by certain objective regularities — laws, which under certain conditions hold for a given segment of reality. With respect to living organisms the cause-effect relation acquires a specific form of means-end relation. However, except in very specific cases of most developed animals and most "intelligent" individuals among them, there is no antecedent *awareness* that a certain kind of behavior is instrumental to a certain favorable state of affairs. Means-end relation is here only a reflex, more or less conditioned or unconditioned. In society a cause can be the *awareness* of a certain objective; an action may be *consciously* undertaken in order to reach an end, no matter how distant.

As to (2): In regard to the values manifested in a process of inquiry, implicitly given in our assumptions, there are two specific features which characterize social philosophy as distinguished from natural sciences and the philosophy of nature:

a) Values in the latter are in most cases epistemological values: truth, and all those requirements which are instrumental to truth, such as precision, clarity, exactness, fertility, applicability, objectivity, and simplicity. They all express the conditions under which our theories might be accepted as corresponding to reality and might be used for the control of reality. In addition to these, in social philosophy there are also non-epistemological values which express various desirable features of men and human relationships in society such as freedom, independence, equality, solidarity, peace, creativity, rationality, participation, and development.

b) In some turning points of the history of natural sciences there were disputes in which opponents differed not so much with respect to empirical data, methods of reasoning and epistemological values but precisely with respect to noncognitive values. Thus the crucial issue in all famous debates about biological evolution was whether self-development was possible in nature, that is, whether new kinds of plants and animals ever emerged without the action of some supernatural agency.

A specific feature of social philosophy is, however, that some of the values of this type which are assumed in our methodology, in our standards of criticism, are precisely the values of those past societies which we are supposed to study and evaluate in an objective way. It is very difficult to give an objective account of ancient Greek society for any West European whose whole culture rests on some fundamental values of ancient Greek culture. Also it is very difficult to say something very objective about the Chinese cultural revolution either for those who participated in it, or for those who are quite ignorant of its underlying traditional and present-day values.

Speaking about value-assumptions the following two questions should be clarified: What are values and what is their ontological status? And how do we distinguish value statements from factual statements?

As to the first question, in order to understand the notion of value one should analyze the tryadic structure *O-R-S* where *O* is an object, *R* a relation and S a human subject. A value is an object related to a given subject. If S in question is an individual, the value in question is *personal*, otherwise it could be a *class, national,* or *religious* value with respect to a corresponding particular group, or it could be a *universal* value — at least for one given historical period — with respect to mankind as a whole.

The object *O* (a material thing or a social event, institution, or human act) is a value with respect to some S if and only if it satisfies a need of S. *Moral* values are human actions which satisfy a need for social harmony, coordination, and social approval. *Aesthetic* values are those patterns of shapes, colors, sounds, or human movements which satisfy a human need to overcome natural limits, to beautify his surroundings, to create and experience imaginary worlds, situations, and human beings. *Political* values are such social institutions and forms of behavior which satisfy human need for security, organization, and participation in communal life.

There are two extreme views about the status of values which should be rejected. One is that values are something purely subjective and emotive and that value judgments are merely ejaculations of our emotive attitudes. Therefore, there is no way either to confirm or to disconfirm them, and there can be no real disputes about them.

The basic difficulty of this theory is a tacit dualistic belief that things and their shapes and colors are simply given and independent of us, whereas our attitudes towards them are quite subjective and arbitrary, varying from one person to the other and from one moment to the next. In fact, objects are not simply given, they are also being created by us: we perceive them in a space reference system selected by us: in shapes, colors, and perspectives which depend upon the nature of our senses, our previous experiences, conceptual categories, and linguistic habits.

On the other hand, values are hardly ever purely subjective: in our emotive reactions and attitudes there are common elements — that is why we are able to agree that some pieces of art have great or even permanent value, that certain modes of behavior (such as keeping promises, supporting the weak, ill, and helpless) are desirable in any society. In fact, some objective phenomena, taken in a predominantly intellectual relation of a subject toward them are being experienced as *things* and connections of things, whereas taken in a predominantly affective relation, they are being experienced as *values.* Any object of human action can be *described* as a fact or *assessed* as a value. The status of value differs from the status of things and facts only insofar as affective experiences of various people in the same situation are considerably more variable than their intellectual reactions. But the difference is one of degree: in spite of all variability there are generally accepted values (ancient Chinese, Indian, Greek architecture, Renaissance paintings and sculptures, Beethoven's music, for example). On the other hand, there are facts which only individuals, contrary to widespread common beliefs, have been able to establish (for example, the discoveries of Copernicus, Galileo, Einstein). While sceptics tend to construe values as purely subjective and relationistic phenomena, dogmatists of various kinds tend to objectify and absolutize them. For example, the German axiological school considers that values *are in themselves,* that they hold in a transcendental way for normal human consciousness in general (Windelband) or that they hold ideally in a sphere of being which is quite outside of and independent from both the material world and the human mind (Scheller). These values are allegedly exemplified in human life, but any such exemplification or total lack of exemplification does not affect them in any way — they are superhuman, absolute, and eternal. Values in this sense are obviously fictions. Real values are historical products, they are relative to historical subjects who spontaneously created them and accepted them, and they change when historical conditions of human life change substantially. Many philosophers reject axiology as a philosophical discipline precisely because it was first developed in such an absolute idealistic way. Nevertheless, one can reject such a mystified approach without overlooking the importance of value considerations.

Now we can address the second question raised above: How to distinguish value statements from factual statements?

One is tempted to say that the distinction between factual and value statements is quite sharp: the former express the results of purely intellectual cognitive operations such as perception, classification, definition, analysis, and inductive inference, they inform us about certain qualitative or structural states of affairs. The latter express needs, the affective attitudes of a subject toward certain objects; they contain an element of choice, of preference; they do not play an informative, descriptive role but are used to express our approval or disapproval, to evoke similar feelings and attitudes in others, to prescribe certain types of behavior, or to encourage others to take an attitude similar to ours.

Although this distinction is rather clear, it is not so sharp as to exclude the possibility of certain cases being ambiguous. Some statements, according to their linguistic form, are indicative sentences which apparently only describe a certain object or assert a state of affairs. Nevertheless, they might be emotionally loaded to such an extent that they perform the function of value judgments. Such are, for example, the following statements, "At the entrance to the gas chamber in Dachau it is written on the door: 'The bathroom' "; "Technological progress in the fifties has been so fast that it has made collective suicide of mankind possible"; and "Armies of great powers invade some countries in order to save them from invasion of foreign powers."

On the other hand, a statement which contains value categories and which, according to its linguistic form would have to be classified as a value judgment, might in fact play the role of a factual statement when its function is primarily to let us know about the norms and values which are actually accepted in a social community and not to express the affective attitude of the speaker. Such are, for example, the statements, "It is good for a philosopher in England not to publish too much" and "Slavery is immoral in Western civilization in the twentieth century."

Such statements are sometimes so ambiguous that only after a careful analysis of the context, of the whole situation, of intonation and other expressive means could one establish whether the intention of the speaker (or writer) has been to evaluate or to make a factual statement.

There is another argument for the view that the distinction between these two kinds of statements is not very sharp. In almost every value statement there is a descriptive element. On the other hand, many factual statements are not free from the elements of emotion, desire, volition. That is only too natural — we are neither purely intellectual nor purely affective beings. Even in the process of the most objective descriptions of facts — in scientific research — our feelings, interests, prejudices, ideological assumptions influence the selection and interpretation of what there is in our perceptive field, and introduce into our formulations an element of emotive color and hardly concealed interest. Objectivity, in the sense of a demand to eliminate all such irrational factors remains only an ideal limit. On the other hand, value statements also contain a descriptive element. People who live in a social community and whose judgments are based on a certain system of norms would consider something a value only if it has certain real features. For example, many people in the West hold that a political system is good only if there are at least two competing political parties. On the other hand, an increasing number of radicals hold that all parties should be abolished in order to have a really good system, participatory democracy. Another example is that there is a prevailing view among Soviet people that a painting could be considered a real piece of art only if it represents real objects. Thus, we see that value statements entail some information. If we know accepted norms in a community, then from the acceptance of some value statements we can conclude something about the properties of objects to which the value judgments refer. Or, if we already know the properties of the evaluated objects we can infer from that knowledge and the given value judgments what the prevailing norms and value-principles are in the given society.

The ontological, epistemological, and axiological principles of a critical social philosophy constitute a coherent unity. A conception about man that distinguishes between his limited actual existence and a totality of man's potential capacities and true needs, a method of inquiry that is radically critical, aiming at the trancendence of given limitations both in theory and in reality, and a theory of value that has human self-realization as its ultimate criterion — obviously support and complement each other. A dialectical humanism is the philosophical foundation of any present-day social philosophy that continues Marxist tradition.

1

Critical Social Theory in Marx

Any theory as a linguistic objectification of human thoughts, experiences, and feelings can become subject to a process of interpretation and practical application which is entirely independent from the intentions of the author, from the historical situation and the cultural climate in which it was born. Karl Marx, while he did not consider this possibility explicitly, did find it necessary in 1882, to exclaim that he was not a Marxist. In the decades which followed, his theory was increasingly misinterpreted and misused.

Marx's theory became the ideology of a whole powerful international movement and, in order to perform that function successfully, it had to be reified and given sacrosanct mythological qualities. As his theory became an important part of contemporary social science, it was very often interpreted and evaluated in the light of the most influential philosophy of positive science, empiricism. On the other hand, whatever empirical philosophers found to be obscure, utopian and metaphysical in Marx, especially his anthropological considerations, became a source of inspiration for modern speculative and humanist philosophers.

Each of these particular groups had their own criterion of relevance in Marx, each made their own selection and projected their own needs and preoccupations into Marx's texts. They all failed to realize the basic novelty of his theory, which is the fact that it is both objective and critical. In most interpretations and further developments of his thought one of these two essential characteristics has been systematically overlooked. Among those who speak in the name of Marx or consider themselves his intellectual followers, some accept only his radical criticism of the society of his time, and others lay emphasis only on his contribution to positive scientific knowledge about contemporary social structures and processes.

To the former group belong, on the one hand, various apologists of postcapitalist society who develop Marxism as an ideology; and, on the other hand, those romantically minded humanists who consider positive knowledge a form of intellectual subordination to the given social framework and who are ready to accept only the anthropological ideas of the young Marx.

To the latter group belong all those scientists who appreciate Marx's enormous contribution to modern social science, but who fail to realize that what fundamentally distinguishes Marx's views from Comte, Mill, Ricardo, and other classical social scientists, as well as from modern positivism, is his ever-present radical criticism both of existing theory and of existing forms of social reality.

The failure of most contemporary interpreters of Marx to grasp one of the basic novelties of his doctrine has very deep roots in the intellectual climate of our time and can be explained only by taking into account some of the fundamental divisions and polarizations in contemporary theoretical thinking.

Basic Modern Theoretical Orientations

The development of science and philosophy in the twentieth century has been decisively influenced by the following three factors: First, the accelerated growth of scientific knowledge which gave rise to a new technological revolution characterized by automation, the use of huge new sources of energy, and new exact methods of management; Second, the discovery of the dark irrational side of human nature through psychoanalysis, anthropological investigations of primitive cultures, surrealism and other trends of modern arts, and above all, through horrible mass eruptions of brutality from the beginning of World War I until the present day; Third, the beginning of the process of destructuralization of the existing forms of class society and the rapidly increasing role of ideology and politics. We must now examine each of these factors in more detail.

As the result of rapid technological development and an increasing division of work in modern industrial society the rationality of science has gradually been reduced to a narrow technological rationality of experts interested only in promoting and conveying positive knowledge in a very special field. In an effort to free itself from the domination of theology and mythology, modern science from its beginnings tended to dismiss unverifiable theoretical generalizations and value judgments. As a consequence, a spiritual vacuum was created which, under the given historical conditions seemed able to be filled by faith in power, faith in success in all its various forms. Philosophy of success, obsession with the efficiency of means, and an almost total lack of interest in the problem of rationality and humanity of goals have become essential characteristics of the spiritual climate of contemporary industrial society.

Increasing our power over nature has created new

historical opportunities for human emancipation, but it has also allowed us to neglect many essential human needs and to extend the possibilities of manipulation of human beings. The universal penetration of technology into all forms of social life has been followed by the proliferation of routine, uniformity, and inauthenticity. The growth of material wealth has not made men happier; data on suicide, alcoholism, mental illness, juvenile delinquency, for example, indicate a positive correlation between the degree of technological development and social pathological phenomena.

Obviously, positive science and technology set off unpredicted and uncontrollable social processes. The scientist who does not care about the broader social context of his inquiry loses control over the product of his work. The history of the creation and use of nuclear weapons is a drastic example of this, as is the abuse of science for ideological purposes. The most effective and, therefore, most dangerous propaganda is not one which is based on obvious untruths, but one which, for the rationalization of the interests of privileged social groups, uses partial truths established by science.

Science cannot protect itself against such abuses if it is atomized, disintegrated, and disinterested in the problems of society as a whole, or neutral with regard to such general human values as emancipation, human solidarity, and development.

The most influential philosophy in contemporary science is positivism, according to which the sole function of science is to describe and explain what *there is,* and, if at least some laws are known, to extrapolate what *might probably* be. All evaluation in terms of needs, feelings, ideals, ethical, aesthetic, and other standards — are considered basically irrational and, from the scientific point of view, pointless. The only function of science, then, is the investigation of the most adequate means for the ends which have been laid down by others. In such a way science loses the power to supersede the existing forms of historical reality and to project new, essentially different, more humane historical possibilities. Its indifference towards goals leads to the growth of naked power, and to adjustment within a given framework of social life, which framework itself remains unchallenged. Behind this apparent neutrality and apparent absence of any value orientation one discovers an implicit conservative orientation. Even a passive resistance to the reduction of science to a mere servant of ideology and politics is acceptable to the ruling elites because pure, positive, disintegrated knowledge can always be interpreted and used in any profitable way: ultimately society can be led to lose its critical self-consciousness.

As to the second factor mentioned above, the discovery of the darker side of man, positivism and other variants of philosophical intellectualism, conformism, and utilitarianism are facing strong opposition among those philosophers, writers, and artists who prefer "the logic of heart" to "the logic of reason," and who rebel against the prospect of an impersonal, inauthentic life in an affluent mass society of the future.

As a reaction to the spirit of the Enlightenment (which has to some extent survived in the form of positivism) a powerful anti-Enlightenment attitude is gaining ground among intellectuals. The world does not make sense; there is no rational pattern by which the individual can hope to master it; no causal explanation which would allow him to predict the future. There is no determination and progress in history; all history of civilization is only the history of growing human estrangement and self-deception. Human existence is absurd and utterly fragile. Confronted with a universe in which there is pure contingency, lacking any stable structure of his being, man lives a meaningless life full of dread, guilt, and despair. There are no reasons to believe that man is basically good; evil is a permanent possibility of his existence.

Such an antipositivist and anti-Enlightenment philosophy (which has been most consistently expressed in *Lebensphilosophie* and various forms of existentialism) is clearly a critical philosophy concerned with the problems of human individual existence. However, this kind of rebellion against the "given" and "existing" reality tends to be as *immediate* as possible and to avoid any mediation by positive knowledge and logic. The basic idea of this obviously antirationalist form of criticism is the following: to rely on empirical science means to be caught up within the framework of the given present reality. On the other hand, as neither historical process nor human existence has any definite structure preceding existence, all general knowledge is pointless. Nothing about the present can be inferred from the past, nor can the future be determined on the basis of the knowledge of the present. All possibilities are open. Freedom of projection is unlimited.

This kind of romantic rebellious criticism is entirely powerless. As Hegel pointed out in the *Phänomenologie des Geistes,* postulated absolute freedom is only freedom of thought; it is the imagined freedom of a slave. Real criticism must start with the discovery of concrete practical forms of slavery, with the examination of human bonds and real practical possibilities of liberation. Without such concrete practical examination, which requires the use of all relevant social knowledge and the application of scientific method, criticism itself is only an alienated form of disalienation.

With regard to the third factor, the beginning of

destructuralization of class society, theories which express the needs and acceptable programs of action of powerful social forces become one of the decisive historical determining factors.

The theory of Marx has played a revolutionary role for the whole historical epoch of human emancipation from alienated labor. It has been and still is the existing theoretical basis for every contemporary form of active and militant humanism.

The critical thought of Marx is the fullest and historically the most developed expression of human rationality. It contains, in a dialectically superseded form, all the essential characteristics of ancient Greek *theoria* — a rational knowledge about the structure of the world by which man can change the world and determine his own life. Hegel's dialectical reason is a really creative negation of the Greek notion of reason and theory: here the contradictions between static, rational thinking and irrational dynamics, between positive assertion and abstract negation have been superseded (*aufgehoben*). The theory and method of Marx is a decisive further step in the process of totalization and concretization of dialectical reason: it embraces not only change in general, but also the specific human historical form of change — *praxis.* The dialectic of Marx poses the question of rationality not only of an individual, but also of society as a whole; not only rationality within a given closed system, but also of the very limits of the system as a whole; not only rationality of praxis as thinking, but also of praxis as material activity, as a mode of real life in space and time.

This theoretico-practical conception of man and human history was not developed further by Marx's followers as a totality, but underwent a far-reaching disintegration into its component parts: various branches of social science, philosophical anthropology, dialectic, philosophy of history, conception of proletarian revolution, and socialism as a concrete program of practical action.

Science without dialectic and humanist philosophy incorporated in its *telos*, in all its assumptions, criteria and methods of inquiry, underwent in socialist society a process analogous to its development in capitalist society: it developed a partial, positive, expert knowledge without discovering its essential inner limitations. The connection of science with philosophy remained doubly external: first, because socialist philosophy had assimilated the principles of Marxism in a fixed, completed form as something given, obligatory, imposed by authority, abstract, torn out of context, and simplified; and second, because these principles, externally applied, do not live the life of science, are not subject to the process of normal critical testing, reexamining, revising, but become dogmas of a fixed doctrine.

That is why Marxist philosophy became increasingly more abstract, powerless, and conservative. That part of it which pretended to be a *Weltanschauung* looked more and more like a boring, old-fashioned, primitive *Naturphilosophie*. The other part, which was supposed to express the general principles for the interpretation of social phenomena and revolutionary action, increasingly assumed the character of a pragmatic apologetic which was expected to serve as a foundation of ideology and for the justification of past and present policies.

This temporary degeneration was the consequence of several important circumstances: such as the fact that the theory of Marx became official ideological doctrine of victorious labor movements; the unexpected success of revolutions in the underdeveloped countries of East Europe and Asia where, in addition to socialist objectives the tasks of a previous primitive accumulation, industrialization, urbanization had to be accomplished; and the necessity, in such conditions, to give priority to accelerated technological development, to establish a centralized system and to impose an authoritarian structure on all thinking and social behavior.

Thus a return to Marx and a reinterpretation of his thought is needed in order to restore and to further develop a critical method of theoretical thinking. Three basic questions should be asked: (1) Is Marx's theory an ideology? (2) Is it philosophy? (3) Is it a science in some sense of the term?

Marx's Theory and Ideology

If by "ideology" we mean any conceptualization of values, needs, and interests, any theory about an accepted ideal, any choice of a general value orientation, any projection of a future for which we are ready to engage, and consequently, a critical attitude toward existing social realities — then there is definitely ideology in Marx's theory. Many of his key concepts are value-laden. For example, the concept of man's *species-being* (*Gattungswesen*) is a normative, not a descriptive notion of man. The idea of *praxis* as a free human activity with definite esthetic qualities, in which man objectifies all his potential powers, affirms himself as a personality, and satisfies the needs of another person — is a key concept in all his criticism of alienated labor in the market economy, and is by all means a value concept. The concept of *exploitation* is both a description in concrete, empirical terms of wages and prices of produced commodities, and the expression of revolt against a certain structure of social relationships. Communism is the projection of an ideal future, not the simple scientific prediction of an inevitable outcome of the historical process. In fact, in Marx's *Economic and Philosophic Manuscripts* there are three different descriptions and evaluations of communism (1) "crude communism" in which "the domination of material property looms so large that it aims to destroy everything that is incapable of being possessed by everyone as common property"; (2) communism (*a*) still political in nature, democratic or despotic, (*b*) with the abolition of "the state, yet still incomplete and influenced by private property, that is, by alienation of men"; (3) communism "as positive abolition of private property, and the end of human self-alienation."

However, what sharply distinguishes Marx's theory from any existing ideology is the *universal* character of values assumed and smuggled into his "essences," and into apparently purely factual expressions. Marx always speaks as a member of the species *man* and even when he appears as the advocate of one particular social class — the proletariat, he means by "proletariat" an idealized social group which has no particular interests clashing with the interest of mankind as a totality.[1]

This contrasts with the usual meaning of the term "ideology," which includes the characteristic that *particular* group interests are expressed and disguised in the form of indicative statements, creating the impression that they refer to obvious facts, and thus demand acceptance as indubitable truths. All ideologies in this sense are dangerous because they create illusions and prejudices, and they are all conservative both because their function is to rationalize and preserve the particular interests of various social elites, and because they are too static and thus necessarily lag behind the facts. Based as they are on interests, emotions, and sometimes most irrational, blind, unconscious drives, rather than on objective observation and critical thinking, ideologies tend, time and again, to reproduce dualistic pictures of the society and the world, with extremely sharp distinctions between good and evil. Such an extremely simplified dualism is not only the result of an obvious bias and the lack of objectivity on the part of those whose interests and needs it promotes, but it is also the consequence of the simple psychological fact that very large groups of people can be moved to act solely by very simple, easily understandable, and emotionally loaded ideas.

Marx's theory is certainly not an ideology in this sense. It condemns capitalism from a universal humanist point of view; it explores the possibilities of building a classless society in which domination of any particular group would be impossible. It is very complex and articulate, requiring a very high level of education to be grasped. Furthermore, Marx explicitly condemns ideology. According to him ideology is false, perverted social consciousness.[2] All genuine theory is a critical self-consciousness and it must play an essential therapeutic role; it must break the mighty intellectual shackles of a reified world and demystify hidden social relationships.

Marx's Theory and Philosophy

Previous considerations have already indicated that Marx's theory both *is* and *is not* a philosophical theory in the classical sense. It is philosophical because it is universal. It is not purely philosophical because pure philosophy, being too general and abstract, can not do much to demystify social relationships or to offer practically relevant solutions to the concrete historical problems embraced by the broad idea of human alienation.[3]

There are two essentially new philosophical constituents in Marx's theory. One is philosophical anthropology, which is at the same time a philosophy of history. The other is a new method of thought-dialectic. The quasi-Marxist philosophy which passes under the name of "dialectical materialism" completely overlooks the former and thoroughly distorts the latter.

Apart from some very general phrases about the greatness of man, alienation in capitalism, freedom as knowledge of necessity, and practice as a "criterion" of truth, philosophers of dialectical materialism have not developed any conception of human nature based upon an in-depth understanding of praxis, involving true, human needs and basic capacities, positive freedom, alienation, and human emancipation. Yet all of these are major themes in Marx's philosophical works. "Dialectical materialism" became a rigid ideological system in a time when some of the most important Marxist philosophical works were not yet known. But there is also method in this neglect: it involves deliberate rejection of these problems for obvious ideological reasons. Only in the light of Marx's humanism can one have an overall critical view of the whole history of socialist society, and only comparing the present-day reality with Marx's humanist project can one fully grasp how much the former is still far from the latter and how little resemblance there is between present-day bureaucratism and Marx's idea of self-government. Knowing what *alienated labor* and *political alienation* are, it should not be difficult to find them in a society which claims to have built socialism a quarter of a century ago. That is why Marx's early philosophical writings had to be classified as Hegelian and not Marxist. However, Yugoslav philosophers and other contemporary Marxian humanists have conclusively shown that the philosophical ideas from Marx's earlier writings underlie all his mature works (such as *Grundrisse der Kritik der Politischen Oekonomie* and *Das Kapital* — although they have sometimes been expressed in a different, less speculative language).[4]

Within this humanist framework dialectic becomes a

philosophical method of a relentless criticism of all existing conditions.[5] To be "radical" in Marx's words means to take things from the root, and "the root for man is — man." The human situation had to be critically reexamined in its totality and human emancipation had to embrace all its particular dimensions: liberation from toil, political liberation, cultural self-actualization, and elimination of super-repression in the instinctual sphere of human life.

Paradoxically enough, Marx never developed either his anthropological theory or a dialectical methodology in a systematic theoretical form. The reason is not, I think, the lack of time, even less the lack of necessary intellectual power. The real reason seems to be Marx's conviction that pure philosophy is, at best, an alienated form of disalienation. He learned this lesson by studying Hegel, Feuerbach, and the young Hegelians, all of whom, in a more or less brilliant way, first reduced man to an abstract being (*Absolute Spirit, Generic Being* or *Self-consciousness*) and then showed how he can be emancipated, but only in the realm of abstract thought.[6]

Those who took some of Marx's statements at face value, who neglected the study of the philosophical background of Marx's theory and came to believe seriously that the genuine, mature Marx was only an economist and social scientist, did not have the slightest chance to understand even his seemingly pure economic works. As Lenin pointed out (in his *Philosophical Notebooks*) nobody can understand Marx's *Capital* who has not studied the whole *Logic* of Hegel.[7] This is even more true for those who are ignorant of Hegel's *Phenomenology of Mind.* These writings are the necessary background against which one can properly understand Marx's conception of man and history, and his dialectic. They are presupposed in virtually every text he ever wrote.

The fact that Marx was a Faustian type of thinker, a philosopher of revolution, precluded the possibility of his developing a purely philosophical or abstract anthropology. Man who is the creator of an open historical process can not himself remain an ahistorical, fixed entity, as in Feuerbach. And if, in every historical epoch, he sets for himself the task of discovering and superseding essential social limitations, he will ultimately find them in the alienated and reified forms of his own practical activity. Therefore, the creation of more rational and more humane surroundings is, at the same time the self-creation of man's own nature, the abolition of some inner tensions and conflicts, and the production of new senses, new powers, new needs, new relationships with other persons. Thus, theory becomes historical and practical. It can no longer remain purely philosophical, it must become concrete. That is why Marx had to make the step from *Economic and Philosophical Manuscripts* to *Grandrisse* and *Das Kapital.*

Marx's Theory and Social Science

In a sense Marx's theory is scientific. The fact that in his mature works, especially in *Capital,* Marx deliberately avoided the use of anthropological conceptual apparatus, developed in earlier works, that he sometimes belittled those writings or that he considered his conception of socialism "scientific," should not be of decisive importance. Marx himself believed that one is what he does, not what he thinks he is. When we analyze Marx's doings, there is no doubt that he devoted most of his life to work which had some definite features of scientific research, even in the strictest empiricist sense. There is ample evidence to support his general statements, his theoretical analysis is made concrete and historical through a most detailed description. Many of his concepts have been given an exact form and are operationalistic. And in the best scientific tradition of his time, he tends to establish laws which govern social processes.

And still Marx's theory is *not* scientific in the sense of empiricist philosophy of science (of, say, Russell, Carnap, Popper, or Hempel). In some important respects it is not scientific at all. Its specific features in contrast to empiricist notion of a theory are the following: First, it contains a highly articulated *a priori* element, and this *a priori* is not only logic, with its deductive and inductive postulates and rules, but a whole philosophical vision about man and his world, a vision in which what is cannot be considered apart from what ought to be. This *a priori* is not an absolute, it has a definite historical character and crystallizes previous experiences, feelings, and intellectual discoveries. But it precedes the collection of new empirical data, provides a criterion for their selection, and endows them with a complex meaning which is both intellectual and emotive. That is why Marx did not need explicit moralistic phrases: even the driest of his descriptions contain an implicit moral connotation.[8]

Second, empirical data cannot be the starting point of inquiry because they are scattered and refer to isolated phenomena. According to Marx, theory must be the study of *whole* structures, of historical situations taken in their *totality.*[9] Marx's critical social theory does not recognize any sharp boundaries among social disciplines, branches, and special sciences. *Das Kapital* belongs not only to economic science but also to sociology, law, political science, history, and philosophy. Nevertheless, although the category of totality plays such an overwhelming role in the methodology of Marx,[10] his approach cannot be properly described as a purely synthetic one. He knew that any attempt to directly grasp a totality without previous analytical mediation usually has a mythological character.[11] That is why analysis was a necessary phase in his inquiry. However, the results of analysis must be reintegrated and taken only as particular moments within the structure of a whole. By proceeding in the process of research from unanalyzed given concrete phenomena (such as population, and wealth) toward abstract universals (such as commodity, labor, money, capital, and surplus value) and then back towards (this time) analyzed empirico-theoretical concreteness,[12] Marx succeeds in overcoming the traditional dualism between the concrete and the abstract, between the empirical and rational (speculative, "metaphysical") approach.

Third, Marx created a conceptual apparatus of social critique which far transcends the limits of a concrete, empirical reality even if it is taken as a whole. The function of this apparatus was not reduced to analysis and explanation, although some of his notions are more or less value free and neutral. Marx's key concepts invariably refer either to structures which *are, but could be abolished,* or to those which *are not yet, but which could be created.* To the former belong such concepts as *commodity, abstract* or *alienated labor, value, surplus value, profit, capital, class, state, law, politics,* and *ideology.* To the latter belong the concepts of *species being* or *social man, praxis, human production, community, freedom, history, communism,* and so forth.

Thus, for Marx, *commodity* is a product alienated from man, an object which was not made by man in order to objectify one of his individual capacities, to satisfy his immediate needs or the needs of another concrete individual, but one which is lost for the producer the very moment it is produced.[13] *Capital* is not only objectified, stored-up labor in the form of money, buildings, machines, and raw materials. It is objectified labor which, at the sufficiently high level of technological progress, appropriates the surplus value (the difference between the prices obtained for produced goods and wages paid for labor which produced those goods). The objective, thing-like form of capital conceals and mystifies a structure of social relationships beyond it,[14] the object (invested money) mediates between those who own and rule and those who produce and who are completely devoid of any rights either to participate in decision-making about the process of production, or to share in produced property. Another example: *the state* is not *any* social organization which directs social processes and takes care of order and stability of the society. The typical feature of the state is its coercive character. The state is an instrument of the ruling class, therefore, it is institutionalized alienated power.[15] Marx believed that the labor movement must abolish the institution of the state very soon after victorious revolution and replace it with associations of workers. A network of workers' councils would no longer be a state because it would not need professional political rulers and a professional apparatus of coercion.

To the other group, those structures which are not yet, but which could be created, belongs the concept of *social man*. This concept does not refer to the individual who lives together with other individuals or who simply conforms to the given norms of a society. Such a person can be very far from reaching the level of a social being. On the other hand, a person may be compelled to live in relative isolation and still profoundly need other persons. He may carry in his language, thinking, and feeling all the essential characteristics of generic human being. In this sense Marx distinguishes between man who regards woman as "prey and the handmaid of communal lust," "who is infinitely degraded in such an existence for himself," and man whose "natural behavior towards woman has become human," and whose "needs have become human needs." This "most natural immediate and necessary relationship" shows to what extent man "is in his individual existence at the same time a social being."[16]

Freedom never meant for Marx only choice among several possibilities, or "the right to do and perform anything that does not harm others." Freedom in Marx's sense is ability of self-determination and of rational control over blind forces of nature and history. "All emancipation is restoration of the human world and the relationships of men among themselves."[17]

Consequently, *history* is not just a series of social events in time; it is a process of permanent overcoming certain limits in the given natural and social surroundings, a process of creating new situations which preserve most of the favorable features of the previous situation, but also contain new institutions, new social structures and patterns of behavior which offer better opportunities for human survival, development, and self-realization.[18]

Thus, all of Marx's important concepts refer to a possible radical change. Insofar as change presupposes something *given,* these concepts have an ordinary empirical component of their meaning; thus they presuppose some neutral, descriptive concepts. However, a change which is not only quantitative but qualitative involves *negation* of the given. On the other hand, it implies the projection of an *ideal* possible future.

In such a way, in contrast to an empiricist, value-free, social theory here we have three different types of concepts:

1. concepts — negations
2. descriptive, neutral concepts
3. concepts — projects

The easiest way to grasp this triplicity is to take concepts which belong to the same category. Thus within the category of *human activity* we should distinguish between (*a*) alienated labor, (*b*) work, and (*c*) praxis. Within the category of *human nature* we should distinguish (*a*) one-dimensional man (*homo faber, homo consumens, homo politicus,* and so forth), (*b*) man in the sense of the totality of social relationships, and (*c*) man in the sense of *species being* (*Gattungswesen*).

Alienated labor is the activity in the process of which man fails to be what he is, that is, fails to actualize his potential capacities and to satisfy his basic needs. Marx distinguished the following four dimensions of this type of alienation:[19] (*a*) One loses control over produced commodities. The blind forces of market enslave man instead of being ruled by him. (*b*) In his struggle for more property and power man becomes estranged from his fellow man. Exploitation, envy, mistrust, competition, and conflict dominate relationships among individuals. (*c*) Instead of employing his capacities in creative, stimulating work, man becomes an appendage of the machine, a living tool, a mere object. (*d*) As no opportunity has been offered to him to fulfill his potential abilities, to develop and satisfy various higher-level needs, his whole life remains poor, one-sided, animal-like, his existence remains far below the real possibilities of his being.[20]

Work is a neutral concept. It refers to an activity which is a necessary condition of human survival and development in any type of society. In *Capital* Marx defines work as a permanent "exchange of matter with nature."[21] Even at a much higher level of technological and social development, when all present-day forms of toil and drudgery would be replaced by the manipulation of machines, when the division into workers, managers, and owners of the means of production would disappear, when socially necessary labor would be reduced to a minimum and lose its compulsory character — man would still have to strive in order to produce indispensable goods and services. *Work* need not be a commodity, need not be meaningless and degrading from the point of view of the worker, but yet, it involves a considerable degree of organization, order, and discipline. Even when fully meaningful, work can only be a means to reach some other end which is entirely outside its sphere.

Praxis is *ideal* human activity, one in which man realizes the *optimal* potentialities of his being, and which is therefore an *end in itself*. Marx never gave an exhaustive definition of this notion, although it plays a key role in his anthropology and is the fundamental standard of his social criticism. Nevertheless, from various scattered fragments one might conclude that, in the opinion of Marx, *praxis* has the following characteristics.

It is the objectification of *specific potential* capacities and powers. In the process of *praxis* man affirms his personality[22] and experiences himself as a subject who can change those features of his surroundings which do not satisfy him. What is specific for *praxis* in contrast to *work* and *labor* is not objectification (or externalization) of human subjective powers in itself, but an entirely different nature of objectification. In *labor* the worker uses only those abilities and skills which he can sell, which are needed in the process of commodity production. Sometimes this is physical energy or the ability to perform continuously one single, simple, physical operation which does not require the use of thinking, imagination, communication, or any other of the worker's capacities. There are many kinds of *work* which need not cripple the worker that badly. And still from the very fact that *work* as such need not be the end but only a means to reach some other end, it follows that: (*a*) the worker might be compelled to employ only those capacities which are relevant to the achievement of the given end, possibly neglecting those in which he is especially gifted and which are potentially most creative; (*b*) as a consequence of a professional division of work, he might continue to employ his abilities quite one-sidedly for an indefinite period of time. In *praxis* self-realization is one of the essential moments: it is the activity in which one actualizes the full wealth of his best potential capacities, an activity profoundly pleasurable for its own sake, no matter how much effort and energy it might require, no matter how pleasant its secondary effects such as success or prestige might be. Another essential characteristic of *praxis* is that, while involving self-affirmation, it also satisfies a need of other human beings.[23] In the process of *praxis* man is immediately aware that, through his activity and/or its product he enriches the lives of others and indirectly becomes part of them. In *labor* and *work* this direct concern for another person's needs might be completely absent. The worker can be either completely self-oriented or concerned only about wages and success. *Praxis* involves a basic intuitive distinction between genuine and false needs. It also involves creativity, but in the broadest possible sense, which might include not only writing poetry, painting, dancing, projecting new architectural designs, composing music, or scientific research, but also teaching, playing, cooking, designing clothes, entertaining people, loving, raising children, and so forth.

Praxis, establishes valuable and warm links with other human beings: in such a way man becomes a *species being*,[24] an individual who is in the same time a social being.

Praxis is *universal* in the sense that man is able to incorporate in his activity the whole of nature and to reproduce the modes of action and production of all other living beings:[25] man has learned from the bird how to fly and from the fish how to swim and dive; a man who belongs to a particular nation, class, race, region, civilization is able to learn and assimilate in his activity the elements of activity of all other human beings, no matter to which social group, region, and historical period they belonged.

Praxis is rational: man does not only act by instinct and by the method of trial and error, but he is also able to discover the structure of natural and social processes in which he takes part, he can make extrapolations for the future, project goals, and look for the most adequate means to satisfy them.[26] *Work* and *labor* are also rational but there might be an essential difference in the purpose for which reason is being employed. (In Carnap's formulation, the *utility function,* which is a necessary component of the concept of rationality, might be different.) In one case the purpose is self-realization and satisfaction of human needs, in another case it might be maximization of income, or the increase of power.

Praxis is *free* in two senses. It is free *from* external coercion, from compulsion to do always the same kind of things, in the same way, under the pressure of some external physical force, or authority, or any kind of necessity. It is free *for* self-fulfillment.[27]

Praxis has definite *esthetic* qualities; it is an activity which, among other things, "obeys the laws of *beauty.*" There can hardly be any beauty in *labor* and there need not be any in *work.* With some element of beauty in their surroundings, workers might produce more, or hard work might be easier and more bearable with some beautiful music in the background. When beauty becomes an end in itself, activity approaches the level of *praxis.*

Such a concept of *praxis* is clearly an ideal limit, a possibility toward which man naturally strives. It is not the ideal in the sense of some pure *Sollen* (*ought*), which exists only in a Platonic sense. It is a real historical possibility in a double sense: (*a*) it has existed in history as a mode of behavior of the most developed individuals, (*b*) all people, at least in some better moments of their life act in that way. However, for the vast majority of mankind those better moments are relatively rare.

Marx did not think that man could be fully liberated from all routine work. The sphere of material production remains a sphere of necessity, of inevitable human metabolism. But he believed, and this belief becomes increasingly well supported by the advance of modern technology — that the working hours could be substantially reduced, and that leisure time would be a time for *praxis*.[28]

The Nature of Marx's Theory

Marx's theory is the result of a critical study of historical possibilities. It is a model, the symbolic expression of an idealized structure — not an empirical description. A theory of this type does not say anything immediate about a concrete segment of reality; however, it establishes tendencies which *under certain conditions* might be manifested *everywhere*. The theoretical structure expounded in Marx's *Capital* is a model in the sense that it does not describe what actually happens in a certain country at a certain moment; it establishes what might happen in all developed capitalist countries under following conditions (among others): (*a*) pure commodity production; (*b*) the existence of a class which, under conditions of commodity production *is* exploited and *an sich* is a potential revolutionary force, but which need not necessarily be aware of its social being and thus become a class *für sich*; (*c*) a perfect market with the balance of demand and supply and without such disturbing factors as monopolies and the intervention of the state; (*d*) a closed national economy, without developed international economic collaboration and influences of the international market; (*e*) investments for profit without taking into account huge nonprofit investments, such as investments into armaments, and space programs.

Marx's laws are, consequently, not expressions of empirically established statistical regularities. They are parts of the theoretical model and they express relations which are expected to hold universally *whenever* the conditions stated explicitly for the model are actually fulfilled. For example, Marx's law of decreasing average rate of profit states that (under conditions assumed in his model) increasing growth of productivity of work leads to the change of the organic composition of capital, a trend which is unfavorable to capitalists and which can be counteracted only by squeezing out of workers more unpaid labor. This leads to growing revolt, to open class conflicts, and eventually, to the collapse of the whole system.

The necessity of this process is relative to the assumed conditions; ultimately it is relative to certain assumed regularities in the behavior of workers and capitalists. Only in this relative sense can we speak about truth or falsity, about confirmation and refutations of this law, and, in general, of Marx's system. The theory of the necessary transformation of capitalism into communism is true if people behave in a certain way, and it assumes that they will behave in this way *if* they become conscious of certain possibilities.

This type of theory which speaks about possible trends and optimal possible outcomes of the historical process under certain conditions would clearly be metaphysical, devoid of any empirical information, if the conditions were not specified and operationalized. Further, if they are stated explicitly, but if there is no reason to believe that they can ever be met, the theory would be entirely uninteresting and practically irrelevant. On the other hand, if the conditions are specified and fulfilled, but the course of events is different than anticipated, the theory would be refuted. Neither of these has been the case with essential parts of Marx's theory.

There can hardly be any doubt that Marx's theory, taken as a whole, is extremely fertile and practically relevant — that is why it has been the subject of so much study and controversy during the entire century since its formulation. It is difficult to find any other of his contemporaries who is still being so widely read and discussed. The reason is, first, that the historical possibilities envisaged by his theory are still open, and second, that the humanist criteria of evaluation and practical choice among possibilities presupposed in his critical anthropology still correspond to contemporary human needs and best express a widespread revolt against the contemporary human condition.

2

Possibilities for Radical Humanization in Modern Industrial Civilization

Modern industrial civilization has increased man's possibilities for a richer, freer, more creative life. As the result of technological development enormous natural and social forces have been set in motion. Yet, the tragic fact remains that slavery and poverty, both material and spiritual, still predominate in our age. While an enormous number of people in backward countries still cannot satisfy their basic needs, artificial needs have been widely created everywhere, not the least of which is a need to possess useless things for the sake of possession, a need for *having* more on account of *being* more.

The old gap between intellectual and physical work is now being gradually replaced by a new one: with the creative work of a few on the one hand, and the utterly dull routine work of a vast majority on the other. In addition, although the standard of living has greatly improved with the help of technology, in most cases this has not made relationships between social groups more humane: while productivity quickly increases, higher wages are still tied to a higher degree of exploitation (defined as the usurpation of value produced by unpaid work). It does not make an essential difference to the worker whether the usurper is a capitalist or a bureaucrat.

Technical civilization has provided means to supersede distances between individuals both in space and time: big cities, fast transportation, highly efficient media of communication make people more accessible to each other. But, at the same time, this development tends to destroy, without providing substitutes, all the sentimental, emotionally laden links which connect an individual with his original natural *milieu.* Modern man feels uprooted and condemned to experience utter loneliness in the midst of a crowd. The more he belongs to a mass society the less he is a member of any genuine human community.

Ever since the Renaissance there has been a strong integrating trend in the civilized world: a spreading of the same technology, economic cooperation and exchange, a fusion of cultures, the creation of international political organization, reciprocal influences in the arts, and scientific collaboration. But simultaneously, very strong disintegrative factors have been at work such as nationalism, racialism, ideological wars, religious intolerance. Narrow specialization and excessive division of labor have helped to sustain sharp boundaries between various spheres of social activity such as politics, law, science, philosophy, morality, and the arts. Consequently, human consciousness is split, an atomistic approach to reality still prevails, direct and particular interests, rather than long-term, enlightened ones, govern human lives.

Due to modern technology and the development of democracy, human freedom has been greatly increased, at least insofar as freedom meaning the possibility of choice among alternatives. However, every choice depends on criteria for choosing, and in our time these criteria are pressed on individuals by highly elaborated and efficient propaganda and advertising techniques. It is tragic how often modern man is most enslaved when he has the illusion of being free.

This discrepancy between illusion and fact is especially evident in the international political arena. Most nations cherish the illusion that their governments are striving for peace. Nevertheless, we have been living on the brink of catastrophic war for more than two decades. Most statesmen cherish the illusion that their decision-making is rational and optimal under given circumstances. However, the result of so many "rational" decisions is a completely irrational situation: the collective suicide of mankind has become a real possibility and it can happen at any moment, whether by choice or by accident.

The Idea of Human Nature

The idea of making the world more humane presupposes a well developed idea of the nature of man, and what it means to exist in an authentic way as a true human person. Any analysis of human behavior in history would lead to the conclusion that, as a matter of fact, man has given evidence of very different and even *contradictory* features. Man has always tended to enlarge his *freedom,* to overcome all historically set technological, political, and social limits. However, slavery is the invention of man, and even a liberally minded person ultimately finds the idea of complete individual freedom unacceptable, both because of the fear of others' irresponsibility and his reluctance to accept responsibility himself. That is why he sets limits and establishes various kinds of *order* in all forms and at all levels of social life.

One of the most distinctive characteristics of man is his *creativity.* In contrast to all other living beings man constantly evolves his tools, his methods of work, his needs and objectives, his criteria of evaluation. Human history, in spite of all its plateaus and oscillations can, on the whole, be considered as a rather rapid progress. But at the same time there is also a tendency in man to resist work and to avoid the effort of creating new things and new forms. The majority of people have always seemed to regard happiness as a state of affairs without work and without change. In addition, man's creativity has always had the negative counterbalance of his destructiveness.

The contradictory features in man are also evident in his social relationships. Man is a *social being* not only in the sense that he prefers to live in a community, but also in a more profound sense: all the features by which he is constituted are social products: language, forms of thought, habits and tastes, education, values, and norms of behavior. Nevertheless, there is also a strong tendency in most individuals to behave occasionally in an antisocial way, to pursue selfish private ends, to isolate oneself from others, to break links with people for no discernible reason, to be possessive, power-hungry, or sociopathic.

The study of man assures us that he is a *rational* being. He is able to analyze things and situations, to weigh alternatives, to derive consequences. He can predict the outcome of a chosen course of action and adjust his behavior to the desired goals. But his goals are too often irrational — they correspond to his passions, urges, and drives. And even when his long-term goals are rather rational in the sense that they have been selected after careful deliberation about his genuine needs and the real possibilities of the given situation, his short-term goals and actual behavior may greatly deviate from them. As a matter of fact, man lives a good deal of his life in complete disregard of his knowledge, even knowing that his course of action is self-destructive. But it should be noted that this basic irrationality of human behavior is only partly the consequence of atavistic impulses, primitive passions, deeply rooted egotistic impulses, or even mental disorders. It is partly the effect of a fundamental human need for an immediate, spontaneous reaction, a need which is in obvious peril in an age of science, technology and overplanning, an age in which those who are not able to calculate and reason coldly seem unfit and unlikely to survive.

One could go on with expounding such antinomies. For example, man is both peace loving and belligerent; he tends to belong to a movement and to have a common cause, but also he often prefers to be left alone; he is very conservative and reluctant to modify traditional patterns of life, but on the other hand, no pattern of life satisfies him permanently. What seems to be essential is the fact that one or the other pole of each antimony may predominate as a result of given historical conditions. But historical conditions are not something simply given and predetermined — they are the result of human practical action taken in partly different previous conditions. The question, then, arises: *Which are the constitutive characteristics of human nature that we should prefer and whose predominance in the future we should secure by our practical action in the present?*

In attempting to arrive at a proper understanding of man, we must distinguish two different concepts of human nature. When we analyze history and establish certain general opposite tendencies of human behavior we arrive at a *descriptive* notion of man which can be expressed by a series of factual empirical statements. But when we prefer some human features over others — such as being social, productive, creative, rational, free, peaceful, and when we classify these characteristics as "truly human," "genuine," "authentic," "essential," "natural," and so on, we arrive at a *value* notion of man, indicating that man is essentially a being of praxis, and that his nature can be expressed by a set of value statements.

These two concepts of human nature have to be justified in different ways and are open to different types of criticism. The descriptive notion of man has to be supported by factual evidence. One who wants to challenge it may try to prove that there is not sufficient evidence to support it, or that evidence is too meager for such an inductive generalization, or that facts at our disposal lead to an entirely different inductive conclusion. Therefore, this is an issue which can be settled by applying the scientific method.

The value concept of man on the other hand, can at best be supported by factual information only insofar as there is evidence that the human traits involved correspond to at least *some* observed general tendencies in the past, and that their realization in the future is not incompatible with all the social forces acting in the present. However, these conditions can be met by several alternative value concepts: they can express the preference for *some other* tendencies in the past, and they can correspond to some other real possibilities in the present. The choice among such alternative value concepts can not be made in a purely theoretical or scientific way. We make decisions on the basis of our fundamental long-term practical orientation to life, which obviously depends not only on knowledge but also on interests and needs, and on a willingness to act in a certain direction. The crucial problem here is: Whose interests and needs are here in question — those of an individual, of a particular social group, or of mankind in general?

The non-scientific aspect of justifying a value concept consists in an effort to show that it not only expresses certain private and particular needs, but also general social needs and interests. This can be done, first, by showing that the vast majority of people really have preferences conveyed by the value concept in question, and secondly, by showing that this concept corresponds to a long historical humanist tradition, that is, to the preferences expressed by the best minds in the past. Of course this method does not lead to irrefutable conclusions. It is impossible to demonstrate to someone that he ought to accept a value only because it had been accepted by others. However, this could be a sufficient basis for *rational* discrimination among various proposed solutions.

Taking into account the great humanist tradition during the last twenty-five centuries as well as actual contemporary preferences which underlie all moral judgment, there can be little doubt that, *other conditions being equal,* and with all necessary qualifications and exceptions, there is a strong tendency to prefer freedom to slavery, creative action to destruction and passivity, consideration for general social needs to egoism, rationality to any behavior governed by blind emotional forces, and peacefulness to belligerency. It would be wrong and dogmatic to say that it is only these preferable qualities that constitute human *nature* or human *essence* or human *being,* as against another ontological level of human *appearance* to which all evil in man would be relegated. In order to establish a sense of direction and a general criterion of evaluation in a humanist philosophy and practice it is sufficient to claim that these qualities constitute what is most valuable in man and what can be considered the *optimal real potentiality* of human being. To fulfill these optimal potentialities is to live a "true," "genuine," "authentic," "humane" life. Failure to fulfill them is what is often called *alienation.*

Radical Humanization

The characterization of modern civilization given at the

outset of this chapter indicates that the vast majority of people, in spite of all achievements, still live a rather alienated and inhumane life.

The process of humanization is often construed in a very superficial way, as simply a greater consideration for the weak, the backward, and the helpless. Humanism is then reduced to a program of aid to overcome material misery, eliminate hunger and illiteracy, and bar brutal forces of political oppression. All this certainly constitutes a part of such a broad concept but a rather nonessential part. For this interpretation of "humanization" does not challenge the very roots of contemporary society; it is acceptable by all those who are interested in preserving the *status quo.* In this sense those who advocate humanitarian programs of aid, liberalization, schooling, and so forth, can be rational and efficient defenders of a basically inhuman system.

If we are dissatisfied with the human condition today as a whole and not just with some of its superficial aspects, if we are ready to search for the deepest roots of the existing forms of human degradation, if we are convinced that a much more fundamental change is needed than the growth of concern over the poor and underdeveloped, then we must further qualify the broad and rather vague concept of, humanization and we would do better to speak in terms of *radical humanization.*

Marx once said that, "To be radical is to grasp things by the root. But for man the root — is man himself."[1]

The last sentence is not tautology if we interpret the term "man" as a descriptive concept in the first case and as a value concept in the second.

To be radical means, then, in the first approximation: to take care of what is most valuable in man, to create conditions in which man would become increasingly a creative, social, free, rational being. However, the main problem is: What are those conditions, and what is their order of importance? If contemporary man is enslaved by alienated social forces, such as states, political organizations, armies, and churches, the question remains: What factors produced these forces and keep them so powerful?

If contemporary man leads a poor life even when he is materially rich, because his needs are poor and focused on an irrational urge for accumulating as many objects as possible, what is the social mechanism that creates such a poverty of needs? If it is true that modern man feels more isolated and lonely than ever, what is there in society which leads to the frustration of all his desires for friendship, love and belonging to a genuine human community? Also what are the objective social causes of all other disintegrative and regressive processes, such as the growth of nationalism and racialism, the atomization of society into professional groups, and the hegemony of politics.

Almost all contemporary forms of alienation are rooted in the existence of social groups which have a monopoly on economic and political power. This monopoly itself is based either on the private ownership of the means of production (in the case of the capitalist class) or on the privileged position in the political organization of the society (in the case of bureaucracy), or both. To be sure, monopoly implies various kinds of usurpation. The usurpation of the unpaid work of other people is usually called *exploitation.* The usurpation of other people's rights in the social decision-making is *political hegemony.*

Contrary to the commonsense ideas, according to which it does not make sense to speak about exploitation above certain level of workers' wages and the standard of living, exploitation is the function of two additional factors. One is the productivity of work: if productivity increases faster than wages, the degree of exploitation may also increase. The second is the social distribution of surplus value: if in society there are individuals and groups whose income exceeds the value of the products of their work, then there is a greater degree of exploitation. This means that one has the right to speak of more or less concealed forms of exploitation, not only in an advanced capitalist country, where the material misery has been greatly reduced, but also in the postcapitalist society where there are strong bureaucratic tendencies.

Contrary to the claims of professional politicians in both capitalist and socialist countries, there is very little democracy in the contemporary world. The fact is that almost nowhere do the vast majority of people really influence decision-making on essential matters. The representatives of people in higher-level social institutions are elected either because of very large financial investments and the support of mighty party machines, or the election itself is so formalized as to be simply a ritual. In both cases the situation is clearly one of the political hegemony of certain privileged groups over the rest of the people who feel powerless and sometimes directly oppressed. When any group usurps the political and economic power of a nation all other citizens and groups are reduced to the position of objects to be manipulated. This is the basis of all other contemporary forms of dehumanization. State, army, political organization, and security service are the instruments of such a manipulation. The function of most ideologies is both to conceal this process and justify it.

Since public opinion is the opinion of the ruling group and since power over people and things is the fundamental value of every exploiting and oppressive group, ordinary people tend to follow the wishes and tastes of the ruling group. Ideological and commercial propaganda play a great role in molding attitudes, tastes, preferences, and, at the same time in producing the illusion that one is free even when his criteria of choice are greatly determined by those who possess the mass media of communication. Monopoly of mass media is one of the essential means of preserving and perpetuating all other monopolies.

Once a *particular* group with a very definite particular interest in acquiring or conserving a monopoly of power starts speaking in the name of the whole society, (and that is what has always happened with ruling groups, including bureaucracy in the postcapitalist society), the very concepts of *general* social goals, values, and interests are undermined. The society loses integrity and a sense of totality. This trend together with the increased division of labor gives rise to innumerable sharp boundaries where links would be desirable: among nations, races, professions, and spheres of social consciousness.

Therefore, to *humanize radically* the contemporary world means to create conditions in which each individual can participate in the control of the enormous social and technical forces which man has at his disposal. An essential condition of such fundamental human liberation is the *abolition of any concentration of political and economic power in the hands of any particular social group.*

The abolition (*Aufhebung*) of private ownership of the means of production and the abolition of capitalists as a class is the first decisive step in this direction. The abolition of politics as a profession which enables a social group permanently to control social operations, and the abolition of bureaucracy as a privileged elite is the second decisive step. Each is a *necessary* condition of a radical humanization, but only both taken together constitute its *sufficient* condition.

Historical Possibilities of Humanization

What are the historical possibilities of such a radical humanization in our epoch? What does it mean that an event or trend is historically possible? We must here distinguish between *a priori* and *a posteriori* concepts of historical possibility. The former is our *hypothesis* about the future based on our theoretical analysis of observed general tendencies in the past. The latter is our *knowledge* about the present based on practical experience. In both cases, to say that a course of events is *historically possible* means that it is compatible with actually given features of a historical situation. There are three essential components of a given situation which are relevant for the concept of historical possibility.

The first is constituted by the objective social facts of the system under consideration in the given moment. Many future events one can think of are excluded by the very existence of certain events and states of affairs in the present, for example, by the level of technological and scientific development, the state of economy, the nature of existing political institutions, and the actual situation in education and culture. On the basis of these factors alone one can speak about the possibility of a peaceful socialist revolution in Italy, a violent one in South America, and the impossibility of revolution in the United States in the near future.

The second factor relevant for the concept of historical possibility is the observed regularity in the past. Since trends in history are not so simple and strict as laws in the comparatively simple systems of nature, exact prediction of future events is not possible. Nevertheless, there are good reasons to speak about *excluding certain alternatives and allowing certain others,* thus making them more or less probable. For example, taking into account the trend since 1937, one can say that no economic crises in the capitalist world comparable with those up to 1929, are possible. On the other hand, regular recessions are highly probable and even inevitable. Also, the trend in the socialist world since 1953, makes a return to extreme forms of Stalinism very improbable and even impossible.

To be sure, in all such estimates both previously mentioned moments must be taken into account. Only when one knows the initial conditions of the system in a certain moment and establishes tendencies of change which took place in the past, can he determine a set of future possible states of the system.

The third factor is unknown or only partly known and predictable, namely, human behavior. History is full of events which would have to be assessed as having very little probability from the point of view of objective conditions and past trends. However, unexpected outbursts of human energy, the unpredictable action of large groups of people, as well as unpredictable mass irrationality, fantastic blunders, or genial solutions of the most difficult problems have caused almost impossible things to happen.

In view of existing technological and economic conditions, social structure, and foreign intervention, both the Russian and Chinese revolutions had very little chance of success. Yet they succeeded. It would have been easy to prevent Hitler's coming to power. But Nazism was sadly underestimated and almost to the last moment of Hitler's final take-over, German social democrats and communists saw the enemy in each other. The Great Antifascist Coalition during the Second World War was a considerable deviation from the logic of international politics between the two world wars. This coalition was due, in the first place, to a substantial blunder in the Anglo-American estimate of Russian ability to resist German attack.

Recent Yugoslav history is full of events whose realization, from the point of view of objective conditions, was rather improbable. The overthrow on March 27, 1941, of Cvetković's government (which signed the pact with the Nazis) was clearly a choice of war against a formidable enemy without a glimmer of hope of survival as a state. The new government surprised many by acting in a completely confused and cowardly way and lost the war in a few days. Although such a collapse usually leads to a general demoralization, in this case it was followed instead by a mass uprising. Two things about this uprising should be noted from the point of view of our problem: first, it cannot be explained by objective conditions, which resembled those in other occupied European countries; second, a cold, scientific analysis of all the objective factors would have demonstrated that the uprising was doomed. Instead, due to the extraordinary behavior of the thousands of individuals who took part in it, it succeeded.

The unexpected role of the subjective factor is the main reason why we cannot draw a sharp boundary line between historical possibility and impossibility. Between those human projects which are clearly possible (although in individual cases they might fail) and those which are clearly impossible (being incompatible with existing natural and social laws in a historical moment) there is an area of vagueness that includes cases where we cannot know if a project is possible until we try to achieve it. From this it follows that the two extreme views about the ontological and epistemological status of possibilities should be rejected: (*a*) the positivist view that the possibilities are *given* and can be known *before* practical action and (*b*) the view characteristic of a number of existentialists — that man's future is quite open and independent of the past, that we are absolutely free to choose, and that only at the end do we come to know what really was or was not possible.

In every historical moment the objective features in a given system of social phenomena allow us to project a set of the possible state of the system in a later moment. The boundaries of this set are more or less vague. This is the *a priori* concept of historical possibility. The attempt to implement a desired possible social project provides practical experience which helps us make necessary revisions and to build up an *a posteriori* concept which is more precise and whose boundaries are sharper. Thus when we think about the historical possibilities of overcoming any existing concentration of economic and political power, we may take into account both general tendencies of the historical process and the practical experience of various social movements in the recent past.

A scientific analysis of the history of capitalist society in our century shows clearly that the role of the capitalist class in the organization and actual management of production, has been decreasing steadily. There can be little doubt that the very institution of private ownership of the means of production — which has played such a great role in the creation of modern industrial society — has now become redundant and that is can be successfully replaced, at least in highly developed countries, by various forms of collective property. The practical experience of successful socialist revolutions demonstrates that socialization of the means of production, in spite of all the difficulties present when social preconditions are not yet ripe, can give rise to a modern society with a comparatively higher rate of technological and economic development.

However, many forms of human alienation have survived in present-day postcapitalist society. This is particularly true when social power is concentrated in the hands of a bureaucracy. By "bureaucracy" is meant a coherent and closed social group of professional politicians which keeps all decision-making in its hands and enjoys considerable political and economic privileges. The growth of bureaucratic tendencies is correlative with a number of regressive processes such as the decrease of initiative at the micro-levels of economic life, the formalization of political activities in which the people grow progressively more passive, the subordination of all spheres of creative work to politics, and the growth of careerism.

There is a certain historical justification for the existence of a political elite in an underdeveloped country, especially in the initial period in which foundations for a new social order have to be established. When this has been done, however, there is no historical need for its survival as a particular social entity. This does not imply either a denial of any kind of elite nor a utopian belief that no rulers and no social organizations are needed to direct and coordinate social processes.

The existence of a moral and intellectual elite is *conditio sine qua non* of a really progressive and humanist social process. But it must not lead to the creation of a closed social group with special rights. There is a vast difference between a ruler who considers himself indispensable and uses force in order to make his subjects happier against their own will, and an ordinary competent man who, having temporarily left his profession to perform certain political functions, considers his office nothing more than an honor, and uses force only against those who break democratically established norms of social behavior. Likewise there is a fundamental distinction between the *state* which has always been the coercive instrument of a particular social group whose interests it protected and promoted by force, and a truly democratic, social organization which needs force only to secure the general interests of the community against antisocial behavior of sick individuals. This type of truly democratic social organization is called *self-management.*

Historically, there is no need for a special social group of professional politicians in a developed postcapitalist society which has attained a considerable level of technological development, productivity of work and mass culture. It would not be difficult to elect excellent deputies to hold office for a limited period of time from a large number of gifted people in various professions who have acquired a certain political experience and skill. Strict responsibility to their voters, observance of democratic procedures in all decision-making, obligatory rotation of duties, lack of any material privileges (salaries for political functions should not exceed the pay scale for any other creative work), and various other measures should discourage any excessive political ambitions and effectively prevent their realization.

Time is perhaps not yet ripe for a complete deprofessionalization of politics and for a rapid replacement of the organs of state by those of self-management both at *micro-* and *macro-*level (in enterprises and local communities as well as in the society as a whole). However, the first experiences clearly demonstrate that even in a semideveloped country such as Yugoslavia, it is really possible to move in this direction and that the result is a large scale liberation of initiative and creativity even among those people in the most degraded social layers who have traditionally been kept in utter ignorance and passivity.

3

Technostructure and Technological Innovation in Contemporary Society

It is often taken as axiomatic that technological innovation is automatically good and therefore desirable. This is a good example of how ideology operates within social theory. A statement about one model having a lower rate of innovation than the other appears as a purely descriptive, value-free statement. But implicitly it expresses and tends to evoke an attitude of condemnation and rejection. That is why critical social theory must start with the question: What is technological innovation and what is its status in the priority pattern of social values? This leads us to the next two questions: What are the basic values of technostructure and what are the social conditions and consequences of technological innovations in socialist countries?

The Social Importance of Technological Innovation

If we accept Joseph Berliner's definition of technological innovation as "the introduction into an enterprise's product line of a physically different product or the introduction of a different technological process for producing an established product,"[1] the concept "innovation" becomes quite descriptive and value free. To be "different" does not specify whether the product or process is better or worse. As a matter of fact, many technological innovations in modern industrial society are, in some respects at least, changes for the worse: cars are less durable, buildings and whole towns are less beautiful, food is less tasty and more poisonous, military arms are increasingly less usable and more dangerous.

Many innovations have been introduced because for some people at least they really are improvements: they bring more profit, more power to dominate and destroy. But for other people these same innovations can signify deterioration rather than improvement.

Therefore the social theorist has to choose from among the following three alternatives:

1. To accept the scale of values of the dominant social groups and, at least tacitly, to approve technological innovation precisely in the forms in which it takes place. This means becoming an apologist for the given social structure.

2. To assume a skeptical value-free attitude and to speak about innovation in a purely descriptive, detached way. This is the position of the isolated individual scientist who is alienated from all existing social forces and who tends to suppress all feelings, all instinctive drives, intuitive fears or preferences, and who prefers to regard his judgments as based on "pure reason."

3. To assume a critical position and approach the problem of technological innovation from the point of view of human needs, not from the point of view of profits, or power, or the desire to dominate. This is the position of the social scholar who is more or less alienated from the existing ruling elites, no matter whether capitalists, political bureaucrats, or technocrats, and who tends to speak as a member of the species man.

This third position seems to be the most cogent. It presupposes, explicitly or intuitively, a critical philosophical anthropology, a theory about genuine human needs and basic capacities for development. From this point of view, many technological innovations can be criticized and rejected, no matter how marketable they might be. Reasons for criticism might include the fact that some technological innovations mean little or nothing from the point of view of human self-development, or that they create unhealthy physical or social surroundings and perhaps even threaten the very survival of mankind, or that their marketing and promotion requires an increasing manipulation of human tastes, attitudes and aspirations, which in itself involves a danger of man's self-destruction.

Under what conditions then, is a policy of discriminate innovation preferable to a policy of simple uniform increase of the total output? A tentative answer should include at least the following elements: (*a*) when the new products satisfy a *greater variety* of vital needs (food, clothes, shelter, and so forth); (*b*) when new technology allows the production of *more* products for *vital* human needs; (*c*) when new technology creates means which increase the possibilities of realizing *higher-level needs* such as knowledge, freedom, creative activity, solidarity, safety, and natural or artistic beauty. For example, political democracy is hardly possible in conditions of general technological backwardness.

The basic condition of human liberation in all its forms is liberation from toil, and the gradual increase of free time — this presupposes technological progress. In conditions both of great scarcity and of great abundance, a policy of permanent technological experimentation and innovation seems to be less crucial: in the former case because the policy of greatest total output might better satisfy the most elementary immediate needs of a greater number of people; in the latter case because, beyond a certain level of satisfaction of basic needs, people develop higher-level needs such as self-fulfillment, cultural development, and political participation which cannot be satisfied in a merely technical way.

Technostructure and Its Basic Values

The whole problem of modern technology cannot be understood properly without a critical analysis of what J. K. Galbraith calls "the technostructure."[2] The social context in which the technostructure operates, its organization and officially accepted ideology may seem very different in Western capitalist and Eastern postcapitalist societies, but it is amusing how similar the basic goals and values of the technostructure really are in all existing social models.

In a private corporation the technostructure has several levels. The board of directors, who represent the stockholders, have nominal power but they are in most cases the passive instrument of the management. Decisions are effectively the work of groups of experts, counsels, auditors, designers, and public relations people. The top management of the corporation can exert more or less pressure on these groups, and can considerably influence their decisions: thus management keeps most of the power.

There are also technocrats within the apparatus of federal government. They are distinct from two other kinds of people in government: the professional politicians who do not have any specialized knowledge but who have spent their lives in various political functions climbing the ladder of state hierarchy, and those who lack both specialized knowledge and long life political experience but who have personality, ambition, lust for power, general organizational talent, and, in some cases, what Weber calls *charisma.*

The obvious tendency in both capitalist and socialist countries is to introduce into government and the state apparatus an increasing number of experts (people like McNamara, Dr. Erkhard, Dr. Maurer, Kissinger) who have both a general scientific culture and specialized knowledge, or a specific know-how in matters of organization, control and general planning. The basic practical attitudes of individuals who belong to the technostructure are very similar in all countries and all kinds of organizations.

The conditions under which the technocracy works are different in various countries. It enjoys considerable autonomy both from the stockholders and from the state apparatus in the United States. This is also true in Great Britain. Even in those economic branches which have been nationalized, the technocracy in the public corporation, in Crosland's words, "has not up to the present been in any real sense accountable to the Parliament, whose function has been limited to fitful, fragmentary, and largely ineffective *ex post facto* criticism."[3]

In India, Ceylon, and some African countries, public enterprises are under state control. Corresponding ministries examine their budgets and expenditures, review policies, question management, keep prices lower and wages higher than autocratic technostructures would permit.

In systems like that of the Soviet Union there are two major sources of outside interference: the state planning apparatus and the Communist Party. Many of the functions of a large private corporation, such as analysis of the market, setting prices, taking steps to insure the supply of raw materials, attracting trained and specialized talent, are performed by the state. The organization of a Soviet firm is much simpler than that of a private corporation. There are no comparable departments such as sales, merchandising, dealer relations, product planning, or procurement. The main preoccupation is with productive and managerial as distinct from planning functions.

For a considerable period of time after the Russian Revolution most managers in Soviet firms were reliable, loyal, and often untrained party officials. This is no longer true. Most of the top positions in a Soviet enterprise are now held by engineers, and, as in any technostructure, they fight for as much autonomy and independent decision power as possible. On occasion they defend the need to ignore or violate orders from outside.[4]

Party and state officials criticize technocratic tendencies very sharply and condemn the more independent-minded managers for behaving as "feudal lords" above the law. In the 1950s Vladimir Dudintsev's important novel *Not by Bread Alone* condemned the bureaucracy of a great metal enterprise for its lack of interest in and later open hostility toward a young gifted inventor. The fact that such a novel could be published should be accounted for not only by the considerable thaw in Soviet culture after the death of Stalin, but also by the fact that all critical arrows in the plays were directed against the factory bureaucracy. It is a regional party official who eventually helps the unfortunate inventor so that justice and reason finally triumph.

On the other hand, the bureaucracy had very mixed feelings about this precedent. Once ordinary people start publicly attacking *natchalstvo* ("those who govern") no one could say where the criticism might end. And, in spite of all tensions and conflicts between bureaucracy and technocracy, they have an indisputable attitude of solidarity when it comes to fending off outside criticism.

Technostructure sees to it that this solidarity is not jeopardized by any overt manifestation of its autonomy. And just as in the West executive managers pay all kinds of lip services to the authority of the stockholders and the board of directors, so a Soviet manager would not waste any opportunity to acknowledge publicly his obligations to the people, the state, and the party. But this is merely a public ritual. In practice, he is accorded large and increasing authority.[5] This is in fact the essence of the whole trend of economic reform and partial decentralization in East European countries. It does not mean so much a return to the market as a shift of some planning from the state to the firm.

The main advantage of the "technostructure" is its specialized knowledge, training, and familiarity with modern, exact methods of management. However, its fatal weakness is the lack of any goal, other than the increase of production.

Those who insist that the pecuniary interest is not the strongest motivation of the technostructure are probably right. To be sure, the managers are far from being indifferent about money and the level of their salaries, but it could be granted that maximization of their own income is not their only or even their main motive. The whole industrial system would collapse if they started minding their own personal return and not the profits of the stockholders.

What then are the goals of the corporation with which one tends to identify? What are the basic values of a manager as a top official of a corporation?

J. K. Galbraith mentions the following four:[6] The first is *an adequate level of profits.* In contrast to the private capitalist the goal is not the maximization of profit since this could be risky and could lead to the neglect of other goals. Instead, the goal is "a secure level of profits which rises in a stable way, which fully satisfies the stockholders and the board of directors, and brings necessary autonomy to the management." This goal is nothing new and for the technostructure it is instrumental and of secondary importance.

The second important goal is *growth; expansion of output.* This is wholly consistent with the personal and pecuniary interest of all participants (owners and managers). What is more important is that expansion means more jobs, more responsibility, more promotion, and more power.

The next goal is of a more general character; it is *identification* of the interest of the firm with the interest of the country as a whole. It should be noted here, first that the underlying logic is invariably: "What is good for General Motors is good for the United States," and second, that the interest of the firm and the whole country is reduced to economic growth.

The fourth important goal is *technical innovation* which is a precondition of growth and which brings a special kind of prestige. Success in scientific research, in its fruitful application, is a valuable social achievement. Consequently, technological *progress* is a generally accepted social value.

The conclusion Galbraith draws from this analysis is that a secure level of earnings and a maximum rate of growth consistant with the provision of revenues for the requisite investments are the prime goals of the technostructure."[7]

The utter emptiness of these goals is striking. One finds two main components in them. One is "a secure level of profits" — in other words, preservation of a state of affairs in which a mere possession of capital secures profit. There was a time when at least a small portion of capital was created by the work of its owner. His imagination, ability, strength of will, and sense of organization helped promote the growth of his capital. But today "A secure level of profits" means profits for people who need not do anything and who, in most cases, have not the faintest idea of what is going on in the enterprise in which they own stocks. To provide them with profits simply because they happen to possess a certain amount of past human labor, objectified in the form of money, is hardly an acceptable social goal.

The second component is growth, expansion, and innovation. This is quite acceptable as a secondary, instrumental goal. But what is the primary goal? What is the purpose of the growth of technology? Technology has always been, is, and will always be a *means*. But to what *end?*

The technostructure is not able to answer the question: What is the ultimate goal of technology? That the goal of technology is the growth of technology itself does not sound very informative or even very intelligent. It is obvious that modern technology has not only produced big cars, supersonic jets, comfortable apartments, good schools, drugs against many diseases, enough "know-how" to produce food in order to prevent any future starvation. It has also brought us nuclear weapons, "I Love Lucy" in color, huge quantities of advertisements of all kinds, and bugging devices, which threaten the right of personal privacy.

Does technological growth mean even more efficient weapons and "Lucy" not only in color but also in the three-dimensional space? Does technological growth promise in future even more commercials, not only in the newspapers and on the television, but also at the concert between the movements of a symphony, between two arias in an opera, or between the pages of a novel? Does more technology mean not only that the FBI will know what everybody thinks, but also that every girl will know about every move of her boyfriend and the husband will be able to listen to every word of his wife?

These questions illustrate the ideological bankruptcy of the technostructure. It wants to take all power but has nothing to offer to man in return. The growth of technology for its own sake is meaningless and dangerous.

If the technostructure has any philosophy, it is a philosophy of complete nihilism, and of complete social irresponsibility.

Technological Innovation in Socialism

In speaking about the conditions and implications of technological innovation in socialist countries we must be quite clear about the distinction between two very different models.

The *Soviet model* might be described as *statism* because the whole process of the planning, direction, and control is in the hands of the state. The basic weakness of the whole system is not so much the fact that it is excessively centralized, but that the central apparatus of power has all the characteristics of the state, according to the classic definition of Marx and Engels. It serves the interests of the bureaucratic ruling elite and uses force in order to preserve the given social structure. Free associations of workers, which for Marx constituted the basis for the new social organization, are not allowed. Planning is strict, pedantic, and imposes tasks on workers' collectives. To the extent to which such planning neglects and arrests initiative it cannot avoid being wasteful. This is clear in the situations which call for change and quick reaction. The huge and utterly clumsy authoritarian apparatus reacts to any kind of information and suggestion coming from below in a much too slow and inefficient way. The fact that the Soviet Union has progressed more rapidly than many capitalist countries is due not to the intrinsic merits of statism, but to several extraordinary conditions:

1. Huge financial means are concentrated in the hands of the bureaucratic apparatus. The decision to invest in new technology or new scientific research often takes a great deal of time, but once the decision is made, the bureaucracy acts on such a large scale and so persistently that it quickly catches up. The Soviet Union's willingness to invest its resources makes possible rapid breakthroughs in a new field such as operations research, computerization of management, application of nuclear energy to peaceful purposes, or space programs.

2. While traditionally mistrusting intellectuals in the field of humanities, the Soviet bureaucracy has built up a cult of positive science and technology. The social status which the leading scientists and managers enjoy is very high. Members of the Academy of Science are enormously admired by the public. Material rewards offered for innovation are surely very limited. But on the other hand, all incomes are limited, and the salaries of the top scientists are second to no other social group.

3. The social status of a Soviet worker has not been radically changed. Everything is being done in his name, but he himself has little opportunity to participate in the decision-making, even at the level of enterprise. Nevertheless, he accepts the new society as his own and tends to be proud of its achievements. There are several reasons for such an attitude. First, his standard of living has been steadily increasing. This has happened elsewhere too, but he sees this as the result of socialism. Second, Russian

patriotism remains a strong integrative force. Third, the Russian worker is not aware of any other possibility and accepts his society as *the* form of socialism. Even to the extent to which he suffers, he takes his suffering as natural and inescapable. Therefore, his alienation does not have that subjective dimension of apathy and vague, accumulated anger which is characteristic of many workers in capitalist societies. As a consequence, he is able to exert more initiative and to introduce more small technical innovations than anybody expects from him.

4. The Russian worker's general level of education has been greatly increased since the days of the revolution. The Soviet system has been relatively successful in providing the large scale subsidy and centralization necessary for mass education and cultural expansion.

The second model, that of Yugoslavia, is a combination of statism and self-management. It is characteristic for this model that the regulation of the process of production at the level of enterprises is in the hands of workers and managers, whereas at the broader level it is in the hands of a bureaucracy. The bureaucracy determines the basic economic instruments such as financial policy, taxes, customs, key prices, capital investments into infrastructure and new branches of industry, aid to underdeveloped regions, and so on. It also determines by appropriate legislation the general framework within which workers' councils can freely move. But workers' councils determine the general policy of the enterprise, decide about distribution of net income, and about such possibilities as merging with other enterprises or splitting off into separate divisions. They also control the technical management and have the right to replace managers. To the extent to which the worker really uses his new rights, his social status sometimes undergoes a substantial change. He ceases to be a commodity. His income is not the fixed price of his labor, but depends functionally on the productivity of the enterprise as a whole, and there is no limit to the amount which he can receive in the form of bonus or surplus income. Therefore, he is directly, materially interested in the achievements of the enterprise as a whole.

Socially and politically, this model has a considerable advantage over statism. While preserving socialized economy, education, and health services, and limiting social differences, it liberates enormous initiative and energy in all micro-units of society. A reduction of the role of the state in economy is naturally followed by a decrease of intervention and control in all other fields: education, science, culture, mass media, and, to a lesser extent, political life. That is why in Yugoslavia, as compared with most other socialist countries, one has the immediate impression of greater dynamism and freedom.

With respect to technological innovation, however, the picture is more ambiguous. There is a certain ambivalence in the basic philosophy of this model. On the one hand, the importance of Marx's humanism is fully recognized in official theory. This should imply concern for the satisfaction of human needs, for the democratization of decision-making, for the abolition of too great economic differences. But, in practice, all economic activity is market-oriented and strongly competitive. There is a strong tendency to forget all humanistic elements and to follow the principles of success, of profit, and of the survival of the fittest. Since 1965, when economic reform was introduced, two opposing positions have emerged. One advocates *laissez faire*, the disappearance of "political" enterprises,[8] elimination of the federal funds for the aid to underdeveloped regions, and reduction of classical socialist welfare programs. It accepts a high level of unemployment as a problem which cannot be solved in the immediate future. The other policy insists on workers' solidarity, on the need for political correction of the undesirable consequences of market economy, on reducing the gap between the advanced and underdeveloped areas within the country. The importance of technological progress is clearly recognized, but only with various qualifications and within a broader social context.

The more market-oriented policy places efficiency and technological progress at the top of the list of social values. And yet even this position (which is much more classical liberalism than Marxism) is quite inconsistent with respect to technology. Efficiency and modernization sometimes require integration into large systems and the abolition of nationalistic barriers. They also require able and knowledgeable management. However, in Yugoslavia champions of liberalism are often ardent nationalists who resist any form of economic integration within the framework of the federation as a whole. Having a vested interest to survive as the political bureaucracy, they are very hostile toward so-called technocratic tendencies and are careful to hire managers who are primarily loyal and only secondarily capable and knowledgeable.

The problem of technological innovation in the Yugoslav model must be seen in the light of a whole complex of favorable and unfavorable factors.

To the former belong:

1. The competitive nature of the Yugoslav economy; new products and new, better technological processes are necessary in order to be able to survive and improve the position of the enterprise at the market.

2. The freedom of initiative of a very large number of producers.

3. The considerable autonomy of the enterprise, and

thus the absence of outside barriers in the process of initiating new projects.

4. The material incentives for technological innovation are greater than in the statist model, although they are limited by progressive taxation and by the moderate egalitarian mentality of the vast majority of people.

5. The surprisingly great openness toward economies of other countries. On the one hand, Yugoslavia imports more than it exports and there is constantly a lack of balance in foreign trade.[9] On the other hand, Yugoslav managers are eager to cooperate with foreign firms, eager to travel and to buy all kinds of licenses for the best that technology offers in their field. As a consequence, each enterprise in a certain field might have a different license.

6. The accepted organization and policies in the field of science favor applied research and direct collaboration of institutes and enterprises. Most Yugoslav scientific institutes are free, independent units with their own organs of self-management. They do not belong either to the state or to the universities or academies of science. For example, according to the existing legal statutes, no one can decide to abolish these scientific institutes. But, on the other hand, neither does anyone subsidize them in a fixed general form. If they wish to obtain social funds for their research they may apply to the federal or republican councils for the coordination of scientific research. Otherwise, they make direct contracts with the enterprises which are interested in their service. That they depend so much on the economy is, from a broader humanistic point of view, one of the basic defects of the whole system. But, at the same time, this is a very favorable condition for technological innovation.

7. Some universities are also very closely connected with big enterprises, for example, the University of Niš with the electronic industry, and the faculty of metallurgy in

Bor with the copper mine in that area. In return for support from the enterprises, the universities organize practical training and specialized research for them. The results have been such that there is a growing tendency to reform the universities, among other things, by bringing them into closer relations with economic enterprises.

8. Finally, although in some respects deplorable, one of the motivating forces for technological innovation is the present mentality of the average Yugoslav who increasingly becomes *homo consumens.* Given the constantly rising income (it is now $650 per capita, and some Yugoslavs are confident that by 1985, it will reach $2000), the impossibility of investing money and becoming a capitalist, and a constant sharp inflationary tendency, a Yugoslav is naturally oriented toward immediate consumption. Having overcome material misery he has become rather selective: he travels a lot and has an opportunity to see and buy foreign products, both abroad and at home. Consequently, he exerts constant pressure on the Yugoslav economy to modernize and to introduce novelties.

Among the most unfavorable factors for technological innovation, one should mention the following:

1. While conducive to numerous small innovations, the decentralization of the financial means makes the national economy as a whole incapable of making necessary breakthroughs in new fields. In fact, there is almost no field in which Yugoslavia as a whole can make a strong, concentrated effort at the present time.

2. Autarchical tendencies within each republic is another unfavorable factor. In the early sixties, self-management was almost identified with decentralization. Experience soon showed that this was an error, a misconception of Marx's ideas about the associations of direct producers. Emphasis on excessive decentralization (even splitting

railways into several regional enterprises) was replaced in the late sixties by an emphasis on integration, on merging small enterprises into bigger, more efficient ones. However, integration hardly ever extended beyond the boundaries of particular republics. Thus, for example, Yugoslavia has built steel factories in each republic, each of them producing less than two million tons, which seems to be the lowest technological limit of rentability. And each republic with access to the Adriatic Sea has its own port but none of them is even close to the lowest limit of rentability.

3. The level of general scientific and technical culture among leading political and economic cadres is unsatisfactory, and the same holds for most factory managers. Therefore, although they are strongly motivated to introduce innovations they are not competent to make good choices. Their decisions either come very late or involve costly errors. One of the basic deficiencies of the present Yugoslav model is that it does not offer a good mechanism for the selection of the best cadres. The reason, of course, is not the self-management, but the limits placed on its further development by the bureaucracy.

4. The existence of a bureaucratic elite is always, in one way or another, an obstacle to a full development of the productive forces of a society. In the Soviet model bureaucracy intervenes too much and in a way which is far from being economically rational. In the Yugoslav model bureaucracy fails to do what is necessary to secure a satisfactory level of economic rationality. It does not use all the power it has and, in fact, officially condemns "administrative intervention." This creates an illusion that Yugoslav society has already realized self-management and that if there is any bureaucracy, it is at least not clearly visible. However, the difference between the two models does not consist in the presence or absence of a monopoly of power

in the hands of the bureaucracy, but in the method of using that power. Yugoslav bureaucracy rules in a much more intelligent, open minded, and flexible way. Instead of using brutal force and the most primitive forms of ideological indoctrination, it applies a much more sophisticated method of rewards and punishments, often giving the impression that those who are ruled are free, and making them responsible *a posteriori.* There are two things here which are unfavorable from the point of view of technological innovation. One is constant delay where prompt action at the level of the nation is necessary. The society as a whole lacks creative, energetic, hard working, democratic leadership and the impression remains that it is poorly organized. On the other hand, the passive presence of bureaucracy as a somewhat tired, sleepy giant who must be asked to approve any initiative at the level of the republics and federation, and whose answers are often negative — thwarts some natural processes of economic self-organization. For example, republican bureaucracies block most of the initiatives which aim at various concrete forms of inter-republic economic integration.

This complex picture, with criss-crossing favorable factors, provides part of the explanation of how it was possible for Yugoslavia to have periods with 15 to 16 percent annual growth rate (1956–60, 1963–64) and also periods of complete stagnation (1967).

The advantage of this model over simple statism is much more obvious in all those fields in which a decrease of state intervention and party control has an immediate beneficial and liberating effect; in education, the social sciences and humanities, culture, the mass media, and political life in various social organizations.

Although the technostructure has some common features in capitalism and socialism, the social and political conditions under which it operates are considerably different, and there are also sharp differences in the conditions which obtain in the two different models of socialism. A critical social philosophy which attempts to build the outlines of a historically optimal society must take into account the various possibilities for technological progress offered by different types of social organization. But it will bear constantly in mind that technological considerations must ultimately be subordinated to humanistic ones.

4

Economism or the Humanization of Economy?

In its efforts to achieve economic progress as rapidly as possible, Yugoslavia is experiencing a serious conflict in terms of societal goals and values. The emphasis on economic development in the past few years has encouraged the development norms and motives such as efficiency, industriousness, technical skill, enterprise, ambition, and material concern.

At the same time, however, Yugoslav society is committed to the project of creating a new basis for human relations, a new culture, and a new morality. It is committed to the fundamental ideals of the revolution such as solidarity, care for the weak and the underprivileged, the abolition of large social differences, the end of exploitation, the right to work, the possibility of individual development as a social and cultural person, and the rational channeling of social processes.

It has not yet become clear how to achieve both economic development and humanization, how to overcome the contradictions in their goals and means. Few people are unaffected by the conflict. People, who for decades have known who they are and what they want, are profoundly confused, incapable of putting the pieces of their being back together, of reuniting thoughts and attitudes. Some who were in the frontline of the revolution have fallen behind in the reform. Others, who watched the revolution from the sidelines, have grabbed front place in the columns of reform. Former partisan commisars become businessmen with capitalist firms; former businessmen begin to interpret for others the true meaning of socialism.

However, even those who have not undergone such an unexpected transformation, and who are convinced that they understand the true nature of the conflicting situation in which they find themselves, interpret that situation in various and differing ways. Some regard the emphasis on market economy as the victory of political realism over utopianism, the triumph of liberalism over conservative forces, or as the latest in a series of inevitable ebbs and flows in history. Others see it as the degradation and downfall of the only possible ideals of socialism, the massive reproduction of a petty-bourgeois way of life, or as a great failure in the selection and realization of the possibilities which history offers. This disparity of attitudes, this incapacity to unite conflicting aims and to overcome the gap between theory and practice, favors many one-sided conceptions whose truth is at best partial and whose moral stance is usually ambiguous.

Among these one-sided attitudes, there is one which is at the moment very influential. It attempts to be more "party-like" than the party program, more Marxist than Marxism itself, and its strength derives from the simple fact that it is fundamentally a rationalization for blind economic forces. It is characteristic of this view, which may be called *economism,* that man is essentially an economic being (*homo oeconomicus*), and a consumer (*homo consumens*), that the essential motive of production in socialist society is the attempt to maximize income and that, therefore, the most important thing for socialism at this moment is *complete liberation* of economic laws and the *undisturbed development* of commodity — money relations.

A critical analysis of economism presupposes a consideration of the entire situational and theoretical context in which the problem of the development of commodity production in socialism is posed. Therefore, one must investigate (*a*) its genesis and its meaning in the modern international socialist movement and (*b*) Marx's attitude towards commodity production and human relations in a society which is based on that production.

Economism and the Classical European Concept of Socialism

The classical European concept of socialism, which during the first decades of this century was the theoretical foundation of the workers' movement throughout the world, and the official doctrine of the Third Communist Internationale, is being seriously challenged today by many socialist thinkers. Typical of this concept was the conviction that:

1. Capitalist social relations were too narrow a framework for the development of productive forces, considering the enormous possibilities offered by modern science and technology.

2. Economic exploitation, political oppression and other forms of human degradation, which are characteristic of the modern world, are chiefly a result of the institution of private property as the means of production.

3. The socialist state is by definition the representative of the interests of the working class and of the widest strata of working people; it is therefore natural for it to have power over all aspects of objectified labor.

4. The maximum of economic and social rationality can be achieved by state planning.

5. The direct concern of the state for science, education and culture assures their maximum rapid and fruitful growth.

6. Social development will gradually but constantly and increasingly lead to the satisfaction of individual human needs, without introducing large economic and social differences.

Almost all of these assumptions have gradually come into question to a greater or lesser degree. Historical experience has largely confirmed that private property is a restrictive factor in modern society. It is true that societies founded on private property can still develop, can even secure a relatively long, lasting period of prosperity, and can, in individual cases (for example, Japan), achieve exceptionally rapid progress.[1] However, after five decades of the practical existence of socialism it must be accepted as a historical fact that, on the average, social ownership of the means of production has assured a significantly higher degree of growth. Nevertheless, the example of Japan demonstrates that social phenomena can never be explained by only one cause. Property relations most certainly exert an influence on the formation of a particular social climate where an accelerated progress is possible. Yet, that certain climate of increased social élan, of integrity, order, and above average individual commitment can also be the result of other factors.

History has particularly contested the uncritical earlier belief in the possibilities and advantages of the state in a socialist society. The oversized sphere of functions and rights adopted by the state has unavoidably made out of it a modern leviathan, an alienated power, basically independent of the people in whose name it acts. The socialist state began to develop according to its own logic and to reproduce much of the irrationality and inhumanity characteristic of the old society. Capitalist profit as the form of appropriating surplus labor has been abolished, but bureaucratic privileges have taken its place. Decision-making has ceased to be haphazard, but has instead become abstract and voluntaristic. State concern for science and culture has permitted the large concentrated investment in material equipment and in the creation of cadres, it has ensured the accelerated development of the natural sciences and of technology, as well as of ideologically neutral art (particularly music), and it has allowed fascinating advances in the field of elementary mass culture. However, that concern, which all too often was transformed into censorship, created a "dead sea" in all those cultural fields whose existence depends on creative freedom: in the social sciences, humanistic disciplines, literature, and art. Since the individual was in every sense dependent on the state, the fulfillment of individual needs did not have high priority. Socialism increasingly resembled a rich society of poor individuals. Bureaucracy took care that economic and social differences did not become too great, but significantly it stood back from the entire rest of society.

Today, this classical concept of socialism is in the process of reevaluation and partial modification throughout Europe, particularly with regard to the economic functions of the state. However, in some of its essential elements it has experienced radical criticism from two opposing sides — China and Yugoslavia.

With regard to her enormous economic backwardness and utterly overstrained program of industrialization, China needed a more rigid model of socialism than the classical one which had originated under European conditions and counted on the niveau of at least semi-industrialized countries. Hence, the great need for a central authority had to be personalized in one leader of supernatural qualities. Maximal efficiency of action, in the absence of technological development, had to be ensured by organization, order, discipline, and unity of thought, in fact, by the complete "ideologization" of the entire culture. Chinese society, with its present low productivity of labor, could not ensure both rapid industrialization and constantly increasing satisfaction of individual needs. China found herself at the crossroads of a dilemma: either enable the present generation to experience not only the collective exaltation of creating a new society and a new revolutionary ethos, but also a significantly higher degree of satisfaction of individual material needs along with a certain slack in the tempo of material development, or seek to conquer the heights of technology with maximum rapidity in spite of all individual deprivation. It is not surprising that the latter course won out. Any slackening of industrialization in a predominantly rural country, such as China, would reproduce a strong petty-bourgeoisie social stratum and make the future uncertain. The centuries-long influence of Confucianism and of Taoism had already prepared people for personal sacrifice and deprivation. The new ideology of dignity in poverty and the subordination of the individual to community requests was already there; it needed only to clear the field of all other alternative ideologies. In fact, this is the meaning behind the so-called cultural revolution.

Of course, the conditions in China are so specific that her experience is not relevant to the development of European countries any more than the experience of these countries constitutes a perfect model for China. Present-day enthusiasm among certain leftists for China and for the Chinese cultural revolution is of a rather romantic nature. It is more an expression of revolt against the situation in the European and American labor movement than an expression of a serious considered belief that the world labor movement should follow China's course of development.

The Yugoslav negation of the classical model of socialism is incomparably more relevant for developed countries. Not only does it contain a thorough critique of the myth surrounding the socialist state, but it has also been effective in building completely new, alternative political and economic structures of self-management.

The key element which allows for a certain continuity to remain between the classical and the Yugoslav models and enables them both to be called "socialist," is the resolute denial of the institution of private property as the means of production. The other basic point of resemblance is that both models apply to a social reality which has not yet reached the level where it would be possible to abolish the market economy.

The main thrust of Yugoslav criticism of the classical model of socialism is its contestation of statism, and its main targets are the dogmas:

1. The so-called socialist state is the unconditional representative of the working class and of all working peoples, and that, consequently, it has the right to dispose of the greatest share of the objectified work.

2. Instead of relying on producers and their true, democratically elected representatives, the state can rationally manage the entire economy of the country.

3. The state must keep control over all scientific and cultural activities.

4. Only the state can ensure the application of the principle of reward according to work and overcome the

forms of exploitation and alienation characteristic of the old society.

In Yugoslavia today, only the most conservative bureaucrats still accept statism as a lasting and satisfactory model for socialist society. However, there are efforts to rehabilitate statism (particularly republican) as a temporary solution, based on the theory that the state is here to stay for a while, and that our bureaucracy is not alien to the working class, but rather governs with its consent and support. It is not exactly clear how it is possible to claim that we *already have* a self-managing society, that there are already self-managing relations in our economy, and at the same time, to justify the continued existence of the state and of bureaucracy. Of course, it can also be the expression of a certain realism and tacit acknowledgment that the realization of self-management has not progressed very far and that a large gulf exists between theory and practice, between propaganda and reality.

If, for a moment, we concern ourselves with the theoretical aspect of the question we will quickly see that there are several alternatives to statism and that, as a matter of fact, very different things are grouped under the title of "self-management."

If we ask ourselves: who, in place of the state, should make the decisions, plan production, and distribute the surplus objectified labor, at least three main answers are possible: (*a*) the immediate producer (in a maximally decentralized system); (*b*) the immediate producer and the organs of the state in the municipalities, republics, and federations; (*c*) the producer and the organs of self-management in municipalities, republics, and federations.

These three answers imply, in fact, three different theoretical models, all of which may claim to be models of self-management because in principle they recognize the right of the immediate producers to participate in decisions regarding the production and distribution of surplus labor. Naturally, the role of immediate producers can vary significantly with each of these models. In addition, a model is not the same thing as reality; for it can be utterly limited by the laws of the market and by varied administrative interventions. In practice, immediate producers rarely enjoy the rights foreseen for them in the system, because, among other things, they are unorganized and confronted with compact oligarchic groups and the apparatus of enormous power. If we bypass all of this for a moment, we could call model (*a*) a system of decentralized self-management, model (*b*) a combined system of self-management and statism, and model (*c*) a system of integrated self-management.

What we have at the moment in Yugoslavia is model (*b*). The further development of self-management, the debureaucratization and deprofessionalization of politics under the conditions of modern technology, which ensures the rationality of only the "big" integrated systems, would be achieved for us under model (*c*).

It is typical of what we can characterize as "economism" that it attempts to achieve economic and social rationality exclusively through the mechanism of commodity money relations, totally eliminating any influence and intervention by political institutions of global society. As a result, economism identifies self-management with decentralization (model *a*), strives towards greater disintegration and atomization of social processes, and, in principle at least, opposes any planning and direction.

From this point of view remuneration according to work is reduced to remuneration according to success on the market. The increase in social differences, the appearance of new socialist bosses and new socialist proletarians, and even the phenomenon of massive unemployment are all seen as normal occurrences within the system. It is natural, according to the postulates of economism, that the skilled and the shrewd should prosper while the weak are ruined. Anything is moral as long as it is not explicitly forbidden by the law. Culture is worth only as much as it brings on the market and science is valuable only insofar as it can be directly applied to industry.

If we abstract the psychological by-products of economism, its cynicism and its total spiritual void, and concentrate on its theoretical base, which is the liberalism of the nineteenth century under the conditions of social property as the means of production, three preliminary remarks are in order.

First of all, economism is unreal and naive. A society built upon its principles cannot long survive in the technological age. A disintegrated industry is incapable of applying modern technology which demands increasingly large investments, a growing degree of communication and cooperation, and an increasingly wider field of operations. The atomized society resulting from economism simply cannot solve any of the larger problems such as hunger, shelter, unemployment, efficient medical aid, the modernization of industry, automation, mass culture, the development of the modern sciences, and particularly, the mobilization of citizens to achieve great social goals. While the process of integration is increasingly progressing in the West, at a time when supranational communities are already in operation, advocates of economism want to expand a program of decentralization.

Secondly, despite some attempts to present economism as the *official* doctrine of Yugoslav society, this is simply not the case. Under the present system, the state either at the federal or the republican level determines the framework of all economic politics. By passing laws, numerous instruments, and decrees, it, as a matter of fact, regulates and, to a certain degree directs, economic processes. According to needs, it even freezes prices and personal incomes, invests, exerts an influence on bank business and the credit system, determines the currency rate, and confirms the form of exchange with other countries. All of this is irreconcilable with economism. Therefore, leaving aside the questions whether or not the state is doing well, what it is doing, and whether or not economism is a progressive or regressive negation of such methods, it is clear that the doctrine is in practical opposition both to the political principles proclaimed in the program of the Yugoslav league of Communists, and also to those politics which have already been carried out in Yugoslavia.

Thirdly, economism resembles statism insofar as both attempt to retain in socialism some of the essential structures of class society. Statism has been working to this end on the political level, conserving, strengthening, justifying, and glorifying the state. Economism tries to achieve the same ends on the economic level, retaining and glorifying the market. Statism created the myth of the "socialist state" and economism has manufactured the myth of "socialist commodity production."

Of course, socialism will need the state for a while yet. Similarly, commodity production and market relations will exist for a long time to come. Undoubtedly the state under socialism is not the same as the state under any previous forms of class society. Commodity money relations with social property as the means of production and involving forms of self-management are not the same as commodity money relations under capitalism.

Nevertheless, the state is an institution of the old class society; it is essentially an apparatus of coercion which makes sense only as long as sharp class differentiation exists and as long as reason remains inferior to power. The same thing is true of commodity production. Marx's criticism of commodity production applies wherever it exists, whether in capitalism or socialism. For Marx, the transition from capitalism towards communism means a process of transcending the institutions of commodity, money, and reified market relations.

If this were not true, economism could pretend to mean something new for socialist theory and practice. As it is, economism cannot be evaluated as anything other than as a not-too-ingenious attempt to restore the long since outmoded bourgeois liberalism of the nineteenth century.

Marx's Critique of Alienated Labor

One needs to get behind the ephemeral individual facts of Marx's *Das Kapital* and the theoretical considerations which more or less relate to the particular forms of capitalist society during his time, to be able to penetrate the furthest depths of this work in order to understand its full meaning. Only then do we see that Marx was far more than an analyst or a critic of a concrete, and today greatly surpassed, historical reality, and that he was, in fact, a theoretician of our society and times as well. He expressed more profound truths about present-day society than many of our superficial contemporaries and many of his disciples who live under the dangerous illusions that, at least in some parts of the world, the questions which Marx posed have already been resolved.

In fact, the problem which represents the basis and the starting point of Marx's entire critique of political economics continues to be the central problem of the present moment and of the entire historical epoch in which we live. Marx condensed this problem into the concept of alienated labor. The term alone was the cause of many misunderstandings and pseudo-conflicts. In itself it is not important. What is essential is the structure to which it refers. The question is what happens to man under certain historical conditions in the process of his work?

Work is the objectification of human powers: while shaping the confined object, man projects onto it his own consciousness, thoughts, desires, needs, and imagination. Through it, he realizes the potential capacities of his being. At the same time, production enables the worker to satisfy needs, his own and those of others. Work, therefore, *could be* an activity through which the individual expresses all of the fundamental characteristics of his human nature, and through which he produces and confirms himself as a man. Man distinguishes himself from other animals in that:

1. He *consciously and purposefully changes the given objects.*

2. He rebels against any form of limitation, be it from the outer world or from within himself, from which it follows that he *aspires to overcome every such restriction, and to perfect and further develop his own self through his creativity.*

3. The motive for work is not only the creation of the *useful* traits of the object which satisfy some direct organic need or increase man's might, but also the creation of those traits. This creation is a *goal in itself.*

4. The product of labor mediates between one individual and another and this establishes a *social relation* between them; the product will satisfy a need of the other man, add to his being in a certain way, and, at the same time, project and confirm the being of its producer.

Work, by its own nature, could be all of this. However, in *modern* history these structural characteristics of work have been manifested only fragmentarily and only in the productivity of individual creators. The work of humanity as a whole, owing to a series of historical conditions, still does not have a humane character.

When the necessity for an increase in the productivity of labor results in the division of labor, in the partition of society into professional groups, in the polarization of physical and intellectual workers, of managers and employees, in the crumbling and atomizing of the entire working process into individual phases, and finally in operations around which the whole life of individual or groups of workers may sometimes be fixed, the entire structure of human work disintegrates and an acute gap between its constituent elements appears: the product no longer has its determined producer and the producer loses all connection with the object he produced.

This is a *two-sided* externalization (*EntäuBerung*); for the product not only escapes from the control of its creator, but it also begins to act like an independent power which treats its maker like an object, like a thing to be used.[2] This phenomenon is possible because behind the object there is another man who uses it to transform the producer into a thing, where human qualities are completely irrelevant except for one: a special kind of commodity which can produce other commodities and which needs for its upkeep and reproduction a smaller amount of objectified work than the amount of objectified work which it creates. This two-sided externalization, which in essence is not a relation of a man to the natural object, but rather a specific relationship of a man toward other man, is alienation.[3]

Marx did not discover the idea of alienated labor; it can be found in Hegel's early works. However, Marx reopened a problem which Hegel had fictively solved and closed. He gave it a real historical perspective within the framework of a general humanistic philosophical vision. While working on *Grundrissen der Kritik der politischen Oekonomie* and on his first draft of *Das Kapital,* Marx rarely used the term "alienation" itself, but the conceptual structure expressed therein was the basis for Marx's entire critique of political economy. Lastly, the experience of the Paris Commune contributed to Marx's definite formulation of his belief that a free community of direct producers, that is, the realization of self-management, is the concrete historical path towards transcending alienated labor.

In his work *System der Sittlichkeit* (A system of morals), written between 1800 and 1802, Hegel had introduced the concept of "general," abstract and quantitative labor which produces goods for the market, as distinct from that special concrete work through which the individual attempts to fulfill his own needs. Abstract labor leads to social inequality, to the increase in degrees of wealth and to ever greater antagonisms. Powers alien to the individual, in relation to which he remains impotent, determine whether or not his needs will be satisfied. The so-called state of justice attempts through proper legal channels to introduce a certain balance, but even this cannot completely avoid giving preference to special interests. According to Hegel, the only possibility for creating a unity of general and individual interests is to transcend the individualistic society, and subordinate to the authority of the state.

We can find a similar analysis of labor in Hegel's *Philosophie des Geistes.* Abstract labor cannot develop the true capacities of the individual. Mechanization instead of liberation only enslaves man: increase in mechanization means a decrease in the value of labor and a further restriction on the worker's capacities. Instead of being the means for the self-realization of the individual, work becomes the means for his degradation and self-negation. The relation between need and labor becomes blind, unestimable interdependence. For a society like this to be able to survive, it is essential, according to Hegel, to have a strong state which will constantly control the wild animal and hold it in check.

Hegel continues this discussion of the problem of labor and the relation of individual to society in his *Die Phenomenologie des Geistes.* His analysis of the reified world in which objects are the incarnation of the subject who created them and in which human interrelations are hidden behind the relations among the objects is of capital importance to Marx's philosophy. Marx adopted from Hegel the idea that man is "the result of his work" and that the "self-creation of man is the process of reification and of its negation."[4] Hegel's analysis of the relationship between master and servant directly prepared the way for Marx's analysis of the relationship between capital and labor. The world is polarized because man's entire being is regulated by work, and men appropriate the work of other men. Such a relationship did not sprout as a result of natural differences between men; it is mediated by the objects which the one produces and the other possesses and disposes of. Hegel indicated the solution to this conflict, but in an abstract, conceptual form: the man whose self-consciousness is awakened, who has felt that behind the appearance of things lies his own self-consciousness, appropriates things and uses them. Yet, at the end of that process he comes to the knowledge that the true object of his desires (*Begierde*) are not things but rather contact with other individuals. Or as Hegel puts it: "Self-consciousness achieves its satisfaction in another self-consciousness."

These ideas have deeper meaning in the modern consumer civilization which reproduces on a mass scale the type of person who can be characterized as a *being-for-things* and not Hegel's *being-for-the-other-man.*

Marx emphasized the enormous significance of Hegel's *Phenomenology of Mind,* but at the same time he pointed out the fatal loophole in this brilliant analysis: all the contradictions of bourgeois society which Hegel so readily perceived and expressed in philosophical language are dissolved only within the framework of pure thought which in itself is one of the spheres of alienation. This amounts to "overcoming" alienation *in an alienated way.* Furthermore, Hegel's entire system remains historically closed and tied to the existing social framework. The monarchist state solves all antagonisms. In this way, reality reaches the level of theory, social institutions become rational (*vernunftig*).

Many Marxists to whom Hegel's works were unknown attributed ideas to Marx which he simply adopted from Hegel. Others immediately noticed that since unbridgeable differences exist between Marx's ideas in *Economic and Philosophical Manuscripts* and their own philosophical convictions, the most convenient thing to do was to dismiss his early works as Hegelian. The ignorance of the former reaction was nowhere near so damaging as the superficial arrogance of the latter. Without the Hegelian analysis of labor and the reified world, not only would there not be the philosophy of the young Marx but there would not be *Das Kapital* either. When Hegel's conservative and apologetic conclusions are discarded and his abstract and mystified form of presentation is left aside, certain profound analyses of real human interrelationships remain. These analyses entered the roots of Marx's thought and reveal their full meaning in contemporary society.

Without this prehistory to *Das Kapital* it is impossible to undertand that work, as Lenin once noted,[5] after having read only Hegel's *Logic* and without even considering

Phenomenology of Mind. What follows is that over the past hundred years there have been few Marxists who have understood how Marx really conceived the transcendence of capitalism.

Contrary to the widespread misbelief that the theme of alienation can be found only in Marx's earlier works under the influence of Hegel, and that he completely discarded this "abstract philosophical phase" in his later, more mature scientific period, it can be irrefutably shown that the basis of Marx's critique of political economy is in his critique of alienated labor, and that, in that respect, there is complete continuity from the *Economic and Philosophic Manuscripts,* written in 1844, *Grundrissen der Kritik der politischen Oekonomie* written in 1857–58 to *Das Kapital.*

Marx's critical position in *Das Kapital* can only be understood in the light of his hypothesis of true human community and true production where each man both "affirms himself and the other man":

1. By objectifying his individuality and experiencing his personality as an objective, sensuous, unquestionable power
2. By the immediate awareness that his work and the use of his product will satisfy the needs of another human being
3. By the mediation between another man and the human generic being; by the knowledge that this labor contributed to supplementing another being, that it became a part of him
4. By creating the life expression of another man through one's own life expression

This is, then, the immediate confirmation and realization of his true being, his generic being.[6]

The analysis of labor in *Das Kapital* is the starting

point for the explanation and criticism of capitalist society, and of any other society which is based on commodity production. The character of labor is contradictory. What Marx in his earlier works called "alienated labor" is now placed under the term "abstract labor." Only abstract labor creates exchange value and only it has a socially acknowledged importance. However, man's labor is here totally crippled, deprived of everything personal, free, creative, spontaneous, or human, and reduced to being a simple supplement to machines. The only socially acknowledged characteristic of that labor will be its quantity and this will be judged on the market and will receive its abstract objective form — money. The fetishism of commodities, the mysticism of the merchandise world are the concepts by which, within the sphere of economics, Marx expresses the same structure of productive relations which he termed in his earlier works "alienated labor." Again, the point is, as Marx says in *Das Kapital,* that "their, the commodity producer's, own historical movement takes the form of the movement of things under whose control they happen to be placed, instead of having control over them."[7] The conclusion which Marx draws from his analyses of the production of relative surplus value reproduces, in condensed form, all of the elements of his criticism of alienated labor in early writings:

> Within the capitalist system all methods for increasing social productive forces are carried out on the bill of the individual worker, all means for developing production degenerate into means for the exploitation of and rule over the producer; they make a cripple out of the worker, a semi-man, they reduce him to the common equipment of a machine, destroy the last remains of appeal in his work transforming it into a real torture; they

> alienate from the worker the intellectual possibilities of the process of labor to the degree in which science is included as an independent force; they deform the conditions under which he works, subject him in the process of labor to a disgusting and pedantic despotism, transform his entire life into working hours and throw his wife and his child under Juggernaut's wheel of capital.[8]

In his *Economic and Philosophical Manuscripts,*[9] Marx distinguished four types of alienation of the worker:

1. Alienation from the product of labor, which becomes an independent blind power
2. Alienation from the production itself, which becomes compulsive, routine, and loses any traits of creativity (which, among other things implies production according to the laws of beauty)
3. Alienation from the human generic being, for whom conscious, free and productive labor is characteristic
4. Alienation from the other man, because satisfaction of another's needs, supplementing another's being, cease to be the prime motive of production.

All of these aspects of alienation can be found in *Das Kapital.*

The fetish character of commodity lies precisely in the fact that "the social characteristics of their own work seem to people to be characteristics which objectively belong to the products of labor themselves, to be properties which those things have by nature." Hence, "social relationships among people assume for them a fantasmagorical form of the relationships among things."

This reification of human relations springs from specific characteristics of labor which produces commodities. Labor can take on the character of a commodity only "when various specific cases of work are reduced to a common character which they all have as the expenditure of working capacity, as human labor in the abstract." This abstract labor ceases to be a need and fulfillment of the human being and becomes the mere necessary means of its subsistence. "The accumulation of wealth at one end is at the same time the accumulation of poverty, hard labor, slavery, ignorance, growing bestiality, and moral decline at the other, that is, on the part of the class which brings forth its own product in the shape of capital.[10]

The alienation of the producer from the other man stems from the simple fact that the purpose of the work is no longer the satisfaction of another's needs, but rather the possibility of transforming labor into money — the general and impersonal form of objectified labor. The drastic forms of alienation among people arise as a consequence of the competition, exploitation, and despotism to which the worker is submitted. In order to increase production and at the same time to prevent a decline in the profit rate, it becomes necessary to squeeze out from the worker an increasingly large amount of unpaid work.[11] Hence, the necessity for the most efficient manipulation of workers possible and the need for an increase in the degree of the exploitation of labor.

Criticism of alienated labor, therefore, is present in both *Das Kapital* and in all earlier works. One who loses sight of this criticism also loses the possibility of understanding the deepest meaning of Marx's message, and opens himself up to the dangerous illusion that many historical problems have been already resolved when all that has been realized are some preconditions and all that has been achieved are some first steps towards their resolution.

A good example of misunderstanding of the essentials of Marx's critiques of capitalist society is the discussion on the disappearance of exploitation in the modern developed industrial society of the West and in socialist countries. One of the frequent arguments used in the West to refute Marx's theory is to point out the fact that, contrary to his predictions, the process of progressive pauperization of the working class did not take place. In fact, its living standard over the last few decades has grown to such an extent that material misery is no longer a primary motive for revolutionary action of workers in advanced countries. This seems to imply that under these conditions exploitation tends to disappear.

However, the quintessence of exploitation is not that the worker is condemned to live in misery because he does not receive equal value for his labor. First of all, Marx assumed that wages in capitalism are more or less equal to the value of labor. Secondly, under the conditions of rapid technical progress and the increase in labor productivity, the degree of exploitation can grow regardless of the fact that wages can also rise.

The surplus value rate is the exact expression for the degree of exploitation of labor by capital. However, the surplus value rate is determined by the ratio of surplus value to variable capital. Therefore, the moment that labor productivity or the total value of produced commodities increases more rapidly than the total sum issued to buy the labor force, the degree of exploitation increases.

On the other hand, contrary to those Marxists who link the phenomenon of exploitation strictly to capitalism, one can say that the mere abolition of private ownership of the means of production does not abolish every possibility for exploitation.

Marx carefully explained in his earlier writings that *private property is not the cause but the consequence of alienated labor,* just as gods are originally the consequence not the cause of religious alienation. Only later does conditioning become reciprocal. In the society which Marx calls "primitive," "nonreflective communism," "man's personality is negated in every sphere," the entire world of culture and civilization is negated and regresses towards the unnatural simplicity of the poor and wantless individual, who has not only not surpassed private property, but has not yet even attained to it.[12] In this kind of society, Marx says, "the community is only a community of *work* and *of equality of wages* paid with communal capital by the community as universal capitalist."[13]

That is why Marx felt that the basic question was that of the *nature of labor* rather than the question of private property. "In speaking of private property, one believes oneself to be dealing with something external to mankind. But in speaking of labor one deals directly with mankind itself. This new formulation of the problem already contains its solution."[14]

The solution, therefore, is to abolish those relations into which the worker comes during the process of his labor, to abolish the situation in which he becomes only one of the commodities in the reified world of commodities. The essence of exploitation lies in the fact that accumulated, objectified labor, that is, capital, rules over live work and appropriates the value which it creates, and which is greater than the value of the labor force itself. Marx expressed this major thesis of his in *Das Kapital,* in the following concise manner: "The rule of capital over the worker is merely the rule of things over man, of dead over live labor."[15]

The specific historical form which enabled the appropriation of objectified labor in Marx's time was the disposal of capital on the basis of private ownership of the means of production. This specific feature clouded over the generality of its content and it is no wonder that to many Marxists it seemed and still seems that the possibility for exploitation existing in a society in which private ownership of the means of production has been abolished is a *contradictio in adjecto*. Nevertheless, it is obvious that private ownership of the means of production is not the only social institution which allows for the disposal of objectified labor. First, in a market economy during the transitional period this institution can be the monopolistic position of individual collectives which enables them to sell their commodities above their value. Such collectives, in fact, appear on the market as collective capitalists and collective exploiters. (Needless to say, within the process of internal distribution this appropriated surplus of value will be assured of never reaching the pockets of the producers themselves, but will rather find its way into the bureaucratic and technocratic elements of the enterprise.) Second, it can be a monopoly over the decision-making in a statist system. To the degree to which a bureaucracy exists and takes over the disposal of objectified labor into its own hands, rewarding itself with various privileges, there is no doubt that this is just another form of appropriating the surplus value created by the working class.

The only way to definitely abolish exploitation is to create the conditions which will prevent objectified labor from ruling over live labor, in which, above all, the right to *dispose of objectified labor will be given to the producers themselves.*

Alienation in the field of material production entails a corresponding form of alienation in the field of public, social life — the state, and politics. Politics are separated from economics, and society is divided into two opposite spheres. One is *civil society* with all the egoism of the concrete owner of commodities, with all its envy, greed for private possession and indifference towards the true needs of others. The other sphere is that of the *political society* of the abstract citizen which in an illusory way personifies within itself the general interest of the community.

Kant and Hegel outlined two basic but contrary concepts of the state and law. Kant's liberal concept starts from the real, empirically given society, characterized by the market and the mutual competition among egotistic individuals, and attempts to reconcile the general interest and freedom of the individual in a negative manner, by demanding restriction of the self-initiative and arbitrariness of the individual. Hegel correctly perceived that simple common coexistence and mutual restriction of selfish individuals does not constitute a true human community. Hegel, therefore, tried to transcend this negative relationship of one individual with the next, seen as his limit, by the assumption of a rational citizen and a rational community in which the individual relates positively to the social whole, and through it to the other individual. However, Hegel himself remained within the framework of the limited horizon of bourgeois society, conceiving rationality as an abstract identification of the subjective spirit of the individual with the objective spirit of the state. The state as the personification of ideal human community is a pure abstraction which fictively transcends the existing empirical reality of bourgeois society.

In his criticism of Hegel's philosophy of law, Marx properly observed that (*a*) such a reduction of a concrete possible human community to an abstraction of the state (the moment of the objective spirit), along with reducing a concrete, historically given individual to an abstraction of the citizen, takes the form of alienation, and that (*b*) this alienation in thought is the result of alienation in the reality itself: The picture of the modern state imagined by the

Germans, was only possible because the state abstracts itself from true people and fulfills the total man in only an imaginary way.[16]

Contrary to civil society, in which there is *bellum omnium contra omnes* and in which only intersecting and mutually contradictory *separate* interests come to expression, in the political state the state-in-general appears as a necessary supplement, and in Hegel's conception it "exists *an sich* and *für sich*." The state, then, is an alienated universal and necessarily entails the formalism of the state, namely, bureaucracy. Bureaucracy attempts to affirm general interest as something special, *beside and above all other private and special interests*.[17] In that way it presents itself as an alienated social power which treats the world as a mere object of its activity.[18] On the other hand, the state and bureaucracy are necessary supplements to the crumbling world of the owners of commodities who all follow only their special and private goals: The state also supports a special interest but creates the illusion of its generality. "General interest can be maintained in face of special interest only as something 'particular' in as much as the particular in face of the general is maintained as something general."[19]

Needless to say, this dualism between the bureaucratized state and special private interests was impossible to resolve by identifying these contradictions in an imaginary way, within the framework of abstract thought.

"The abolition of bureaucracy," says Marx, "is possible only when general interest becomes reality," and when "special interest really becomes *general* interest."[20] And that is only possible when the individual man begins to live, work, and relate to his fellow man in a human way "only when man ceases to separate his *forces propres* as a social power from himself in the form of political power, only then will human emancipation be achieved."[21]

Marx explained this conception more clearly in *Grundrisse.* Here he compares political with religious alienation; in both cases man projects his general human generic characteristics and needs either into an out-of-this-world being, or into the state. Both are a necessary supplement to the incomplete social reality and can wither away only when man liberates himself from the idiocy of tying his entire life to one calling or to wage labor.

Marx shows in *Das Kapital* that all the basic rights guaranteed by the state to its citizens have a formal and alienated character. *Freedom* is merely the citizen's right to dispose of his commodity. *Equality* is in reality merely the application of the principle of equality to the exchange of commodity.[22] Everyone looks out for himself and not for the other. General good can only be realized "behind the back of the individual" by the "invisible hand," as Adam Smith says. For Marx, the question is how to strive for the general goals of the community consciously and freely, in the most rational and most human way possible. For that, the state is no longer necessary. "Freedom consists in transforming the state from an organ which dominates society into an organ which is completely subordinate to it, and even at the present, the forms of the state are more or less free to the degree that they limit the freedom of the state."[23]

In his early work *The Poverty of Philosophy,* Marx offered the theory that "in the process of its development the working class will replace the old civil society with an association which excludes classes and their contradictions. Then there will no longer be political rule in the traditional sense, because political rule is precisely the official expression for the class contradictions in civil society."[24] In the

Communist Manifesto Marx says that achieving democracy is the first step in the workers' revolution. The state is nothing more than the proletariat organized as the ruling class.[25] Marx's concept of the fate of the state during the revolution is particularly clear in his analysis of the experiences of the Paris Commune. He talks throughout of "destroying state rule," of "smashing" it, of its being "superfluous." With enthusiasm he accepts two, "infallible means," as Engels calls them, for preventing bureaucratism. First, "the Commune appointed for its officials persons elected by the general vote, persons who are directly responsible and at any time replaceable by their electors." Second, "public office, whether it concerns high or low positions, had to be performed for worker's wages."[26] For the first time in history, if only for a short period, the state was replaced by self-management.

In his "Paris Manuscripts" of 1844, the road was not yet clear to Marx as to how to overcome alienated labor. He only makes a rough draft here of the general vision of a society in which all individuals develop freely and realize themselves as complete personalities. Social relationships are no longer those of envy, competition, abuse, or mutual indifference, but rather relations in which the individual, while fulfilling the needs of the other man, while fulfilling and enriching his being, directly experiences his own affirmation and self-realization.

Marx gives a concrete historical dimension to this general vision of transcending alienated labor in his *Grundrisse.* It was entirely clear to Marx that new, more humane relations of production will occur only in an advanced society, in the production relations which, thanks to the scientific and technological progress, have already become universal, no matter how reified. Only when man is no longer directly governed by people but by abstract forces, by reified social laws, will the possibility be created to bring these reified conditions of existence under communal social control.

In *Das Kapital,* Marx's solution for the problem of alienation of labor is quite clearly outlined, for example, in the discussion on the fetishism of commodities. "The form of the process of social life, i.e., of the process of material production will cast off from itself the mystical loggy veil only then when the product of freely associated people is under their conscious, planned control. But this requires such a material basis and such a set of material conditions which in themselves are the wild product of a long and painful history of development."[27] One should particularly underline that famous passage in the third volume of *Das Kapital* where Marx says:

> Freedom in the field of material production cannot consist of anything else but of the fact that socialized man, associated producers, regulate their interchange with nature rationally, bring it under their common control, instead of being ruled by it as by some blind power; that they accomplish their task with the least expenditure of energy and under conditions most adequate to their human nature and most worthy of it.[28]

The idea of self-management is enriched and made concrete through Marx's analyses of the experiences of the Paris Commune. All the elements of self-management are already given here, namely:

1. The regulation of the process of labor should be left in the hands of the workers themselves; it cannot remain the monopoly of any special profession of managers who concern themselves with that only, and who, as the only historical subjects, will manipulate all other people like objects.

2. Producers must be *associated,* and that association must be *free.* Self-management is not, therefore, a synonym for the atomization and disintegration of society, as some of its opponents like to represent it and as it may appear in practice when mistakenly understood. Self-management assumes integration and this integration must be free and voluntary.

3. The control of production carried out by the associated producers must be *conscious* and *planned;* the exchange with nature should be regulated in a *rational manner,* and not abandoned to the rule of blind powers. Self-management, therefore, assumes constant direction, the elimination of uncontrolled economic forces. That presupposes the development of culture and science, and a clear understanding of the goals of development, for without that it is useless even to speak about rationality.

4. This communal control and direction of material production should engage as little human energy as possible, for managing things, and above all people, cannot be a goal in itself, but only a means for securing truly free, creative, and spontaneous activity.

5. The kind of self-management which Marx had in mind is possible only with a relatively high degree of development in a society. According to him, it "requires the kind of material basis which is the result of the long and painful history of development." However, if something is ever to get a developed form, it must *start* to develop in time. That is why Marx investigated so seriously and with such interest the experience of the Paris Commune and derived conclusions from it for the practice of the workers' movement. That is why history will certainly justify the efforts in Yugoslavia to begin with the introduction of the first, initial forms of self-management even if in unripe conditions.

6. Still, in observing the conditions under which the exchange with nature is to take place, Marx does not consider the greatest success and efficiency, the greatest increase in power over nature, the greatest material wealth as the most important things. For him, the most important thing is to carry out this process under those conditions which are the *most adequate and the most worthy of the human nature of the worker.*

Marx concludes the third volume of *Das Kapital* with that with which he began in "Economic and Philosophical Manuscripts" and that which he explained in considerable detail in those earlier manuscripts.

There is no Marxist economy, there is no revolutionary theory without a theory of man and human nature.

Only to the degree that social relations become increasingly humane can one talk of real historical progress.

Economic Rationality and Humanism

It is perfectly clear, then, what Marx's viewpoints were concerning the fate of commodity production during the transitory phase. He had a good enough sense of history not to expect its disappearance immediately following the workers' revolution. But it was equally clear to him that the occurrence of alienation of labor and fetishism of commodities was characteristic of *every* commodity production and not just that performed under capitalism. The transition from capitalism to communism was for him basically the process of the gradual supersession of reified market relations. In his opinion, the self-management of associated producers was the only way to realize this historical possibility. That is unquestionably the case, and if in addition one could observe that this model of Marx's is fully applicable to our own conditions, any engagement for the "liberation" and affirmation of the market and ("socialist") commodity production as a strategical principle, would obviously have a counterrevolutionary character.

Many problems and disputes arise from the fact that, due to unforeseen historical circumstances, socialist revolutions broke out at a much lower level of material development than that which Marx had in mind, so that the new societies also had to carry out the historical tasks of capitalism: the abolition of feudal relations and structures of behavior, the original accumulation, industrialization, urbanization, and the development of commodity production to the level at which its radical abolition would be historically possible.

In that complex and dramatic situation, petty-bourgeois and most conservative bureaucratic forces see only two alternatives from which to choose: (*a*) either the complete liberation of "business initiative" and a maximal thrust for a market economy regardless of all that this would mean in the social, cultural, and moral spheres: (*b*) or the substitution for uncontrolled forces regulating the economic process *via* the market, by a conscious regulation and direction on the part of the "socialist" state apparatus.

There is no doubt that this dilemma is entirely wrong. The first alternative would lead to a restoration of the social relations of bourgeois society with the essential peculiarity that private ownership of the means of production would be replaced by some kind of group property. The second alternative would lead to the restoration of Stalinism, with the possible exception that the once primitive bureaucratic apparatus could be replaced by a symbiosis of educated bureaucrats and technocrats.

The disputes which have occurred in Yugoslavia over the past few years are centered around the question: How is it possible to develop commodity production and at the same time to continue to develop socialist interpersonal and intergroup relations?

There is no doubt that in any semideveloped society, commodity production with all its implications (division of labor, exchange of products according to the laws of value, and the market as *one* of the essential regulators of production) is still necessary.

It is questionable, however, whether a virtue should be made out of the unavoidable, whether one should make an epochal revolutionary transformation out of something which is not characteristic of socialism, and which appears as a demand resulting from the immaturity of historical conditions and from economic, political, and cultural underdevelopment.

It is especially contestable whether socialist human relations can be built up if, in many important spheres of production and social activity, the roads toward a gradual transcendence of commodity-money relations are not already being uncovered at the present moment.

One who takes a critical attitude toward economism need not in the least deny: (*a*) that people will liberate themselves from forced routine labor and production for the market only at a much higher level of technological development; (*b*) that only in a society of abundance will people *definitely* cease to be obsessed by the bare motive of possession and emancipate themselves for the development of the whole spectrum of deeper and more refined human needs; (*c*) that the historical phase of commodity production cannot be jumped over in this ascent towards an affluent society; (*d*) that during this phase the market must continue to play its role as one of the essential objective indicators of economic efficiency and rationality.

However, economism, even when it tries to remove itself from Adam Smith and *laissez-faire* liberalism, is amazingly indifferent to the fact that one-sided liberation of the laws of commodity production must necessarily lead to a dangerous strengthening of all those social structures which in socialism should, in fact, be weakening. Labor would increasingly take on the character of alienation and reification, the rule of objectified over live labor would become more pronounced, exploitation in the form of bureaucratic privileges would be joined by the classical forms of exploitation in the form of income not based on labor, social differences would increase instead of decrease, culture would be abandoned to the mercy of the market, and, in the last analysis, to that low and primitive level of needs for cultural goods which was inherited by an undeveloped capitalism.

In such a situation, petty-bourgeois ideologists, who regard their almost total disorientation and ideological meandering from Smith and Bentham to Proudhon and the Marginalists as the discovery of new socialist roads, become more numerous, louder, and more aggressive. They will deny that Marx ever gave a general critique of commodity production, "he was concerned with capitalism *only*." They will angrily protest against any criticism, no matter how qualified, of the market economy. How could anyone be so absurd as to even think that commodities by their "fetishism could infect *socialism itself*?" According to them, "nothing, literally nothing" would be lost by our society if the private sector would be allowed to spread out and to employ a larger number of persons. (It is not the same thing, it seems, to be exploited under capitalism and under socialism!) In a situation in which a stratum of socialist *nouveaux riches* appear who obviously did not earn their high incomes on the basis of labor, but by abuse, corruption, and unlawful property transactions, there is a growing pressure in the mass media and constant lobbying in political circles to open the gate to private capital investment and profit appropriation (in the form of share dividends). The future of Yugoslav socialism depends on its capacity to resist this growing degenerative tendency.

If critical thought is up to the mark, if its goal is to transcend rather than to destroy the present, it already contains within itself the positive solution. I will attempt, however, to formulate in a condensed, explicit form what is meant by the humanization of economics, and how a connection between the rationality of economics and concrete Marxist humanism is possible under today's circumstances.

1. While economism tolerates very extensive and arbitrary administrative intervention by the state in economics and in some fields where it is totally unnecessary, for example in science and in culture, it, on the other hand, proclaims the liberation of economic laws from any kind of social interference even when coordination and direction are necessary for assuring economic rationality at the level of global society, and for preventing and correcting socially unacceptable consequences of commodity-money relations.

It is essential, therefore, to make a typology of various kinds of interventions from the center, and to distinguish between those which are irrational and functionless (and which should be much more radically abolished than economism has so far suggested), and those which are necessary for either economic rationality or for socialist humanism. The latter, if properly understood, will not be mutually exclusive.

1. True rationality is the maximum efficiency in the realization of consciously chosen social goals which are historically possible and which suit real social needs.

2. True social rationality, towards which socialist society should strive, cannot be reduced to a simplified and

one-sided formula of the "liberation of economic laws." Commodity-money relations must be freed from arbitrary interventions by the bureaucratic apparatus, particularly those which prevent interrepublic integration and favor one economic group at the expense of the other. However, if the adequate investigation and regulation of uncontrolled market forces has become an objective need in the whole world, then that must be particularly so for socialist society. Socialism cannot permit mass unemployment, increase of social differences outside certain limits, increase in the lagging of the backward and undeveloped, stagnation and even decline of production, dangerous disproportion and instability, and drastic forms of disharmony and anarchy. If such occurrences are, particularly since 1929, the object of constant concern and control of social-political institutions in the capitalist world, it is ridiculous and paradoxical to declare such intervention in socialism as "extra-system interference" and as "centralistic control."

3. In fact, socialism today must go a step further. Society must gradually undertake certain measures toward *transcending commodity-money relations.* Even in capitalism, that historical process is to some extent already achieved: there is an increasing quantity of goods and services in the fields of education, culture, social security, medical aid, food, and dwelling which are no longer commodities. If socialism does not wish to enter history as a form of social organization which successfully secures retarded industrialization, it must show and show *now* how it is possible to organize production for human needs, and not for profit, how remuneration can be correlated to work, and not to mere success on the market, and, finally how the rule of objectified things over live labor can be abolished.

4. The crucial question is: *Who* is to take over all of

these functions of directing, correcting, and creating new productive relations? The competence of the state must definitely be decreased, even though it will still, for some time to come, maintain certain managerial functions. A growing responsibility for regulating social processes and formulating socialist politics must be assumed by the higher-level organs of self-government which should fill the great vacuum between the enterprise and the federation.

Yugoslav society is still insufficiently organized. But instead of offering the perspective of better organization based on democratic, self-managing principles, economism refers us to the market laws. If economism does not really believe in Adam Smith's "invisible hand," it is still its duty to show concretely how the immediate commodity producer can effectively influence the decision-making process in global society, and how it can effectively assure a *higher* degree of rationality than that already being achieved in capitalist society.

If it were to do that, however, economism would no longer be economism. Then it would be a threat to bureaucratism. As it stands, economism attempts to remove from the daily order of things, or at least to postpone, the question of creating those democratic institutions which should replace bureaucratic institutions. Essentially, this is an ideology which consciously sacrifices socialist humanism in order to assure eventually a higher degree of economic rationality and thereby to rescue bureaucratism. Thus, a politic of conscious abolition of bureaucratism is necessary in order to assure economic rationality and to rescue and further develop socialist humanism.

5

The Principles of Politics in Liberalism, Fascism, and Socialism

Behind the obvious differences between the theory and practice of liberalism, fascism, and socialism, one can discover the common feature of traditional politics as the "sphere of alienation," a ruthless, immoral, pragmatic struggle for power, in which one individual and social group tends to reduce other individuals and social groups to mere objects. This fact raises the question of whether in the future, politics as such could be transcended altogether and under what conditions social relations and processes could be regulated in a way which is no longer political in the traditional sense. Nevertheless, while we still live in political societies, the differences between various twentieth-century political systems are still of great theoretical and practical importance.

Comparing the political doctrines of liberalism, fascism, and socialism, one may immediately notice one fundamental distinction: the aim of politics and the *raison d'etre* of political institutions is from the point of view of the first: the isolated individual; from the point of view of the second: the nation or the race; from the point of view of the third: the class, the proletariat.

Most liberalist political theorists have held that the primary purpose of the government is to establish and to preserve an order within which all individuals will be secure and free to exercise certain basic rights: to express their views, to assemble, to elect their representatives in the political institutions, to choose where they wish to live and work, to own property, to compete on the market and so forth. The social life is obviously split into two different spheres: the political and the civil. A certain amount of order and collectivity in the former is a necessary condition for freedom and individualism in the latter. The state is construed as an institution which stands above all social groups and above all conflicting class, national, racial, religious, professional, regional, and other particular interests. It takes care of the general interest of the whole social community, and of the interests of all individuals as abstract citizens. It is assumed that the price which the individual has to pay for his security and for freedom in the sphere of civil life is obedience, loyalty, and subordination to the existing law and to the decisions of the existing government.

There is a certain ambiguity in the theory of bourgeois democracy regarding the extent to which the state is an alienated power. From the very concept of a democratic state it follows that the state, in one way or other, should express the general will, rule with the consent of its citizens, and be primarily an instrument for promoting their interests. All the classical works of democracy subscribe to the thesis that ultimate sovereignty rests with the people. And still, a more careful study leads to the conclusion that the classical theory of democracy recognizes that in reality the state is more or less an alienated power, a social structure which rules over people and which is controlled by them only to a limited extent.

Locke realized that the prince and the government

may abuse the rights yielded to them on the basis of a social contract, and that they may actually oppress the people. There is no democratic mechanism by which people can really control the rulers and replace them. The idea of democracy can then be saved only by recognizing the right of people to rebel and to use force to overthrow the government. However, in order to calm those conservative opponents who tend to construe democracy as a state of permanent anarchy, Locke explains that people prefer to bear small injustices rather than to rebel. Thus, real riots can be expected only when abuses reach the level of a permanent tyranny. It is clear that for Locke, democracy does not mean active participation of each citizen in the process of decision making and it does not mean self-management. The very fact that management remains in the hands of a group of people who rule *in the name* of others and with the active or tacit consent of others, in reality often leads to tension, conflict, abuse, and injustice, which has to be tolerated within certain limits.

Grotius spoke explicitly about the formation of the state as *alienation* of certain individual's rights and powers. And Rousseau was well aware of the fundamental problem of bourgeois democracy: it is not and, especially in a big country, it cannot be *direct participatory* democracy. On the other hand, he was extremely skeptical about representative democracy and did not see how people could effectively control their representatives and prevent them from becoming an alienated power. Consequently, his theory of general will is very ambiguous: if the general will is the will of all or of a majority, it is difficult to see how to determine actually what is the general will. National elections cannot be held to decide every important issue. On the other hand, if the general will is not constituted by common elements in individual wills, if it is objectified and identified with the real general interest of people, then at best, it becomes a redundant concept which has not contributed anything to the theory of democracy, because it does not add anything to our knowledge as to how to implement the general interest of people in the operation of the state. At worst it might be used by a totalitarian regime for its self-justification.

Jefferson was well aware of the necessity of alienation of the state, especially with respect to young generations, that he saw the only solution in occasional uprisings and in the reexamination and the change of all laws every twenty years.

However, generational conflict is only one type of conflict between the state and a part of the population. Furthermore, the conflict between generations is usually only a manifestation of a much deeper conflict: between privileged and underprivileged social forces. Young people are not yet strongly committed to one of the classes, they do not yet have firmly entrenched interests and are much more open to humanist and egalitarian aspirations. Therefore, youth tends to be strongly critical toward the existing order and existing forms of social injustice, and at least partly and temporarily, the young come into conflict with the state, which is dedicated to preserving the given order.

The bourgeois state even in its ideal, theoretical form suffers from a fundamental weakness: it assumes the separation of the people into rulers and ruled citizens. Real political life is open only to the former: they struggle, they make decisions, they draft and pass the laws, and they stipulate sanctions to implement their decisions. The latter live a fictitious political life: at best they are informed about what has been decided and they give their consent, they are presented two or more candidates and they vote for one of them, they read in the newspapers what new bills have been passed and have become binding for them. They can express their dissatisfaction by writing letters or abstaining, but, being unorganized, in most cases they cannot have much impact on the centers of political power. They can vote for a different candidate in the next election, but there is no guarantee that if elected he would prove more satisfactory.

In practice, in the context of a society divided into "haves and have-nots," the separation of the rulers from the vast majority of those ruled becomes a much more serious matter. The basic function of the state, to preserve by force the given order, fully coincides with the interest of privileged social classes to preserve the *status quo*. The state becomes essentially a coercive apparatus, which at best combines maximum possible rationality and a minimum of necessary violence in order to direct social processes within the limits of established social structure and the established form of distribution of social wealth.

This is not to deny the importance of political liberties existing in a bourgeois society. Nor it is to deny the enormous importance of the recognition of certain basic human rights which are integrated in the written constitution and law of each democratic state. However, within the context of a society with enormous social differences the practical effect of the recognition of these liberties and rights is far from what the theory of bourgeois democracy promises. The whole conception of political liberty which has been assumed by that theory is extremely *naive* and *superficial.* The assumption is that one is free when he can choose among various existing beliefs and vote for one of political parties and candidates. This is freedom only in comparison to situations where there are no choices whatsoever. But this is very superficial, limited, and sometimes even illusory freedom. Those who control big national political organizations and mass media of communication have overwhelming influence on the formation of habits, the formation of policies, and the selection of candidates. Economic power brings with it political power. And vice versa, political democracy is impossible without economic democracy.

Bourgeois democracy survives under two conditions: (*a*) if it successfully avoids economic crises, secures steady economic progress, and minimizes the political interest of the workers by fully transferring all their attention to day-to-day economic struggle for increasing wages and better work conditions and(*b*) which is a precondition of (*a*): if it introduces gradual social modifications reducing drastic forms of social inequality, while preserving basic structural social differences which effectively keep the vast majority of population in an underprivileged position.

In the absence of these two conditions, social conflicts acquire such a sharp antagonistic form that a society has to face two other solutions each of which starts with the abolition of previous democratic forms:

One is *facism* which uses most brutal forms in order to prevent the further development of class conflicts and which tries to mobilize all social classes for the promotion of national and racial interests.

The other is *socialism* which tends to bring the class conflict to its logical end, to resolve it by smashing up the bourgeois state and by creating a new proletarian state. The task of this temporary, purely transitory instrument is to effect the change of the whole economic structure and to prepare for the abolition of politics and the state itself as a coercive apparatus.

Unlike parliamentary democracy, fascism disregards the interests of individual citizens completely. The individual is completely subordinated to the totality, and the totality is the nation. In that spirit Mussolini spoke of a "superior law" and an "objective will" that "transcends the particular individual and raises him to conscious membership of a spiritual society." He also says that the fascists conception is "against individualism"; it is for the state, and for the individual "only insofar as he coincides with the state."

To be sure all this talk about individuals *spiritual* existence within the state to which he is completely subordinated is a mere mystification. The greater the emphasis on the "spirituality" of a society the more one can expect to find behind that rhetoric a politics devoid of any spirituality, reduced to a naked struggle for power and control over human beings.

The concept of universal will is taken here in a sense quite different from the one accepted in democracy. It is no longer the will of *all* or of *majority* — it is the will of a *few* or even of *one* who succeeds in unifying the multitude and leading it in the struggle for power.

Mussolini admits that the fascist state is totalitarian: "Everything is in the state, nothing human or spiritual exists, much less has value outside the state." "Outside the state there can be neither individuals nor groups (political parties, associations, syndicates, classes)." This means that literally no political activity, which is not controlled and directed by the state and the ruling party would be tolerated.

Of course, even fascists avoid saying that they are against liberty and democracy. "Fascism is for liberty. And for the only liberty which can be a real thing, the liberty of the state and of the individual *within* the state." "The fascist state has limited useless or harmful liberties and has preserved those that are essential." The logic of that essential liberty has been philosophically clarified by Gentille

— this is one of those disgusting examples where the dignity of theoretical thought has been fully used and abused in order to create the appearance of profundity and some hidden rationality beyond quite simple and odious things: "Force and consent are inseparable, the one implies the other. The authority of the state and the freedom of the citizen constitute a continuous circle wherein authority presupposes liberty and liberty authority." This is a disastrous kind of feedback — there is nothing easier than to produce consent by force which will be then reinforced by the consent. What essentially characterizes fascism is not mere totalitarianism, mere destruction of all liberties and glorification of the state. The *structure* of political power is one thing, its *historical meaning* is another. The purpose of fascist totalitarianism is twofold: (*a*) to destroy the labor movement, and to try to force a unity of the whole nation under bourgeois rule, which is otherwise unattainable while class struggle is going on within the nation and (*b*) to mobilize the whole nation for expansion, for conquering other nations and their territories, in other words, to compel the whole nation to fight for typically bourgeois interests.

To a superficial liberal observer it seems that there are striking political similarities between fascists and socialist political systems. In both the state apparatus is extremely powerful and controls all economic, social, and cultural life. In both there is a one-party system. Both tend to develop a cult of the leader. Both tend to glorify the national army. Both tend to intervene militarily and to invade other countries in their own national interest.

But even if we disregard, for the moment, very important differences, the enumerated phenomena are not the same in both cases.

1. The state in postcapitalist countries is no longer an instrument in the hands of bourgeois and petty bour-

geois forces, but the product of a revolution initiated by a well-organized *avant-garde* of the workers' movement. It is true that, historically speaking, the *avant-garde* underwent a process of considerable transformation and emerged as a new ruling elite — a bureaucracy. That is why it did not tend to wither away as Marx, Engels, and Lenin had forecast but increased its scope and power. Still, the primary task of the postcapitalist state is not expansion, but accelerated industrialization, urbanization, and as fast an increase in the standard of living of the population as is possible under the existing condition of struggle with the leading capitalist countries. The goals of present-day socialist states closely resemble the goals of advanced liberal capitalist countries. To be sure, they are vastly different from the goals of an advanced socialist society, which according to Marx would be: free production, elimination of the subordination of individuals in the division of labor, abolition of antagonism between mental and physical labor, universal participation in political decision making, and gradual transcendence of the narrow horizons of bourgeois rights.

2. Some contemporary ideologues of liberalism which reduce democracy to multi-party systems often identify fascism and existing forms of socialism because in both, political power is in the hands of one party, and the existence of any other rival political organization is strictly forbidden. Granted that any such political structure can be labeled as a "dictatorship," still one should not fail to notice some essential differences both in original purpose and in the subsequent trend of development.

Communist parties were created by genuine revolutionaries, individuals who rebelled against existing oppression and social injustice and who in most cases sincerely wished to liberate people of all classes, nations, and races from slavery, poverty, and meaningless drudgery. Fascist parties were created by fanatic nationalists and racists who were ready to use drastic means in order to preserve existing social structures and existing differences, who saw the solution to the problem of poverty and unemployment in grabbing the possessions of other nations and races.

Having an absolute monopoly of political power was for fascists a matter of principle, a consequence of basic natural, biological inequality. For victorious Marxists, at least in the beginning, it was a necessary evil. There is vast empirical evidence that they really believed that both the state and the party should wither away after a brief transitional period. Unlike anarchists, they had enough of a sense of history to realize that a more just, classless society can not be built without some organized power which would abolish old privileges and economic differences and which would lay down the institutional basis for a new culture. According to the Marxist doctrine, the role of the party after the revolution was not supposed to be ruling and controlling all spheres of social life, but political education and the creation of a new social consciousness. The historical fact is that in most socialist revolutions there was a phase in which very strong emphasis was laid on education and search for a new culture. The fact is also that even in a very militant and rigid type of political party such as Lenin's Bolshevik Party there was an initial phase (1917–20) of considerable internal democracy and an unsuccessful attempt to collaborate with other working class parties.

The liberalist critics of socialism sometimes give very superficial accounts of the whole process of transition from a revolutionary vanguard to an authoritarian bureaucracy. At worst, liberalism sticks to the conspiracy theory according to which communists are really not interested in liberation or abolition of exploitation but *solely and from the beginning* in seizing power for the sake of power. At best there is the view, expressed for example by Bertrand Russell in his *The Theory and Practice of Bolshevism*, that keeping political power for a long period of time in the conditions of general backwardness, and facing a hostile and noncooperative peasantry, will bring about considerable changes in the consciousness of the new rulers, no matter how sincere their revolutionary ideals might be in the beginning. There is an important grain of truth in this conception. It is also methodologcally interesting: it starts from a basic assumption of Marxism, namely, that the consciousness of people is conditioned by the objective social conditions of their life. Then, it supplements the current doctrinaire Marxist analysis in economic terms only, by incorporating political power into the concept of objective social conditions. There is no reason to think that the productive forces and the relations of production are always the decisive social infrastructure. Many Marxists have tended in their analyses to neglect the phenomenon of political power as an *objective* and, in certain historical conditions, *decisive* basis of all other social occurrences, including economic development.

And yet, the liberalist critique completely overlooks the fact that in addition to general backwardness and a potential power hunger in some individual revolutionaries, there was another decisive causal factor which compelled victorious revolutionaries to stay in power longer and to be more rigid than they themselves intended. That factor was the counterrevolutionary intervention of foreign powers: sending armies, supporting any kind of domestic resistance, organizing the military, economic and political blockade of the new revolutionary republic. Quite contrary to fascism, in postcapitalist countries a one-party system and political dictatorship is in many cases not the cause but the consequence of the hostility of the surrounding capitalist world.

It should also not be overlooked that even in a communist party which has eventually become a center of alienated political power, in which monolitism, rigid discipline, and hierarchical order have completely replaced initial democratic forms, the ideology still remains basically humanitarian. No matter how much humanism might be abused by bureaucracy it cannot but continue to affect the ordinary behavior of people, to introduce warmth and friendliness into human relations, to encourage egalitarian attitudes, to emphasize the importance of science, culture, education, rationality, and to discourage racialism, open chauvinism, aggressiveness, glorification of war, and all those patterns of behavior which were so characteristic of fascist ideology, which were necessary psychological prerequisites for national expansion and creation of new empires.

3. The existence of the cult of the leader in the time of Stalin, especially in late thirties and until his death, was imitated in the forties and early fifties in almost all socialist countries, and still exists in some of them. This is definitely one of the most negative phenomena of the postrevolutionary developments, one which certainly resembles similar cults in fascism. There is nothing in Marxist theory nor in the life of the first two international communist organizations to indicate the possibility of such authoritarian practices in a postcapitalist society. It is true that Marx had a great influence in the First International, but he obviously was the best brain and the strongest personality there and he was *primus inter pares*. That was a natural relation based on natural talent, strength, and knowledge, not on the power derived from the control of the police and the army. It is true that Marx was rather intolerant toward some of his

opponents, especially Proudhon, Bakunin, Lassalle, and Herzen. But he had to fight for his views, and victory was never guaranteed. Engels had a very prominent place in the Second International especially in the German Social Democracy but he was essentially an adviser not a leader. Lenin definitely was a great leader, the creator of a movement, a man without whom the October uprising would not have happened; he was an overwhelming authority. And still nobody feared him, he had to fight for his views, he always had opposition and several times he was defeated, which still did not jeopardize his leading position.

Compared to Lenin and even to some other leading Bolsheviks, Stalin was a rather insignificant figure. He was not an original mind and was not highly respected as was Lenin. He was not a brilliant speaker like Trotsky, he did not enjoy the reputation of being a theoretician like Bukharin, he was not so well known as Zinoviev. How did he succeed? The answer to this question has an objective and a subjective component.

From the objective point of view there were certain historical conditions which made the appearance of a dictator possible and even desirable.

First, by the end of the Soviet civil war, in 1920–21, the new state faced an almost unsolvable task: it was too backward for socialism, and too ravaged for normal life. It was quite alone, surrounded by a hostile world, devoid of any feeling of security. The European proletariat did not rise to arms as expected; there were uprisings in Hungary and Bavaria but no successful revolutions. On the other hand, there were strikes of hungry workers and uprisings of peasants and sailors in Kronstadt. The Soviet state had to adjust to the entirely new situation. Several Bolshevik leaders thought that there was no alternative but to give up political power and go into the political underground. However, if the revolution was to survive, somebody was needed to introduce order and create a new faith in the possibility of building up socialism in *one* isolated country, to mobilize not only toiling masses but whole nations for the new patriotic task of defending and building up a new socialist fatherland — the Soviet Union. Stalin was the proper man to do the job. His career had been dedicated to the organization, discipline, and running of the Bolshevik party. While Trotsky commanded the Red Army, while Zinoviev worked in the Comintern, while Lenin elaborated basic policies, Stalin worked as organizational secretary of the party and secretary of the Committee for the National Question. All kinds of *apparatchiks* whom he selected and appointed to their posts became key figures in introducing order. While in earlier years Trotsky consistently advocated his theory of permanent revolution, and Lenin preached his view that socialism in only one country was impossible, Stalin kept silent. After Lenin's death, Stalin was the only leader who could stand on his complete conviction that socialism can be and must be built in one country. And he was the only one who was ruthless and cruel enough to demand extreme efforts and extreme sacrifices to achieve the almost impossible task of accelerated industrialization without any capital and without any aid from outside.

Second, after the end of civil war and the end of the NEP there were a number of alternatives open. In the preceding period it was considerably easier to decide what to do: there were hardly any choices. There was a lot of struggle and waste of energy, but again one did what one had to. When the country recovered, that was no longer the case and there were several possibilities. Opposition from the left required more workers' democracy, more initiative in encouraging proletarian revolutions abroad; opposition from the right demanded better opportunities for the peasants and small entrepreneurs; the center under Stalin considered that a strong central state power must refrain from any adventure abroad and concentrate all forces on accelerated industrialization and collectivization of agriculture. Stalin sounded more realistic than Trotsky and more revolutionary than Bukharin. However, this ambitious program of building up an entirely new economy required the unity of the country, and above all full unity of purpose, efficiency, and discipline within the party. For years, after Lenin's death during the NEP, in the absence of any big project, the party was split and spent most of its energy on bitter debates among its factions. By the end of the twenties and when the time came for a new revolutionary offensive, the rank and file were tired of debates and a majority were prepared to conform to any order, to suppress any dissension, to forget about its own freedom for the sake of efficiency.

Here we have to take into account an important social psychological factor: namely, the escape from freedom, an almost masochistic striving of whole collectives of people to escape their unbearable feeling of aloneness and insecurity, to find a powerful person with whom they could identify, to whom they could surrender the burden of freedom and responsibility. For many centuries the Russians identified themselves with the tzars, and it is not mere chance that it was a Russian, Dostoevsky, who first drew attention to the phenomenon of the escape from freedom in *The Brothers Karamazov*, in the famous parable of the Grand Inquisitor. Jesus Christ returns to earth in the sixteenth century and arrives in Spain. The Grand Inquisitor recognizes him and orders the guard to arrest him. That night he visits Jesus in the prison and in a long conversation tries to justify himself — the inquisition — and even the arrest of Jesus. The essence of his argument is that Jesus tried to set mankind free but mankind does not want and can not bear freedom. Freedom makes demands upon it that it cannot meet; it is, therefore, a major cause of suffering. In fact, mankind craves authority, mystery, miracles, and someone to worship.

One has to choose whether to grant mankind what it wants, although this alternative is degrading and demands doing some horrible things. Or one can choose to accord mankind freedom with all its nobility, in which case the decision is cruel for it will torment men. Jesus is that cruel man; he deserves to be charged with inclemency and self-indulgence. The Grand Inquisitor, on the contrary, chose to be humane, to take that terrible gift from mankind, out of compassion and out of mercy, to give mankind authority it wanted. This task is not pure and gratifying; it requires acts which will make him repulsive. But this only shows the depth of his compassion.

This text in which one could easily put Stalin in the place of the Grand Inquisitor and substitute Marx for Jesus, is not only a brilliant irony but also a penetrating analysis of a pattern of mass-behavior which is typical for all Caesaristic political structures. There are historical situations in which very broad masses of people suffer from collective insecurity and anxiety which can be overcome only by a far-reaching depersonalization, the identification with a great leader, and membership in strict organizations and institutions. In such a situation a leader can easily emerge, even if he is not a typical *charismatic* leader, even if he lacks any magic charm and any ability to immediately fascinate large masses of people. Stalin lacked some of the qualities of a charismatic leader: there was nothing magnetic in his personality, he was a poor speaker, and a rather poor demagogue; he did not mix much with ordinary people; and for years he did not move out of the Kremlin. But he had some other abilities which helped him to defeat all his rivals and eventually to become the most powerful leader in recent history. He was cold, rational, extremely clever, and ruthless, but he also had an enormous ability to sense what kind of policy could enjoy support by party cadres, what kind of policy, although bold and demanding, would still be within the limits acceptable to the masses in a given moment.

The myth of Stalin was built up by a bureaucracy which needed him. The bureaucracy endowed him with superhuman and supernatural qualities of wisdom, clairvoyance, courage, steel-like strength of will, and absolute dedication to the working class (which he, in fact, rather despised). The mass media helped to disseminate that image and to reinforce it. Thus, Stalin created bureaucracy. And bureaucracy created him.

Radical social change makes personal dictatorship possible but not inevitable. There are several signposts which, if heeded, can prevent a dictatorial takeover:

1. One must know in advance that certain types of objective historical situations are very favorable for the emergence of leaders who gradually become dictators. Such a situation occurs when a society is in a state of obvious stagnation; the liberal government is too weak to introduce necessary reforms; and the labor movement, while sufficiently strong to intimidate the bourgeoisie, is too weak or too split to seize power. In this situation there is considerable danger of a development toward facism.

Another situation is that in which a socialist revolution has been attempted in a backward, predominantly agrarian country, thus requiring a prolonged use of force and political propaganda in order to mobilize all national resources for accelerated industrialization. Under these conditions a radical social change might be the best solution, but one should be aware of the political consequences in advance and should not expect much political democracy during a relatively long transition period.

2. Contrary to the widespread tendency to glorify political leaders and to identify fully with them, an entirely different political education of the masses is necessary. The people should learn to develop an objective and critical attitude toward their leaders so that they would be loyal to ideas and programs rather than to individual leaders. Such a political education and corresponding change in political attitudes becomes possible and successful only when society reaches such a level of general development as to guarantee everyone a minimum of legal and economic security, and a minimum of general culture necessary for critical thinking. A very important condition for a widespread resistence to any kind of authoritarianism, demagoguery and cult of individual charismatic leaders is free access to the *mass media.* A society which enters a period of radical social change must not allow any kind of monopoly on the mass media of communication. The only possible answer to the monopolizing of mass media by the ruling elite is the creation of unofficial, underground mass media.

3. A society which is in the process of social change must not allow creation of social structures which permit bureaucracy to become the dominant political force.

Even if a dictatorship is successfully avoided, the problem of how people can have real influence in the conduct of government remains. In both socialist and democratic nations the most common form of political organization is the political party. One can seriously question the role of political parties today and several criticisms can be leveled which indicate that they are not suitable for achieving maximum political participation of the people.

Are Political Parties Obsolete?
First, there was a more or less satisfactory democratic political life without political parties. Political parties in the present-day sense of the word did not exist in Germany and France before the middle of the nineteenth century or even as late as the 1870s. The existence of political parties is not a necessary condition of democracy, and they should be gradually replaced by various forms of direct democracy, at least to the extent to which it is possible in very large communities.

Second, the concept of a party as the only form of political organization can be also attacked from the point of view of contemporary experiences with political parties. They increasingly have become centers of alienated political power. They are conveyer belts of increasingly powerful political bureaucracies, and the ordinary citizen is increasingly losing the ability to influence the leadership and the party apparatus. The average citizen does not really participate in the political life, he does not take part in the basic decision-making, he is only invited to give his consent to certain programs and even these programs do not bind the elected candidates. Electoral campaigns are increasingly expensive. Money comes from the wealthier social groups and it is natural that the groups which finance party activities will also have more influence in determining policies after the election of executives. Under such conditions parties do not sufficiently represent various interest groups; rather they represent different tendencies within the economically most powerful interest groups. Therefore, in spite of the competition between two or several parties in a two- or multiparty system there is not much choice for a large number of citizens. The leading parties are all similar and their programs and candidates are also similar.

The result is apathy and a widespread lack of interest in politics.[1] In the long periods between elections, the political arena is left only for political professionals and a limited number of nonprofessional elected representatives. Political education, if there is any, is reduced to brainwashing and mobilization for the next election.

A third possible line of attack on the party as the form of political organization is a criticism from the point of view of present-day optimal possibilities. One can argue that parties as mediators between unofficial and official holders of power are no longer necessary as links between people and government. In a historical period when the vast majority of population lacked energy, education, and time for political activities, parties and party bureaucracies played an important role in organizing people politically, in formulating programs, in controlling governments, and in reconciling conflicts. In an advanced industrial society, once the productivity of labor has reached such a high level that every citizen can satisfy his basic material needs for food, clothing, and lodging, can receive a good education, and have a considerable amount of leisure time at his disposal, professional politicians will no longer be needed as organizers, propagandists, ideologues, and leaders. They will be needed only as experts in the state apparatus in the limited number of jobs where special knowledge and skills are required.

With a withering away of professional politics as a special field in the social division of work, the nature of political organizations might be profoundly changed. One party, in the political systems of the Soviet type, two-parties in systems similar to the United States and Britain, and several parties in systems like those in France and Scandinavia might be gradually replaced by a pluralism of flexible *ad hoc* political organizations which would represent various different interest groups, which would offer incomparably more opportunity for the direct participation of each citizen, and which would offer a much wider range of programs and candidates. The distinguishing characteristics of these political organizations would be the absence of permanent party machines and party bureaucracies. They would no longer be instruments of the privileged elites which keep concentrated economic and political power in their own hands. Instead, they would become forms of genuine political democracy both direct and indirect.

Thus a thesis that parties are obsolete in an advanced industrial society does not mean denial of all kinds of political organization. Nor does it mean that all political functions performed by parties must be rejected. Many of these functions are necessary for political democracy: (*a*) articulating needs, interests and aspirations of various social groups; (*b*) laying down alternative long range and immediate social goals; (*c*) formulating programs for the implementation of these goals; (*d*) integrating large segments of population on certain common goals; (*e*) political education of the masses; (*f*) finding compromise solutions for conflicts among various nationalities, races, religious, classes; (*g*) recruitment and choice of gifted (nonprofessional) political leaders and functionaries; (*h*) the organization of electoral campaigns for the representatives of the given social group or segment; (*i*) control and criticism of the government.

However, not all of these functions demand constant political organization. A good deal of political life in a democratic community could and should be free, spontaneous, and unregimented. And if some of these functions sometimes need organizational effort, the political organization should not have the fixed form of a party, with establishment politicians, who in some respects are similar in all parties in power, no matter whether they serve Breshnyev or Nixon, Franco or Mao.

One of the main arguments for the existence of the parties such as they are today, is that they secure a necessary amount of continuity. What does continuity mean in this context?

If it is continuity of a certain ideology — we see that many parties hardly have any ideology (Democratic, Republican), or they have given up a good deal of their ideology in practice a long time ago (Bolsheviks, Marxism). On the other hand the Fabians had a distinct ideology without ever representing a separate party. Marx himself did not found a party.

If it is continuity of a certain program, of some important social ideas about further development of the country, then these ideas will survive anyway, provided that they are really important and express the real needs of the country and the people. Otherwise a party could secure their continuity only in an artificial way by molding people's beliefs and attitudes through the tremendous force of mass media. In the absence of parties, ideologies, party propaganda, and compulsory political education provided by the powerful party machines — people would be in a better position to examine critically various views and solutions and form their own beliefs and attitudes.

Finally, continuity might also mean the lasting power of party heads, charismatic leaders, or bosses behind the scenes. But it is exactly this kind of continuity which should be eliminated. In the final chapter, we will examine in more detail how government without political parties can be an effective means of achieving true political participation by all the people.

6

The Concept of Revolution

Throughout previous chapters we have spoken frequently of revolution. In view of the manifold ways in which this word is used and abused today, it would be well to examine at some length what is involved in the concept of revolution, particularly within the context of Marxist thought. There are two kinds of questions which arise in connection with the Marxist concept of revolution. The first kind refers to the *theoretical basis* of this concept: how to understand the concept of revolution, and whether revolution is a necessary form of the transition from one type of society to the other, and more specifically, from capitalism to communism. The second group of questions has a *concrete historical character:* Under what conditions are revolutions possible in the contemporary world, and what are their types and phases of development?

The meaning of revolution depends to a large extent on the context in which it is used. While revolution always means an important, radical change, what we regard as "important" and "radical" and, in general, what we recognize as *real change* will depend on the context. If tomorrow a general were to be ousted from power by some other general in Brazil or Bolivia, many world newspapers would write about it as another of those numerous Latin American "revolutions"; but there need not be any reason to regard such a change of regime as a real social change, least of all as revolution.

On the other hand, nobody would hesitate to call the overthrow of the Temporary Interim Menshevik Government on October 25, 1917, a true revolution. However, many authors call the rapid transition to industrialization and a planned economy in Russia in 1930 the *second* Soviet revolution, just as the transition to self-management in Yugoslavia in 1951 is sometimes regarded as the *second* Yugoslav revolution.

Obviously in the first case, under revolution we understand only a radical change in the nature of government, while in the second and third cases we think of a profound change in the economic sphere or in the social structure in general. The problem, then, is whether we shall regard as revolution any radical change in a certain sphere of society or whether we shall apply this concept only when a radical transformation of the totality of society is involved, that is, when the transformation of those social structures and institutions, on which all forms of social life essentially depend, is involved.

This question is by no means so academic as it may appear. If the seizure of power by the party of the working class is *revolution* and not merely the first step in revolution, then all that follows is peacetime development, and the society that we find the day after the "revolution" is already a *new* society in which the emphasis is already on *positive growth* rather than on a series of further *negations.* True revolutionaries are often faced by imprisonment in this "new" society; as a result of revolution, only the jailer has changed. If revolution means a radical abolition of old social relations and their replacement by new and more humane relations in which the area of human freedom has expanded and the prospects of a richer and fuller life for every individual have increased, then revolution is a process which must continue in a variety of forms throughout the whole transition period. During that period there is no room for self-complacency, apology, and ideological rationalization of the existing structure. The vision of a possible more humane future must be a constantly present criterion for critical assessment and direction. Any stabilization can only be temporary and conditional and must necessarily lead towards corresponding forms of self-abolition and transcendence. Any temporary adjustment of people to the existing conditions must be accompanied by the adjustment of the conditions to human needs whose realization has become historically possible.

The concept of revolution, as a much deeper and more radical transformation than the actual seizure of power and change of class character, is not new; nor would we have to single it out if it had not been systematically repudiated in practice by bureaucratic groups in socialist countries.

However, two questions connected with this concept remain unsolved even at the theoretical level. The first is: if revolution is a radical social transformation affecting not only the sphere of politics, but also the economy, culture, and everyday life as a whole, can it consist only of a series of violent changes, catastrophes, and convulsions? Or is it an ensemble of changes which can be peaceful, gradual, and "evolutive"? The problem is that certain very abrupt, convulsive changes have not brought any great actual transformations (for instance the "big leap forward" in China in 1959 or the general strike in France of May, 1968), while certain very important social changes have been brought about peacefully: decolonization after World War

II, the introduction of planning and the managerial revolution in contemporary capitalism, the reduction of major social differences in Sweden and other Scandinavian countries, and the transition to self-management in Yugoslavia. But if we accept the second alternative, the question arises: Have we not expanded the meaning of the concept of "revolution" so much that it loses all informative value? Important changes take place in every historical epoch. Then is not every historical epoch revolutionary in a certain sense? Obviously this approach to the concept of revolution can be avoided only if (*a*) we distinguish the epoch of *growth* from the epoch of *transcending* a total social structure and (*b*) if we establish precisely the *basic limit* of a social structure which will be abolished during the period of its transcendence. The establishment of such a limit is at the same time a general, basic definition of the sum total of changes which constitute a revolution, regardless of whether they are violent or comparatively peaceful.

Marx and the Concept of Revolution

In Marxist literature the question of socialist revolution has frequently been reduced to the question of the *collapse* of capitalist society. A basis for this reduction can be found in some of Marx's texts — those in which he speaks as a political activist and concentrates on the immediate tasks of practical struggle. However, Marx's general theoretical views provide a basis for a much wider and more articulate concept of revolution.

In his earliest writings (1843–45), Marx speaks about revolution in terms of a "revolt against degradation" (the same words had already been used by Hegel) and complete human emancipation. According to him,

> The possessing class and the proletarian class express the

> same human alienation. But the former is satisfied with its situation, feels itself well established in it, recognizes this self-alienation as *its own* power, and thus has the *appearance* of a human existence. The latter feels itself crushed by this self-alienation, sees in it its own impotence and the reality of an inhuman situation. It is, to use an expression of Hegel's, in the midst of degradation the *revolt* against degradation, a revolt to which it is forced by the contradiction between its humanity and its situation, which is an open, clear and absolute negation of its humanity.[1]

Marx's standpoint here is not one of abstract moralizing humanism: it does not expect emancipation to be the consequence of a higher moral consciousness; it is the result of a social development which is unconscious and involuntary. The proletarians are not the agents of emancipation because they are morally superior and have noble and unselfish social aims.

> On the contrary, in the fully developed proletarian, everything human is taken away, even the *appearance* of humanity. In the conditions of existence of the proletariat are condensed all the conditions of existence of present-day society in their most inhuman form. Man has lost himself, but he has not only acquired, at the same time, a theoretical consciousness of his loss, he has been forced, by an ineluctable, irremediable and imperious *distress* — by practical *necessity* — to revolt against this inhumanity. It is for those reasons that the proletariat can and must emancipate itself. But it can only emancipate itself by destroying its own conditions of existence. It can only destroy its own conditions of existence by destroying *all* the human conditions of existence of pres-

ent-day society, conditions which are epitomized in its situation. It is not in vain that it passes through the rough but stimulating school of *labor*. It is not a matter of knowing what this or that proletarian, or even the proletariat as a whole, *conceives* as its aims at any particular moment. It is a question of knowing *what* the proletariet *is*, and what it must historically accomplish in accordance with its *nature*.[2]

In this way Marx overcomes two difficulties implicit in any conception of a radical social change: (*a*) Does not a change for the better involve the existence of a morally superior consciousness and will, and how are these to arise among the most degraded and uneducated social groups? (*b*) Does not every change lead only to the substitution of one ruling class for the other?

As to the former, Marx's solution is that the necessity of revolting against degradation and inhumanity gives rise to an objective mass movement which may open the way to a new society independently of any conscious goals. As to the latter, capitalism, according to Marx, has brought about a new and unique situation: for the first time in history an oppressed class, the proletariat, cannot emancipate itself without abolishing itself, and without destroying *all* the inhuman conditions of existence.

The difficulty with this view is the tacit assumption that the revolt against degradation is *inevitable*, that the proletariat *must* emancipate itself, that emancipation is a *necessary* result of an objective social process.

In its economic development, private property advances toward its own dissolution. . . . The proletariat carries out the sentence which private property by creating the proletariat passes upon itself, just as it carries out the sen-

> tence which wage labor, by creating wealth for others and poverty for itself, passes upon itself.[3]

The problem is how one can become free without freely choosing freedom? How can a necessary process ever bring about a consciousness which is more than a consciousness of necessity? How can a reified society ever lead to emancipation and give rise to a behavior which is no longer reified?

The dilemma is: Either one has to wait for such a total deterioration of the workers' conditions of existence that an eruption of revolt will follow with the *necessity of a natural law,* and this eruption will wipe out the forms of old society. Or emancipation is only a *historical possibility,* and workers have to become aware of it, to choose it, and to engage in it to the extent of risking whatever they have already achieved.

The first alternative presupposes (*a*) that workers' conditions of existence necessarily deteriorate, (*b*) that there is a strict determination in social processes, and (*c*) that the very destruction of an inhuman social form necessarily leads to the abolition of alienation. All three assumptions turn out to be false. (*a*) Workers are still degraded and alienated, but their conditions of existence slowly improve, they may even be "satisfied with their situation," may "feel themselves well established in it." (*b*) Unlike natural events, a rebellion is never strictly determined, and it cannot be predicted with certainity. Human suffering does not have either a lower limit, beyond which collective rebellion becomes inevitable, or an upper limit, beyond which it becomes impossible. (*c*) There is no *greatest* possible evil for men. The destruction of one definite evil may liberate, but it may also lead to an even greater evil. As a matter of fact, some contemporary revolutions have destroyed some conditions of alienation (for example, private property), while at the same time they have strengthened other conditions of alienation (such as, the state, and political authority).

Therefore, if one prefers to accept Marx's conception of revolution as human emancipation, one has to abandon the language of *necessity* and speak in terms of *historical possibility,* and one has to do justice to the subjective, conscious, goal-oriented human activity instead of relying on an implicit unconscious echatology of the historical process.

Another essential weakness of Marxist thinking about the problem of revolution has been a readiness to overemphasize the importance of a *political* revolution, and a failure to realize its essential limitations, and inherent dangers.

In his article "On the Jewish Question," written in 1843, Marx made a clear distinction between *human emancipation* and *political emancipation:*

> Political emancipation is . . . a dissolution of the old society, upon which the sovereign power, the alienated political life of the people rests. Political revolution is a revolution of civil society.[4]

It overthrows the political power of a ruler and his servants, "it makes state affairs — the affairs of the people," it "makes the political state a matter of general concern."[5] In this early period, French revolution was obviously the model of a political revolution for Marx. That is why he took political revolution to be the dissolution of the old civil (feudal) society: "The political revolution therefore *abolished* the *political* character of civil society. It dissolved civil society into its basic elements, on the one hand *individuals,* on the other hand the *material and cultural elements* which formed the life experience and the civil situation of these individuals."[6]

The essential feature of the political emancipation is the fact that it polarizes men into *egoistic individuals* with private interests and liberty to engage in business, and *citizens,* parts of the political state where they have definite, recognized rights and where their relations with other individuals are regulated by *law.*[7]

While the former is "man in his sensuous, individual, and *immediate* existence," the latter "political man is only abstract, artificial man, man as an *allegorical moral being.*" Therefore, Marx concludes:

> Human emancipation will only be complete when the real, individual man has absorbed in himself the abstract citizen, when as an individual man, in his work, and in his relationships, he has become a *social being,* and when he has recognized and organized his own powers (forces propres) as social powers, and consequently no longer separates this social power from himself as political power.[8]

One year later, in his articles in *Vorwärts,* Marx generalized the concept of political revolution and made a distinction between *political* and *social* revolution. "Every revolution breaks up the *old society;* to this extent it is *social.* Every revolution overthrows *the existing ruling power;* to this extent it is political."[9]

Social revolution is more profound and more important than the mere political revolution. A worker's own labor excludes him from social life, which is the true life of man, and this exclusion is "much more complete, more unbearable, dreadful, and contradictory than the exclusion from political life. So also the ending of this exclusion, and even a limited reaction, a *revolt* against it, is more fundamental, as *man* is more fundamental than *citizen, human life* more than *political life.* The industrial revolt may thus be *limited,* but it has a *universal* significance; the *political* revolt may be universal, but it conceals under a *gigantic* form a *narrow* spirit."[10]

This narrow spirit is characteristic of any one-sided political thinking. "Because the proletariat thinks politically it sees the source of bad social conditions in *will* and all the means of improvement in *force* and the *overthrow* of a particular form of state."[11] As a consequence, workers waste their forces "on foolish and futile uprisings which are drowned in blood." "Their *political* understanding obscured from them the roots of their social misery; it distorted their insight into their real aims and *eclipsed* their *social instinct*."[12]

Another much more serious consequence of a reduction of revolution to its mere political aspect is the emergence of a new ruling group. In 1971, while reading the lines written by Marx in 1844, one has the impression that they refer to our time and that Marx explains there the causes of bureaucratization of all socialist revolutions in the twentieth century (which were all predominantly political ones).

The standpoint of a political revolution is

> that of the state, an *abstract* whole, which *only* exists by virtue of its separation from real life, and which is *unthinkable* without the *organized* opposition between the universal idea and the individual existence of man. Revolution of a political kind also organizes, therefore, in accordance with this narrow and *discordant* outlook, a ruling group in society at the expense of society.[13]

As early as 1844 Marx saw quite clearly both (*a*) that socialism cannot develop *without* political revolution and (*b*) that socialism cannot develop if the revolution *stops with* its political phase: "Without *revolution socialism* cannot develop. It requires this *political act* as it needs the *overthrow* and the *dissolution.* But as soon as its *organizing activity* begins, as soon as its *own purpose* and spirit come to the fore, socialism sheds *political* covering."[14]

What happens, then, with politics in the process of socialist development? What does it mean to say that the individual man becomes a *social* being, and has no more need to separate his own *social* power from himself as *political* power? Marx gave a concrete answer in 1847 in his *Poverty of Philosophy:*

> The working class, in the course of its development, will substitute for the old civil society an association which will exclude classes and their antagonism and there will no longer be any political power, properly so-called, since political power is precisely the official expression of the antagonism in civil society.[15]

This is one of the very early formulations of the idea of self-management. The road to it has to be opened through what Marx called in that text "total revolution," which is the most complete expression of class struggle, and, at the same time, the end of a society founded on the *opposition* of classes.

Nevertheless, while he retains a critical attitude toward politics and any political power, Marx keeps insisting that the general reconstruction of society must start with an overthrow of the old political order. Furthermore he emphasizes that political revolution must have a violent, bloody form:

> Let us not say that the social movement excludes a political movement. There is no political movement which is not at the same time social. It is only in an order of things that are no longer classes and class antagonism,

that *social evolution* will cease to involve *political revolution.* Until then, the last word of social science, on the eve of every general reconstruction of society, will always be:

> "*Le combat ou la mort; la lutte sanguinaire ou le neant. C'est ainsi que la question est invinciblement posée.*"
> (George Sand)[16]

In the *Manifesto of the Communist Party* Marx maintains that a "more or less veiled civil war is raging within existing society, up to the point where that war breaks out into open revolution, and where the violent overthrow of the bourgeoisie lays the foundation for the withering away of the proletariat."[17]

In this militant text there is a strong emphasis on the cataclysmic character of the workers' revolution.[18] Contrary to his earlier views, he speaks here about "the conquest of political power by the proletariat" (not about the abolition of political power as an alienated *social* power).[19] It is true, he says, "the Communist revolution is the most radical rupture with traditional property relations: no wonder that its development involves the most radical ruptures with traditional ideas" (about freedom, property, family, nationalism, religion and morality).[20] But he also, for the first time, speaks about the formation of the workers' *state* as the result of the overthrow of the bourgeois political power:

> . . . the first step in the revolution by the working class is to raise the proletariat to the position of ruling class, to win the battle of democracy. The proletariat will use its political supremacy to wrest, by degrees, all capital from the bourgeoisie, to centralize all instruments of production in the hands of the state, i.e. of the proletariat organized as the ruling class. . . .[21]

Granted that this evolution of Marx's views toward the idea of "proletariat as a ruling class" and toward the idea of a workers' state (which, in a series of steps has to revolutionize the old mode of production and transform profoundly the old social order) was a practical necessity and a sign of Marx's growing sense of reality, the question remains: If political power is *alienated* power (presupposing a ruling elite which mediates among citizens) how is this new alienation to be overcome? How is this new state to "wither away," what is there in the state itself (even one of this new type, "organized, armed proletariat") to secure a process of gradual self-abolition?

Theoretically Marx has seen the way out and the solution is still valid:

> When in the course of development, class distinctions have disappeared, and all production has been concentrated in the hands of a vast association of the whole nation, the public power will lose its political character. Political power, properly so called, is merely the organized power of one class for oppressing another. If the proletariat during its contest with the bourgeoisie is compelled, by the force of circumstances, to organize itself as a class, if by means of a revolution, it makes itself the ruling class, and as such, sweeps away by force the old conditions of production, then it will, along with these conditions, have swept away the conditions for the existence of class antagonisms and of classes generally, and will thereby have abolished its own supremacy as a class.
>
> In place of the old bourgeois society, with its classes and class antagonisms, we shall have an association, in which the free development of each is the condition for the free development of all.[22]

It is clear from this passage that for Marx the ultimate goal of a communist is a *radical economic and political democratization:* a full freedom of development for each *individual* (not class or party, or any other mediator among individuals). However, it is not at all clear how to dismantle organized political power once it has been established on a new ground. It is true, Marx never speaks about the power of the party, or of the *avant-guarde* of any kind — he keeps speaking about the power of the whole workers' class. But experience has shown how easy it is for a small group within a class to monopolize the power of the whole class, and to manipulate the vast majority of the class. Marx could not have foreseen Stalinism. But Rousseau was aware of the inherent difficulties in the formation and expression of the general will. He strongly suspected that there was always a danger of people's representatives alienating themselves from the people. Unfortunately, Marx was not so suspicious and he did not realize that this problem, far from being specific for liberal bourgeois democracy, holds for any organized human society. Only much later in his analysis of the Paris Commune, did Marx learn from experience how the problem has to be dealt with.

> The Commune was formed of the municipal councillors, chosen by universal suffrage in the various wards of the town, responsible and revocable at short terms. The majority of its members were naturally working men, or acknowledged representatives of the working class. . . . From the members of the Commune, downwards, the public service had to be done at *workmen's wages.* The vested interests and the representation allowances of the high dignitaries of state disappeared along with the high dignitaries themselves. Public functions ceased

> to be the private property of the tools of the Central Government. Not only municipal administration but the whole initiative hitherto exercised by the state was laid into the hands of the Commune.[23]

In the decades which followed, few people bothered to put all the pieces of the Marx's theory of revolution together. His more sophisticated, philosophical ideas about human emancipation and politics as a sphere of alienation were forgotten, or even rejected (as immature, Hegelian, or youthful utopian visions); the later insights from his historic writings were overlooked. What survived vividly in the consciousness of many generations of Marxists were simple ideas from the militant, programatic, popular texts. Socialist revolution was widely accepted to mean a violent, political overthrow of the bourgeois rule and the establishment of the workers' state ("the dictatorship of the proletariat"), which is supposed to *build up* a new "socialist" society (whatever this term might mean).

Marx later allowed the possibility of a peaceful socialist revolution under certain conditions (in England and Holland during his time).[24] Engels even went as far in the revision of his and Marx's earlier views as to prefer legal, parliamentary means of struggle to "illegal and *revolutionary* tactics" [!].[25]

This new more flexible approach was received with considerable interest in the international social-democrat movement but it was ignored by the Third International. Nevertheless in both cases the revolution was construed as a sudden, catastrophic event which requires many years of preparation, organized resistance and political education — directed and controlled by the well-organized revolutionary *avant-garde* — *The Party.*

Concepts of Revolution in Contemporary Conditions

The view of the German social democrats was best expressed by Bebel at the Erfurt Congress when he said that "the capitalist society itself is preparing the ground for its own ruin at full speed and we have only to wait for the moment when power will slip from their hands." In the same style Kautsky said innumerable times that the party could do nothing better than get itself ready for the decisive *mass* revolution when the suitable moment arrived.

This apparently radical theory, with all its mechanical determinism and the optimistic assumption that capitalism itself inevitably leads to revolution which only has to be met in readiness, was in fact the expression of a practice which was already highly reformistic.

In 1896, when Bernstein published his series of articles in *Neue Zeit,* he merely openly expressed this reformism and tried to prove that the existing facts did not offer any ground for hope of an inevitably approaching downfall of capitalism. For the growing poverty of the mass of workers did not come about nor did such a concentration of capital as was to be expected according to Marx's theory, nor, in his view, were economic crises unavoidable — these were the basic premises of the thesis of the inevitable collapse of capitalism. Regardless of how right Bernstein factually was (and in many respects he was not, especially in his assessment of economic crises), his basic reformistic thesis "goals are nothing, movement is everything" contains a revolutionary element. For if a movement is socialist at all, it must by itself possess a revolutionary character and not only *prepare* for a future event which alone will be regarded as revolution. The questions are: What actually makes a movement socialist? What is the totality which lends revolutionary meaning to every action within a movement?

Rosa Luxemburg transcended the reformism of both Bernstein and the social-democratic center by her concept of revolution as a *series* of catastrophes:

> The more capital, by means of militarism throughout the world and at home, liquidates the noncapitalist classes and aggravates the living conditions of all working people, the more does the daily history of the accumulation of capital throughout the world become a continual chain of political and social catastrophes and convulsions which, combined with periodical economic catastrophes in the form of crises, will prevent the continuation of capitalist accumulation . . . even before capitalism reaches the natural limits of its economic development.[26]

Rosa Luxemburg too found it necessary to emphasize what is not indispensable in the theory of revolution. What Marx understood as the epoch of the "fundamental transformation" of society she presented as a series of catastrophes. The far more vital question of what constitutes the "fundamental transformation," was either not at all specified or was dealt with in an inadequate manner. The basic change is reduced to the abolition of private ownership of the means of production and to the introduction of planned production in the place of anarchic production.

This defect can also be found in three leading theoreticians of the Soviet society — Lenin, Trotsky, and Bukharin. Their idea of revolution is incomparably more concrete and contains radically new elements: fatalism and faith in the decisive role of the spontaneous movement of the masses have been replaced by activism and the belief that the historical process can be guided in a revolutionary direction, even though all the historical conditions for the transcendence of capitalism have not yet matured.

As early as 1905–06, Helphand (Parvus) and Trotsky

developed the theory of permanent revolution, according to which, even in an undeveloped country like Russia, the proletariat can take over the leadership of the masses and win first a democratic revolution and then abolish private ownership of the means of production and begin building socialism. Lenin, who had long believed that the democratic and the socialist revolution must be separated by a long historical period, took the view in the spring of 1917, that the latter can quickly follow after the former, primarily owing to the special conditions created by war. Thus, revolution need not begin in a country with highly developed productive forces, but it can begin in a country which forms the weakest link in the chain of imperialism.

In his *Program of the Communist International* of 1928, Bukharin distinguished three kinds of revolutionary movement: the classical proletarian revolution which breaks out in a developed country; a combination of proletarian revolution and peasant rebellion which occurs in semideveloped capitalist countries; and finally, the revolutionary movement of several oppressed classes in colonial and dependent countries.[27] Each of these movements increases the general crisis of capitalism. Finally "the capitalist system as a whole reaches the point of its final collapse and the dictatorship of financial capital is replaced by the dictatorship of the proletariat."[28] Consequently, the establishment of the dictatorship of the proletariat is the essence of socialist revolution.

In practice, at last in the beginning, the dictatorship of the proletariat was understood to be a truly democratic form of government — with very broad freedoms within the party and in the press and public life. In 1917, the Bolsheviks offered the Mensheviks and the Social Revolutionaries participation in the government. Negotiations broke down and no coalition came about because of the Social Revolutionaries' demand that Lenin and Trotsky should not be included in the government. However, even during the most difficult and critical days of the civil war a legal opposition still existed in Russia, while in the party itself decisions were adopted only after bitter struggles between individual groups formed *ad hoc*. Lenin, the undisputed leader of the party, found himself more than once in the minority group. One of the first decrees of the Council of People's Commissars after October, 1917, was the abolition of the death penalty, despite Lenin's opposition. The first public appearance of Stalin, Commissar for Nationalities, took place at the Finnish Social Democratic Party's Congress in Helsinki in mid-November, 1917, when he proclaimed Finland's independence.

But as a result of the well-known coincidence of tragic historical circumstances, the dictatorship of the proletariat soon began to take on a new aspect. The Bolsheviks could neither realize awakened hopes nor could they give up their efforts at a moment when success seemed at hand. They had promised the country peace in the belief that the proletariat of the Central Powers would cease fighting against a Russian government of workers and peasants and turn their arms against their own rulers. However, the Germans continued advancing. When the Bolsheviks captured General Krasnov after his abortive march on Petrograd, they set him free on his word of honor that he would not resume fighting. The general gave his word but soon afterwards set himself at the head of White Army forces in the South. This meant taking up arms.

The independence of Finland meant in fact the reestablishment of the power of the Finnish bourgeoisie. Bukharin and Derjinski accused Stalin of making concessions to the bourgeois nationalism of small nations. Soon afterwards (in February, 1921) the Red Army occupied by force the Georgian Republic and drove out the Menshevik government.

In June, 1918, the Mensheviks and the right-wing Social Revolutionaries were outlawed because of the cooperation of some of their members with the White Guard. Following a series of revolts and assassinations and after the murder of Uricky and Volodarsky and the serious wounding of Lenin by the Social Revolutionaries, brutal mass terror began.

In March, 1921, the revolt of sailors began in Kronstadt, then one of the Bolsheviks' principal strongholds. The sailors called for the promised freedom, the authority of the Soviets, and the discontinuation of the dictatorship of the Bolshevik party. The Red Army had to fight against proletarians. The revolt was suppressed in blood. Then followed the struggle against the "Workers' Opposition" within the party itself. The Tenth Congress (1921) adopted a resolution prohibiting opposition groups within the party. A Central Control Commission was set up with the task of carrying out periodical purges.

At the party congress, the first to be held in the absence of the ailing Lenin, Stalin, replying to a critic (Lutovinov) who demanded more freedom of discussion within the party (and who soon afterwards committed suicide), used for the first time a phrase which was to be faithfully repeated by all Stalinists in suitable circumstances, that is, that "the party is not a debating club."

At the Thirteenth Congress Trotsky, forced to his knees under the relentless attacks of the Stalin-Zinoviev-Kamenev triumvirate, was to utter another famous phrase — without which Stalinism would hardly have been possible:

> One *must not* be right against the party. One can be right only with and through the party because history has not created any other way for the realization of what is right. The English have a proverb: "My country, right or wrong." With much more historical justification we can say: "My party right or wrong in any particular situation."[29]

In October, 1926, the first *public self-criticism* of a whole group of party leaders — Trotsky, Zinoviev, Kamenev, Piatakov, Sokolnikov, and others — occurred. A year later, Bukharin with tears in his eyes, was to ask the Politbureau for forgiveness because of a single private conversation he had had with Kamenev. By the end of 1929, all rivals, the famous October leaders, had been eliminated, Trotsky expelled from the country, and others removed from leading positions.

The dictatorship of the proletariat had turned into the dictatorship of the leader. This is not the place to discuss in what measure this transformation was objectively founded on any need for centralist methods in the process of accelerated industrialization in a very backward country. The important thing is that this process was accepted by Marxists as more or less normal. In the existing theory of revolution there was nothing that would obviously contradict what happened during the practical implementation of the first successful socialist revolution. Private ownership of the means of production was actually abolished. Forced industrialization was designed to create an affluent society. Anarchic capitalist production was replaced by planning. Did not Stalin express the will of the party of the proletariat? Was the party not the *avant-garde* of the proletariat?

In the Soviet Union, China, and Yugoslavia, in Cuba and other socialist countries, however, certain relations, institutions, and structures have survived which are also present in all forms of class society and which have not been essentially changed by revolution or been clearly proposed as objectives of revolution.

First, various, more or less concealed, forms of exploitation have survived. The idea of exploitation was narrowed and reduced to that special form which develops in the productive relationship of capitalist and worker. However, *in its most general meaning* the usurpation of the surplus of value on the part of individuals and social groups remains unaffected in any society where the principle of remuneration according to work is not consistently applied and commodity production prevails. It is irrelevant whether this usurpation is perpetrated by individual capitalists or by collectives on the basis of market monopoly, momentary favorable market conditions, or favorable import-export regulations. It does not matter whether the surplus of labor of the working class is usurped by capitalists in the form of profits and on the basis of ownership of the means of production, or by bureaucrats in the form of excessive salaries and privileges on the basis of unrestricted control of social objectified work.

The phenomenon of the alienation of political power has also survived. The initial successes of revolution, primarily the seizure and stabilization of the new revolutionary authority, are possible only insofar as the *avant-garde* of the movement really expresses the mind and will of the working class and the mass of people who support the movement. However, the new authority fails to realize many of its proclaimed objectives; then it decides that it must act in the interest of the proletariat even though against the momentary wishes of the proletariat. The measure in which administration and political activity become a profession, permanently restricted to a small number of chosen,loyal, and deserving individuals, will determine the extent to which politics will become an alienated activity. Then the political institutions of the new authority cease to be a form of real mediation of the will of the revolutionary masses and become institutions for manipulation and coercion. Thus, in the sphere of economics and in the sphere of politics the individual still has more or less the status of an object. The self-management system in Yugoslavia has introduced the process of transcending this state of affairs. This process is still in its initial phase, and is more of a reformist than a revolutionary nature. It is developing slowly. It has earnestly tackled but not yet radically transcended the economic and political monopolies of bureaucracy. Its future is uncertain. If it does not develop quicker after the disappearance of the generation of great revolutionary leaders who came to power in 1943–45, self-management will be reduced to only an appendage of a basically statist system.

The most essential thing in the concept of revolution is neither the use of force, nor the existence of a mass movement, nor a change of the nature of government, and not even the collapse of the social system as a whole; none of these is a necessary or sufficient condition for a real progressive transformation of social relations. *The essential characteristic of revolution is a radical transcendence of the essential internal limit of a certain social formation.*

Consequently, the basic theoretical question of revolution is the establishment of this essential internal limit. Only when we establish which basic social institutions make a society nonrational and inhuman, only when we establish the historical possibility and the paths for abolishing these institutions and replacing them by others which ensure more rational and more humane social relations, can our idea of revolution become sufficiently clear and concrete. Only then can we avoid becoming victims of the fallacies of *false avant-gardism.* These fallacies appear in two basic forms. One form is *pseudo-avant-gardism* which regards a movement whose objectives in fact are not radical as revolutionary. It also regards as revolution an ordinary reform of a system which only has certain external radical qualities such as extreme leftist phrases, a romantic negativist symbolic, an organization which condemns the existing society as a whole, without a clear idea of which of its key institutions have to be transcended, abolished, or preserved as part of the new and more progressive institutions of the future society.[30]

The other form of *false avant-gardism* is the *myth of the old avant-gardism* which emerges when a social group successfully completes the initial part of revolution, seizes power, changes its social being, and assumes a conservative role while, at the same time, trying to preserve its former revolutionary ideology. This is dictated not only by the need to preserve illusions about itself, but also by the need to maintain spiritual contact with the mass of the people in whose name it originally acted. Both needs are satisfied by careful cultivation of traditions from the past revolutionary period on the one hand, and by ideological mystification of the existing relations on the other.

Admittedly it is difficult to avoid the fallacies of *false avant-gardism* and to pinpoint the internal limits of an existing social formation. Reality has several different strata and thus, also several different limits and possible negations, and each of them depends on our general systems of values on the one hand, and on a correct assessment of real historical possibilities on the other. The establishment of the essential internal limit of a social formation depends on the following premises:

1. A social formation has its particular economic, po-

litical, social, and cultural dimensions. It is, therefore, possible to restrict oneself to only one of them and refer separately to political, economic, social, or cultural revolution. What we are primarily concerned with here is *the totality of society*, and thus *integral revolution* which would embrace all these spheres (which, after all, cannot be sharply divided from one another). But even if the question is put in this way, the fact remains that social reality consists of different strata: market economy in general, capitalist market economy, a specific form of capitalism.

The internal limit of various particular forms of capitalism (liberal, monopolistic, state capitalism) is the control of objectified work based on private ownership of the means of production. The abolition of this limit certainly has a revolutionary character, but private ownership may be replaced by state ownership. The internal limit of capitalism as such is production for profit and the appropriation of profit by the owners and professional managers. However, the ultimate basis of any contemporary society (its deepest stratum) is commodity production; its internal limit is the fetishism of commodities and the alienation of labor.

Thus an answer to the question on revolution presupposes the specification of the problem: Do we have in mind the transformation of private capitalism or of capitalism in general or, the most radical transformation, of class society based on commodity production and alienation of labor?

2. How the question of revolution is to be posed depends, however, on how we understand the relationship of practice and the existing historical reality. The opposite extremes are the opportunistic positivism of *Realpolitik* and the voluntaristic utopianism of revolutionary romanticism.

The former assumes that practical activity should be

adjusted to what is necessary in the social process or what is the "objectively dominant, prevailing tendency." If the majority of the workers are really interested exclusively in a higher income and higher living standards, then not only can the beginning of revolution be linked exclusively with a possible catastrophic weakening of imperialism on an international level, but the social transformation itself will not be understood radically enough. It will be conceived primarily as a change of the nature of government. The commodity monetary relations will be largely left untouched because the producers "objectively tend to behave as commodity producers." The bureaucratic structure of society will be left untouched because the workers "objectively tend to leave the burden and responsibility of decision-making to experts, managers, and professional politicians." No real cultural revolution will take place because the mass of people "objectively prefer entertainment music to Mozart and western films to Shakespeare." Revolutionary action which bases the concept of objective historical possibilities on the law of large numbers ends in reformism and not infrequently in counterrevolution.

Romantic utopianism, on the other hand, admits no social determination and takes the line that before action all possibilities are open, that the spirit of utopia rather than the spirit of critical knowledge should be followed and that thus one must commit oneself to what is the most humane, regardless of how objectively possible it is. The idea of what is historically negative becomes very broad and truly radical: it embraces not only production for profit, but also commodity production in general; not only deformations of modern technology, but also technology in general; not only bureaucracy, but also any organization and institutionalism; not only a positivistic understanding and application of science, but also all planning and rational calculation. In relying on the logic of the heart and pleading for full liberty and spontaneity, extreme radicalism can help to create undreamed of new possibilities, expand accidentally the area of real human freedom, and play the highly important role of catalyst by attracting attention to cleverly concealed real problems, exposing all the brutalities of the existing authority, and awakening immense latent energies. But all this is a matter of chance. To dispute *everything* in a society means to dispute even what in existing historical conditions, at least for a time period, should be preserved in the new society. This leads to a failure to pinpoint what really can be transcended. Revolution understood romantically is either revolution in thought only, or, if an attempt at political realization, only a preliminary catalytic phase of real revolution.

Historical reality is not only what dominates, but also what is rare and exceptional; not only what now factually *is*, but also what tomorrow *can be if we become committed in a definite manner.* Whether something can or cannot be is a matter not only of intuition and imagination, but also of the rational assessment which should precede action. Neither are all possibilities open, nor are they all excluded except one. Everything can be that is not excluded through the action of certain social laws in a certain historical situation. Naturally, laws must not be reified: they are only regularities of human behavior which can be changed if this behavior ceases to be spontaneous, or haphazard, and becomes conscious and premeditated. Since the behavior of all people in every aspect cannot be changed so radically that all laws cease to be valid, many logical possibilities are in fact not realized. Among those which are open, revolutionary commitment attempts to achieve not those which are the most probable, but those which are the most humane and most rational, even though they may border almost on the limit of impossibility.

3. The establishment of the essential negation of a social formation thus depends on three kinds of assumptions: (*a*) on the specification of the system whose negation is involved; on this will depend what can be regarded as essential and what is inessential; (*b*) on critical knowledge of the historical situation in which the given system exists. Only by considering the existing lawful tendencies of human behavior can we say which social institutions and structures can be transcended; (*c*) on a certain value orientation which rests on the concept of real human needs and, in the last resort, on a critical philosophical anthropology. Only when we have a definite idea of what man is, what in given historical conditions he can be, and which of his essential needs can be realized, can we establish what is negative in existing reality and what are the institutions which prevent man from being what he can be.

Every practical activity explicitly or implicitly starts from a certain idea of the negative things which should be eliminated. For positivistic realism, the negative is what impedes growth and the effective functioning of the existing. The anthropological assumption here is that man *is* what factually predominates in his present behavior, that his needs can be established by empirical study of his choice between alternative possibilities. Naturally, a complete neglect of such empirical facts would lead to a radical departure from reality. On the other hand, however, the uncritical acceptance of empirical facts means definitely remaining within the limits of the existing, and giving up revolutionary activity which should transcend those limits. Every producer is able to participate in economic and political decision-making, even though empirical investigations may establish the phenomenon of escape from freedom and a one-sided preoccupation with income. Every man has the ability to find pleasure in works of art if he acquires the necessary education. Certainly, if society is not organized so that it enables every individual to reach the level which society as a whole had already attained, any "objective" investigation will show that a huge majority of the people "freely" choose to remain on the level of folklore and shoddy entertainment.

Utopian romanticism, on the other hand, starts from an abstract and unhistorical anthropology. It does not put the question of what man can be *in a definite historical situation* by transcending one form of society and entering another which, though more humane and more rational, still has certain essential inevitable limitations. In the absence of mediation by such concrete historical knowledge, utopian romanticism poses the question of the realization of unlimited and unconditional freedom, creativity, social solidarity, and human spontaneity. This leads to disputing the existing society *in toto;* all its institutions are on the whole negative, because they put limitations on this unlimited, absolute ideal.

Philosophical anthropology which draws inspiration from Marx (both from Marx, the author of *Economic and Philosophical Manuscripts,* and from Marx as the author of *Das Kapital*) has a historical character. Its view of man and human needs is concretely general and many-layered. It contains not only the idea of what man could be when definitely freed from coercive physical work, and when class society and commodity production are abolished, but also of what man could be *tomorrow* while human material production, the division of labor, the market and professional politics still exist. As long as such social institutions continue to exist, man's freedom and his need to assert in a practical way, all his potential abilities will be limited. But even today man could free himself of the anarchy of commodity production, he could more freely choose his profession and find more enriching ways to spend his leisure time. Even today everybody could share in decision-making and management, and the present unlimited competencies of professional politicians could be reduced to the activity of experts who analyze data, propose alternative solutions, and work out practical measures, leaving to elected members of self-managing organs to adopt vital decisions.

In the light of these considerations, the question remains: What are the basic elements of the Marxist concept of revolution under modern historical conditions?

Revolution is the negation of the essential internal limit of modern capitalism. This essential limit is not simply private ownership of the means of production, as it seemed to most of Marx's followers, but a whole structure which can be characterized as follows: on the basis of private ownership of the means of production, a social class, the bourgeoisie, has unlimited control of the entire total of objectified work, organizes the production of goods exclusively for profit, lets the market determine the value of all goods, including the value of labor which is reduced to the level of ordinary goods, and thus acquires the possibility of appropriating the total surplus of value. Revolution must radically transcend this structure. It must abolish private ownership of the means of production, but must not allow any other social group (for instance, the bureaucracy or technocracy) on some other basis (for example, on the basis of the monopoly of political power) to control objectified work and appropriate a major proportion of the surplus of value. Commodity production and the market can be transcended only gradually, and this requires a whole historical epoch. However, in conditions of a developed industrial society the initial steps towards its abolition must be undertaken immediately. The commodity production can be gradually transcended by production for man's needs. Payment according to success in the market can be transcended by payment according to intensity, degree of skill, and creativity of work in that measure, and producers themselves can assume control of productive forces and objectified work. The laws of the market can first be corrected, in order to avoid undesired social differences and other nonrationalities, and eventually they will lose their meaning in a free society.

In view of the dual nature of negation, two stages of *communist* revolution can be clearly distinguished. The first stage abolishes the class system of society and the exploitation of producers (either by the bourgeoisie or the bureaucracy) and by this very action it transcends the classical form of the state, replacing it with a developed integrated system of self-management. The second stage is the abolition of commodity production.

The typology of the forms of socialist revolution could be as follows:

1. In a developed capitalist country the proletariat seizes power by force and establishes a dictatorship of the proletariat which possesses all the characteristics of socialist democracy. There is no historical record of any such revolution. The May events in France in 1968 showed the possibility of this classical form of violent proletarian revolution.

2. In a developed capitalist country which is nearing the affluent society a number of gradual transformations take place which lead towards a reduction of social differences and growing participation by the workers. Power begins to pass into the hands of the people in a legal parlia-

mentary manner (as in Sweden or Chile) or as a result of the inability of the capitalist-bureaucratic government to settle the existing problems on the domestic and international plane (such as war, the Negro problem, and automation in the United States).

3. In a semideveloped capitalist country in which the bourgeoisie has displayed fatal deficiencies, such as an inability to solve agrarian or national questions, revolution may be the only means to overcome crisis and accelerate general development. The combined forces of the workers and peasants and, in certain cases, also of all other patriotic forces, including a part of the bourgeoisie, seize power and adopt a triple task: (*a*) to remove the remains of feudalism and introduce democracy, (*b*) to accelerate industrialization, and (*c*) to bring about socialist transformation.

The Russian, Chinese, Yugoslav, and Cuban revolutions belong to the third type. None of them has so far been completed. Parallel with major successes in removing the feudal heritage, in promoting industrialization and urbanization, and in developing new forms of democracy, these countries' general initial low level of development and cultural backwardness led to a certain degree of bureaucratization. This bureaucracy has slowed down and, in certain socialist countries, almost completely halted the process of radical transformation of social relations. This is the essential limit of all societies which are moving toward socialism today.

The world has not yet seen a revolution of the anticipated classical type, although recent events have clearly shown that it is too early to regard it as historically transcended.

Developments in some of the most highly developed capitalist countries allow us to describe them as a profound transformation of society which has some features of socialist transformation. However, it is impossible to say whether this transformation will continue and lead to a definitive negation of the essential internal limit of capitalism or whether perhaps, various hybrid social forms will emerge which have the characteristics of both capitalism and socialism.

On the other hand, in backward colonial countries anti-imperialist movements and regimes exist which are trying to omit certain capitalist forms and undertake certain socialist measures such as nationalization and planning. In certain cases these processes may be regarded as a preliminary stage of socialist revolution. Social relations in those countries are too undeveloped for socialism to mean anything more than a vision of a far distant future.

The Possibility of Socialist Revolution

Revolutions are not necessary processes in a sense of reified necessity. Praxis must be taken as the essential moment of social necessity. There are two essential forms of reification of necessity in Marxist literature — one scientific, another philosophical.

The former consists of the *reification of scientific laws.* Laws are taken as empirical description of the relationships or tendencies which are entirely independent of human will and human action. What is overlooked here is the methodological fact that scientific laws have a definite meaning only within the framework of a theoretical model. However, every model is an ideal structure and establishes relations and tendencies which would be manifested everywhere *under given conditions.* Of course, conditions can be changed by the practical activity of man. Human ability to adjust, or a widespread feeling of satiety or boredom, might introduce unexpected breaks in the continuity of a historical process. Therefore, there are no laws which express the *inevitability* of socialist revolution. There are only laws which establish the necessity of the abolition of capitalism *if* the bourgeoisie and proletariat behave in accordance with their objective interests, that is, if the former continues to struggle for the increase of the rate of profit and if the latter retains the ability of revolutionary action because the degree of its being exploited increases.

Another form of reification of necessity can be found in a speculative conception of the *dialectic of history.* Necessity in the historical process is here assumed at the level of essence (as opposed to mere facticity), becoming (as opposed to more being), and reason (*Vernunft*) as opposed to mere intelligence (*Verstand*). However, human praxis — in contrast to abstract thinking — is always open, spontaneous, creative, and free. It has a certain structure but it is more or less flexible, multivalued, poli-deterministic and it cannot be construed as a simple deductive scheme.

Therefore, the true question is not whether the socialist revolution is necessary but whether it is *historically possible, under what conditions* it is possible, and *what should be done* in order to realize this possibility.

The general problem of the historical possibility of socialist revolution entails a whole cluster of specific problems with respect to various kinds and various phases of revolution.

Out of this cluster I shall choose the following problem which is essential for the revolutionary theory and praxis in socialism: What are the possibilities of preventing the bureaucratization of the victorious *avant-garde* of the labor movement? What are the possibilities of overcoming an already constituted bureaucratism? (Bureaucracy here means a closed social group of professional politicians which has a monopoly on political and economic power and which appropriates a part of surplus value in the form of various privileges.)

The answer to these questions depends on the level of general development of a society.

A society which is not yet industrialized and urbanized, which has not yet developed commodity production, which is still disintegrated and divided, in which various strong particular interests contend against each other, in which the culture of broad masses is still on such a low level that every democratic institution soon acquires a degenerated form and becomes a mystification of real social relationships, such a society can hardly avoid bureaucratism. Bureaucracy appears as a social force which eliminates various remnants of feudalism, undertakes the measures of an accelerated economic, social, and cultural development, performs the regulative economic functions, coordinates and integrates in the name of general social interest (but without ever forgetting the affirmation of its own particular interest). Bureaucracy satisfies certain essential needs of revolution in backward social communities.

In a developed industrial society in which there is a high degree of socialization of production, it is possible to reach such a high degree of integration of society even in an early stage of the revolution that there will be no need for a particular profession of rulers and protectors of public interest. Such a society can create a model of management in which the monopoly of bureaucratic power will be prevented by introducing the following structures: (*a*) the organs of immediate self-management in various types of communities (for production, education, health services, etc.); (*b*) intermediary councils for coordination and arbitration elected by all interested communities; (*c*) organs of self-management of the global society responsible for the definition of general goals and for fundamental decision-making.

It is assumed here that the representatives of producers and other strata of society would be elected in a democratic way, without special privileges, and would be replaceable at regular intervals. The only remaining professionals would be *experts* and *administrators* who would be strictly subordinated and responsible to the elected bodies.

A developed society which already possesses the possibility of creating all these institutions of self-management should make resolute efforts to prevent all those processes which lead to bureaucratization such as: (*a*) fusion of the victorious party and state; (*b*) professionalization of the leading political functionaries; (*c*) privileges for performing political functions; (*d*) monopoly of the mass media of communication; (*e*) public property being used for the private benefit of permanent leaders; (*f*) allowing the cult of certain personalities. Analogously to the norms of ancient democracy it should be a matter of revolutionary ethics to remove potential charismatic leaders from the positions of power and influence and to transfer to them other important social functions.

What are the possibilities of overcoming bureaucratism where it already has deep roots?

It is by no means certain that socialist revolution will be continued in such societies in a not-to-distant future. A society which permanently pays more attention to the growth of technology and efficiency than to social relationships, which would calmly adjust to a bureaucratic-technocratic form of management, would lose those subjective forces which are necessary for a further development of socialist revolution. No automatic process will in itself abolish the existing forms of human alienation. Huxley's *Brave New World* or Orwell's *1984* are real historical possibilities if men thoroughly adapt themselves to a bureacratic society.

On the other hand, forces which rebel have to face the following difficulties:

1. Bureaucratism cannot be abolished by an act comparable to nationalization of the means of production. A whole alternative democratic system of management would have to be built from the bottom up. The initial forms of participation and self-management should be fought for while bureaucracy is still in power.
2. Bureaucracy cannot be abolished by force because, in contrast to the bourgeoisie, it immediately controls the apparatus of force and tends to keep it as strong as possible.
3. Bureaucracy has an almost absolute monopoly over the mass media and it usually succeeds in concealing its true nature and presenting itself as the only historical subject of revolution.
4. As a consequence, all counterrevolutionary forces would join any attempt to overthrow its rule by force.
5. In a society which is not yet sufficiently integrated every change of regime would mean only the substitution of one bureaucratic group for the other.

What are then the chances of de-bureaucratization?

In the first place, the development of modern society undermines the foundations on which the existence of bureaucracy rests much faster and in a more radical way than was the case with the bourgeoisie. Modern economy requires integration into big systems and pulling down all artificial barriers. Every insistence on these barriers appears irrational and self-defeating. A large number of clerks must now be replaced by electronic computers. The primitive reports of half-educated apparatchicks must be replaced by critical scientific analyses. Due to a high percentage of educated and cultured people who enjoy considerable leisure time, a need for creating or maintaining a special profession of political rulers increasingly disappears.

Under these conditions bureaucracy might continue to rule only by brutal force or due to a thorough demoralization of former revolutionary forces.

However, nowadays it is not possible to rule by brutal force for a very long time. Every political power is doomed once it is compelled to abandon its own legality and to disperse the myth of the existing order as the natural and progressive one. Faced by inumerable forms of passive resistance, bureaucracy would have to solve a large-scale and almost insoluble task. Besides, bureaucracy is never a unique monolythic group and is usually polarized into a more or less rigid and aggressive faction and a liberal faction which tends to replace force and compulsion by various flexible forms of control and manipulation. The rationality of associated producers is being opposed by *Staats raison* in the former case, *raison* of the market in the latter. To be sure, confronted with an immediate danger, all factions and all national bureaucracies quickly build up a unified front. In Czechoslovakia we were witnesses of an international bureaucratic intervention comparable to former international capitalist interventions.

In an early phase in the struggle against bureaucracy, while the critical social self-consciousness is still in *statu nascendi,* the most important means are *truth,* bold *demystification* of existing social relationships, *dethronement* of deified persons and institutions, and above all a *great moral strength.* It should be borne in mind that bureaucracy sometimes survives long after it has lost any historical justification because it succeeds in breaking psychologically the most active progressive elements in society.

What is needed in this phase is a *critical* science: a *new revolutionary culture*, a *powerful democratic public opinion.* Above all a *new morality* is needed — a morality of human dignity, solidarity, stoic persistance, and spiritual superiority which can struggle with a strong material force.

Thus conditions are created for a broad antibureaucratic movement of the whole mass of the proletariat. The conflict among bureaucrats and workers always exists at least in a latent form and for at least two reasons. First, because bureaucracy as a matter of fact appropriates a good part of the surplus value created by workers' unpaid labor. Second, it prevents any really efficient workers' participation in the process of social management.

When workers become aware of the true nature of their social position, when they overcome the barriers of ignorance and ideological mystification, one might reasonably expect that workers will demand the abolition of the remaining forms of exploitation and the abolition of all those social structures which transform their representatives into bureaucratized professional rulers.

Such a radical negation of bureaucratism is a matter *of a whole epoch.* There is nothing to guarantee its success. It is an objective historical possibility which can be realized only with enormous amounts of human energy.

But there is no alternative if we want to make room for genuine human emancipation and for any other profound change in the field of social superstructure and individual psychological life.

7

The New Human Society and Its Organization

Positivist, Utopian and Critical Projects of the Future

The future need not necessarily correspond to the vision which results from what scientists and technologists describe by extrapolating dominant tendencies in the present and by applying laws of statistical possibilities to conscious human beings. On the other hand, there is little chance that the future will coincide with those dreams, no matter how noble and humane, which assume that all possibilities are open and that we are absolutely free to choose among them.

All possibilities are open in logic, but not in history. Human nature is not an abstract, fixed, transcendental entity. But neither is it something which can be created by any arbitrary decision of a free individual. In each historical epoch there is a general structure of human being, as a crystallization of the whole past history of human praxis. This structure is a concrete dynamic totality which underlies all of the more specific determinants, those of class, race, nation, religion, profession, and individual character. It is constituted by conflicting general features and tendencies of human behavior and thus it is dynamic and open for further change.

What follows, then, is that the future is neither divorced from the past and present, nor strictly determined by them. There are several possible futures, with various degrees of freedom, order, rationality, affluence, and internal harmony. In a reified world in which human individuals behave like isolated atoms, concerned only with their immediate particular interests, without any critical grasp of the whole, without any project for changing global society, the future would be the outcome of the struggle of blind alienated social forces. Mankind would be condemned to the *most probable* future, no matter how deeply inhumane and frustrating it might be.

It is one of the essential characteristics of the present historical situation that, while we still live in a reified world in which man has lost control over the forces he himself has produced, and has been turned into a mere object of historical process, some essential material and subjective conditions have been created for a radical abolition of reification. It is historically possible to overcome the anarchy of the market economy, to supersede alienated political power and put an end to the existing forms of mass manipulation. It is possible to liberate increasing number of individuals from degrading routine work, to free them for real praxis, for creation of a new culture, for active participation in all social decision-making. There is little hope that these possibilities will be realized by chance, by the free play of statistical laws, or even by *ad hoc* efforts of individuals and small groups. They can be brought to life only by a social movement, by a conscious and coordinated practical engagement of large social collectives, which break away from a long apathy and indifference, and rebel against the misery, the injustice, the oppression, and the stupidity of the whole compulsory framework of their daily lives. Such a social movement is by all means a mutation, a creative "jump" in the behavior of the large masses of people, who for a long time have tried to accept the unacceptable and to bear the unbearable. In order to succeed, it must be carried through by an extraordinary emotive energy, imagination, initiative, and spontaneous faith in a just ultimate cause. It also needs a sufficiently articulate and concrete revolutionary theory, which mediates between the vision of an ultimate goal and a clear critical awareness of the existing reality. Such a revolutionary theory shows the way out and brings into focus those features and institutions of the given social structure which constitute its essential historical limitation and the starting point of all subsequent revolutionary transformation.

From the preceding considerations it follows that truly revolutionary contemporary thought about the future cannot be either utopian in the traditional sense or scientific in the sense of a positive science, although it contains an element of both.

Traditional utopias from Plato and Augustine to Joachim di Floris, and from More and Campanella to Fichte, Owen, Fourier, Cabet, and Saint-Simon, were all dreams about a *perfect* society. But they were not and could not be completely divorced from history. They express real human needs and to a certain degree they bear the stamp of certain social structures of their time. Thus one finds the influence of Spartan aristocracy in Plato's *Politeia,* early feudalism in Augustine's *De Civitate Dei,* egalitarian tendencies among citizens of new free towns in More's *Utopia,* absolutism of eighteenth-century manufacture in Campanella's *Civitas solis,* new industry in Cabet's *Voyage en Icarie* and Saint-Simon's *Reorganisation de la societe europeanne.* Nevertheless, in a sense, they are all definitely ahistorical. They assume the possibility of the complete satisfaction of human needs and of the ultimate resolution of all contradictions. This amounts to projecting the definitive end of history. The ideal which they describe is hardly mediated by a criticism of the given social reality. The way to it is not visible. Utopias appeal to reason or a sense of justice as the social forces necessary to carry them out had not yet appeared on the historical horizon. Essentially, a utopia in the traditional sense is a free exploration of optimal but unreal human possibilities. Therefore, it does not have the strength and effectiveness of a practical force.

And still, there is no revolutionary thought without a utopian element, in the sense of a "*Seins-tranzcendente*" and "*Seins-sprengende*" orientation.[1] Its fundamental values such as equality, freedom, universal solidarity, social justice, and the fulfillment of an individual's capacities, cannot be justified by positive knowledge. They are a continuation of a great humanist and utopian tradition and an expression of dreams, desires, and hopes of the best minds in the history of mankind. Nothing guarantees the realization of ultimate revolutionary goals; such long-range anticipations clash with many alternative possibilities and cannot be corroborated beyond certain limited initial probability. By working for them, by participating in the creation of a new faith of millions of people,[2] we take an enormous responsibility: there is no certainty that our undertaking will not bring about a considerably different society from the one anticipated, or raise quite new and unsuspected problems, or eventually turn out to be a tragic defeat and the loss of noblest human energy. However, only by taking such a risk can we consciously make history and create possibilities which could never be brought to life by blind economic and social forces.

The basic weaknesses of purely scientific projections of the future all stem from the fact that these tend to be reduced to *mere extrapolations of dominant* objective tendencies in the present social reality.

In the first place, futurology as a positive, value-free science remains silent on those crucial social problems where it fails to notice any clear cut tendencies. Thus we are flooded by information about the incredibly high standard of living in the "postindustrial society," about new materials, new instruments and machines, new successes of biology and medicine, and new methods of controlling people. But we are being told little or nothing about human relationships, social structure, new social institutions, and distribution of political power.

Second, there are contradictory tendencies in the contemporary social process. Some lead to survival and continuation of the *status quo*, some to destruction of old forms.[3] Those which dominate at the moment give birth to opposite tendencies which may become dominant before long. Therefore, extrapolation is possible in various directions, contradictions may be overcome in various ways. The question as to which of the various possible futures is optimal for men of our historical epoch cannot be answered within the scope of a positive science devoid of any fundamental value assumptions, without asking further questions: What could man be, what ought he be in the conditions of a technologically advanced society? Apologetic positivism, which tacitly or explicitly accepts the values of the ruling elite of the existing society, makes its projections within the framework of the given. This is why it sees in the future only the quantitative growth of technique, goods and services, comfort, and state power.

Third, the tendencies of human behavior are not the

same as the laws of *things*. From a formal point of view in both cases there are certain regularities which sometimes can be expressed in a rather exact way and by the same kind of symbols. But a scientist without imagination and feeling for processes which develop deep under the surface of social phenomena, might easily become the slave of objective tendencies,[4] habits, aspirations, and patterns of behavior which come about as a consequence of a widespread feeling of satiety and boredom or of utter frustration, revolt, or despair.

And still, modern radical thought about the future, if it really should become a guide for praxis, must be scientific in the sense of *critical* and not simply positive science. The essential point where a critical science differs both from a positive science and a fruitless neoromantic criticism of all science and technology is its dialectical conception of the given. The *given* always contains an essential inner limit, an inner negation. It is not only constituted by processes which tend to conserve certain social forms, but also by those which challenge them, erode them, and eventually lead to their collapse and supersession.[5] The task of a critical scientific analysis is then, (*a*) to show which institutions and structures make social relationships irrational and inhumane, (*b*) to show what real historical forces could possibly abolish them, and (*c*) to clarify how these forces could be strengthened by appropriate practical collective engagement. This is the only way to make it clear under what historical conditions, with what concrete objectives and by what actions a radical change is possible, and what course must be taken from the initial transformations towards the realization of the ultimate goal. Thus a critical radical theory appropriates maximum freedom within existing historical limits. It is both a theory and a will to praxis.

Human Nature and New Values

The fundamental assumption of all revolutionary thought is that it is possible to build up a genuine community of free individuals who have equal opportunities for development, creative work, and satisfaction of their basic material and spiritual needs. The traditional utopian way to defend the possibility of such a community was its derivation from an overoptimistic conception of human nature.

This method was applied, although for other purposes, in Plato's *Politeia.* His theory of a strict hierarchical structure in an ideal state, with division into three separate orders (the statesmen, the soldiers, and those who carry on the business of providing for material needs), was derived from his conception of the three essential powers of the human soul: reason, spirit, and appetite, with the corresponding cardinal virtues: wisdom, courage, and temperance.

However, in the Hellenistic utopias of Euemeros and Iambulus there are no castes, no slavery, no division of work, no state power, and the people live in a state of permanent bliss in their distant, isolated islands. Stoic philosophers (Zeno, Chrysippus, and others) even then dreamed of a universal world-state without wars, laws, courts, money, and power over people. An inherent goodness of human nature is obviously presupposed.

In More's *Utopia* there is no private property. All individuals are equal and willingly work physically for six hours daily. There are no crimes, no penalties, no egoism, no conflicts, and everybody is happy. According to More it is want and certain social conditions which make people bad. "While there is still private property, while money is still the measure of all values, it is hardly possible to lead a just and happy policy. . . . While money still survives, poverty, drudgery, and anxiety will weigh as an inescapable burden upon the greatest and best part of mankind." More is convinced that most evils would be uprooted by the abolition of money. "Because, who does not see that fraud, theft, robbery, fight, quarrel, riot, murder, treason, and poisoning, which are now through daily punishment being more curbed than dammed up, would all have to disappear with the elimination of money, and that in the same moment fear, sorrow, anxiety, bother, and tension would vanish too."

One century later Campanella expresses a similar belief: when there will no longer be private property all selfishness will become pointless and pass out of existence. People will no longer fight for wealth but for glory. "The Solarians assert that poverty makes people mean, cunning, thievish, homeless, and lying. On the other hand, wealth makes them impudent, haughty, ignorant, treacherous, boastful, and heartless. In a genuine community, however, all are both rich and poor at the same time — rich because they do not wish what they don't already have in common, poor because nobody possesses anything, therefore, things serve the Solarians and do not enslave them."

This basically overoptimistic, perfectionist view of intrinsic human goodness, dominated the history of European thought until the twentieth century.

It was expressed in the seventeenth-century theory of the state of nature and natural rights. According to Locke, the state of nature is "a state of perfect freedom and equality" and also a state of "peace, goodwill, mutual assistance, and preservation."[6] This same overoptimistic view underlies the eighteenth-century philosophy of the Enlightenment. In the well-known words of Rousseau: "Man is *born free* and everywhere he is in chains."[7] Man is also conceived as an essentially social, productive, and rational being, capable of an indefinite progress in the future.

"There is no limit set to the perfecting of the powers of man," wrote Condorcet. "Doubtless this progress can proceed at a pace more or less rapid but it will never go backward."[8]

This optimistic spirit of the Enlightenment found a place in the thought of Marx. It is true that Marx rejected the then current concept of human nature as abstract and ahistoric. One of the implications of his dialectical approach might have been the discovery of internal, contradictory features in the *Gattungswesen* of man which includes good and evil, sociability and class egoism, rationality and powerful irrational drives, creativity and destructivity. Marx's description of early capitalism implicitly suggests something must have been basically wrong with man if he were able to build up that kind of social relations. His description of early communism is surprisingly realistic: "Crude communism is the culmination of universal envy and leveling down. . . . Universal envy setting itself up as a power is only a camouflaged form of cupidity which reestablishes itself and satisfies itself in a different way."[9] And still, in spite of the fact that both his philosophical method and his empirical knowledge pushed him toward recognition of a dark side in human nature, Marx remained ambiguous, with one pole of his thought in the Enlightenment, but the other in the twentieth century. The dilemma which he had faced remains unsolved. That dilemma could be formulated in the following way.

If human essence really is "the ensemble of social relationships,"[10] then this is a concrete and historical conception embracing all the basic contradictions of its time. However, in this case the question arises: Is there a human nature *in general* or is it relative to a specific historical epoch? If it does not make sense to speak of human nature in a general sense, with respect to the whole history of mankind, then the concept not only becomes relativistic, but also purely descriptive value — neutral and inadequate as the anthropological basis for an activistic and critical social thought and praxis. A historically given totality of social relationships can be critically assessed and transcended only when confronted with a vision of possible, more humane social relationships, and this presupposes a general value-concept of human nature.

But, on the other hand, if a general value-concept of human nature is assumed as the fundamental criterion of all critical assessment and the ultimate goal of human praxis, than there is a serious danger of a naive, romantic, and utopian idealization of man.

There is no doubt that for Marx a general idea of human nature was not only possible but also necessary. He makes a distinction between "constant drives which exist under all conditions and which can be changed only in their form and direction they take" and the relative drives and appetites which "owe their origin to a definite type of social organization."[11] Then, arguing against Bentham, in *Capital,* Marx said that "he that would criticize all human acts, movements, relations etc. by the principle of utility must first deal with human nature in general, and then with human nature as modified in each historical epoch."[12]

A careful study of Marx's early anthropological writings leads to the conclusion that evil is excluded from his concepts of *human essence* and *human nature* and referred to a historically transient phase of alienation. As long as private property and exploitation still exist, and relations among men are still dominated by selfishness, greed, envy, and aggressiveness, man is alienated from his essence. These negative features of empirical man — such as they have existed so far in history — are not part of human nature; as long as they characterize human relations man is not yet truly human. However, "communism is the positive abolition of *private property,* of *human self-alienation,* and this is the *real appropriation of human* nature through and for man. It is, therefore, the return of man himself as a *social,* i.e. really *human* being, a complete and conscious return which assimilates all the wealth of previous development."[13]

Although Marx, contrary to the often repeated objections of his critics, did not consider communism the ultimate goal of history but only the necessary form and the dynamic principle of the immediate future,"[14] he did say that communism was "the *definitive* resolution of the antagonism between man and nature and between man and man."[15]

The experiences of the twentieth century, however, do not give us reason to believe that evil in man exists only in the sphere of "facticity" and only in the time which precedes genuine human history.

Our century will go down in history not only as an age of technological rationality, efficiency, and liberation, but also as an age of incredible eruptions of human irrationality and bestiality. The scope and character of bloodshed and mass madness — in the two world wars, during Stalin's purges, in Korea, the Congo, Algiers, Biafra, and still in Vietnam, Laos, and Cambodia — can no longer be explained by the romantic, dualistic picture of a latent positive essence and a transient bad appearance. Evil as a human disposition must lie very deep. Obviously it is also a latent pattern of human behavior, which is the product of the whole previous history of the human race, always ready to unroll as soon as favorable conditions arise. It will certainly be transmitted to many future generations and will need a very long period of time to vanish in its present forms.

What further complicates the picture is a variety of new unexpected forms of evil. Life in abundance and comfort has removed many sufferings, illnesses, fears, primitive forms of struggle, and oppression, but it has created a whole new pathology. The most developed societies have the highest percentage of suicides, mental illnesses, rapes, juvenile delinquency, drug addicts, and alcoholics. Industry and civilization have made man more rational, powerful, and efficient in some important spheres of human life; but at the same time they have reduced warmth, sincerity, solidarity, spontaneity in human relations. Emotional hunger in material affluence, desparate loneliness amidst the crowd, boredom in spite of a huge variety of entertainment for sale, utter powerlessness amidst gadgets which multiply senses create the situation to which modern civilized man often reacts by developing strongly aggressive and destructive dispositions.

Another surprising and indeed alarming twentieth-century experience is an obvious deterioration of motives and a sharp moral decay within the leadership of many victorious revolutionary movements. For most ordinary participants of those movements this phenomenon was so astounding that they never grasped what happened. By now the sociological dimension of this process is clear: it is the transformation of the revolutionary *avant-garde* into a privileged bureaucratic elite, and it takes place whenever the society as a whole is not sufficiently developed and integrated. The anthropological dimension, though, remains obscure if only positive features have been projected into the notion of human essence. That great revolutionaries, makers history, could have been tragically defeated due to a general immaturity of historical conditions — sounds plausible. That so many of them were able to become great demagogues and tyrants seems incompatible with the whole traditional utopian anthropology.

The alternative offered is a negative pessimistic utopian conception in which evil is a permanent, constitutive feature of human life. There are constantly in man: anxiety, fear, hatred, envy, egoism, feeling of guilt, and lust for self-affirmation and power. All forms of modern culture: psychoanalysis, social anthropology, existentialism, surrealism, expressionism, and other trends of modern literature and arts, have strongly emphasized this darker side of human nature. Thus a strong anti-Enlightenment and antirationalist attitude has emerged and prevailed in many countries, especially in immediate postwar periods. That is why, nowadays, any projection of a happier and better future society must answer the question: Is it still possible to believe in man, is he not basically irrational and sick and lost to unknown, uncontrollable evil forces in himself, which, like Furies, destroy every good intention, every noble project?

The only answer which can be given by a modern dialectical thinker is: stop considering man a *thing!* He is neither a good nor a bad thing. It is not true that there is a *logos* of historical process which will inevitably make empirical man increasingly similar to an ideal harmonic, all-round entity. It is also not true that man is confronted by such a chaotic world, outside and within himself, that all his conscious striving to change, to create his world and himself anew is merely a labor of Sisyphùs.

The former is not true because all known social laws hold only under definite conditions and with many deviations in individual cases. While these conditions last and while the individual is isolated he has no power to change the laws. However, associated individuals can, within the limits of their historical situation, change the conditions and create a new situation in which new laws will hold. In spite of considerable uncertainty whenever such a radical change takes place, as a matter of fact, some implications of the conscious collective engagement can be predicted. This kind of fact supports the view that both historical process and human nature have a definite structure — no matter how many — valued, and open for further change. For the same reason the second extreme conception is also not acceptable. Human freedom cannot be construed (*à la* early Sartre) as a total lack of any fixed content in man, lack of being something, therefore a burden and a yoke. The world is not condemned to stay eternally absurd as Camus believed. Man is not a complete stranger in his world and he differs from Sisyphus insofar as he is able to change both the world and his own nature. At least some stones remain at the brow of the hill. At least in some historical moments large masses of people act in a way which leads to considerable modifications in human nature.

Change is possible because human nature is nothing but a very complex and dynamic whole, full of tension and conflict between opposite features and interests.

There is, first, a discrepancy and an interaction between interests, drives, and motives which belong to different levels of socialization: individual, group, generation, nation, class, historical epoch, and mankind as a whole. Thus, great personalities — by their character, their exceptional influence on the behavior of their class, nation, generation, and sometimes the whole epoch — contribute to the constitution of human nature as a concrete universal. Conversely, one of the fundamental effects of culture is to make individuals internalize and appropriate universal human values in a particular local, regional, national, class form.

Second, there are in man internal contradictions between positive and negative, good and evil, rational and irrational, desire for freedom and reluctance to assume responsibility, creative and destructive, social and egoistic, peaceful and aggressive. Both are human, and it is possible for these conflicting features to survive indefinitely. But it is also possible that man will act during a prolonged period of time in such a way that one would prevail over the other. We have a chance to choose, within certain limits, what kind of man we are going to be. While practically bringing to life one of several possible futures we, at the same time, consciously or involuntarily mold our own nature by fixing some of our traits, by modifying others, by creating some entirely new attitudes, needs, drives, aspirations, and values.

A historical fact which is often overlooked is that some values which have been very important in the recent past have lost their meaning and serve now to inspire revolt among the new generation. At such a moment a sudden mutation in human behavior can be observed. This is especially the case with those values which originated in powerlessness and all kinds of privation, and which have influenced human behavior for such a long time that many theoreticians took them for lasting characteristics of human nature. For example:

1. Material scarcity has brought about a hunger for goods, a lust for unlimited private property. This intemperate hunger, this typical mentality of a *homo consumens* developed especially when, for the first time in history, in industrial society, conditions were created for mass satisfaction of material needs. However, it loses a good part of its meaning in the conditions of abundance in a "postindustrial" society. In the scale of values some other things become more important. One can already observe this ten-

dency in advanced industrial countries where people increasingly give preference to traveling and education over food and clothing.

2. A situation of powerlessness and insecurity against alienated political power gave rise to a lust for power and obvious overestimate of political authority. This kind of obsession developed on a mass scale in the most civilized countries in our century due to the introduction of various forms of semidemocracy, such as, a type of society in which political power is still alienated and established in a strict hierarchical order, but at the same time open to a much larger circle of citizens. On the other hand, the rise of the will-to-power is caused by the destruction of other values: it is a substitute for a will to spiritual and creative power, it is an infallible symptom of nihilism and decay. However, it loses any meaning to the extent to which the basic political functions would be deprofessionalized and decentralized to the extent to which every individual would have real possibilities of participating in the process of management.

3. In a society in which a person is condemned to a routine technical activity which has not been freely chosen by him, and does not offer opportunity for the realization of his potential abilities, the motive of success naturally becomes the *primum movens* of all human activity, and pragmatism becomes the only relevant philosophy. Nevertheless, one can already envisage conditions under which basic changes in human motivation might take place. If an individual were to have a real possibility of choosing his place in the social division of work according to his abilities, talents, and aspirations, and if in general, professional activity were reduced to a minimum and to a function of secondary importance with respect to the freely chosen activities in the leisure time, the motive of success would lose its dominant position. Success would no longer be

regarded as supreme and worthy of any sacrifice, but only as a natural consequence of something much more important. This more important and indeed essential thing is the very act of creation no matter whether in science, art, politics, or personal relations. It is the act of objectification of our being according to "the laws of beauty," the satisfaction of the needs of another man, the forming of a genuine community with other men through the results of our action.

In general, the scarcity, weakness, lack of freedom, social and national insecurity, a feeling of inferiority, emptiness, and poverty to which the vast majority of people are condemned, give rise to such mechanisms of defense and compensation as national and class hatred, egoism, escape from responsibility, and aggressive and destructive behavior. Many present-day forms of evil really could be overcome in a society which would provide to each individual satisfaction of his basic vital needs, liberation from compulsory routine work, immediate participation in decision-making, a relatively free access to the sources of information, prolonged education, a possibility of appropriating genuine cultural values, and the protection of fundamental human rights.

We are not yet able to predict today, however, which new problems, tensions, and conflicts, which new forms of evil will be brought about by the so-called postindustrial society. For this reason we should be critical toward any naïve technocratic optimism which expects all human problems to be solved in the conditions of material abundance.

A considerable improvement in the living conditions of individuals does not automatically entail the creation of a genuine human community, in which there is solidarity, and without which a radical emancipation of man is not possible. For it is possible to overcome poverty and still retain exploitation, to replace compulsory work with senseless and equally degrading amusement, to allow participation in insignificant processes within an essentially bureaucratic system, to let the citizens be virtually flooded by carefully selected and interpreted half-truths, to use prolonged education for a prolonged programming of human brains, to reduce morality to law, to protect certain rights without being able to create a universally human sense of duty and mutual solidarity.

Participatory Democracy and the Problem of Bureaucracy

The key problem which mankind will have to face for a long time is how to prevent the recurrence, even in new social models, of considering people as things.

This problem is of fundamental importance for any radical vision of the future. For the existence of alienated concentrated economic and political power in the hands of any ruling elite — of military leaders, private owners of the means of production, managers, professional politicians, or even scientists and philosophers — would impede any radical changes in the sphere of human relationships. The division of people into historical subjects and objects would entail a hypertrophy of the apparatus of power, a conservation of the ideological way of thinking, a control over the mass media of communication, a limitation of political and spiritual freedom. Consequently, a permanent concentration of power in the hands of any particular social group would be an essential limiting factor of the whole further development.[16]

Fortunately, scientific and technological progress with all the far-reaching consequences in the economic, social, and cultural plane opens the historical possibilities for a radical supersession of those institutions which in past history have allowed certain privileged elites to rule over people, such as the state, political parties, army, political police, and security service.

These institutions are necessary to hold together, to protect, regulate, and direct society only while it is dismembered and disintegrated, which is the case with all backward and even semi-industrial societies. While there are a multitude of clashing particular interests — of various enterprises and economic branches, various regions and nationalities — a particular force is needed which will mediate, arbitrate, and direct in the name of the general interest, although the general interest has not yet been constituted. But one of the most important consequences of the present scientific and technological revolution is the dissolution of all artificial barriers and the integration of small, relatively autonomous economic systems into big ones.

Until recently big systems required big bureaucratic apparatuses. However, a profound change is taking place while we are entering a new phase of the technological revolution — the era of cybernetics. All routine administrative operations, including the analysis of information and the search for optimal solutions within some given programs, will be performed much faster and in a more accurate way by electronic computers. A considerable part of bureaucracy would thus lose any *raison d'être.*

Of all the various strata of contemporary bureaucracy the only one which will surely survive are the experts who make and test the alternative programs within the framework of the goals, criteria, and established priorities of the accepted general politics. It is essential that the only remaining professional politicians, highly skilled administrators and executives, be strictly subordinated to the elected political bodies. They will still maintain considerable power and influence. Unlike other citizens they have free access to all information. They have more time than others to study the data and to try to establish certain general trends. By mere selection and interpretation of data, by the choice of certain possibilities and elimination of others in the process of the preparation of alternative solutions, and finally, by a biased presentation of the results of accepted programs, professional politicians will retain a considerable capacity to induce a desired course of action. In order to check this capacity and keep it within certain limits, several possibilities are open.

First, the subordination of professional politicians to the corresponding assemblies and councils of self-government must be as complete as to allow full responsibility and immediate replacement of any official.

Second, professional political experts will have different roles and to a certain extent different interests. They should not be allowed to form a political block or to control any kind of political organization. Their function of expertize will be best performed if they eliminate any personal or group loyalities and any ideological considerations, and if they would be obliged to follow the principle of technological rationality, that is, to try to find the most adequate means for the goals laid down by the elected representatives of the people.

Third, their whole work should be critically examined by the independent political scientists. Future society must pay very serious attention to the critical scientific study both of politics in general and of actual political practice embracing also its economic sociological and psychological aspects. In contrast to the present-day "politicology" which is either apologetic or focuses on remote events, future society will need a political theory which will try to discover limitations in the actual practice and which will not only study phenomena *a posteriori,* but will also make projections and prepare solutions parallel to the work of the experts in the state apparatus.

Fourth, the most important and indeed revolutionary change in the political organization of the future society should be concerned with the determination of general policies, with the definition of general goals, and with the criteria of evaluation of possible alternative political programs. These key political functions must be radically democratized: the very idea of politics implicit in them will be fundamentally altered. According to Weber,[17] politics is (*a*) the set of efforts undertaken in order to participate in ruling or in order to influence the distribution of power either among the states or among different groups within one state; (*b*) this activity is basically the activity of the state; (*c*) the state is "a relationship of domination of man over other men, based on the means of legitimate violence." Politics in this sense, as compared with true *praxis,* was characterized by Marx as the sphere of alienation. Political activity could, then, become praxis under following conditions:

1. The political praxis is the domination of man over things. The things, however, in the human world are the products of objectified human work. Therefore, political praxis is essentially a control and a rational direction of the social forces which, in fact, are *les forces propres* of social man.

2. The criterion of evaluation among various alternatives of this process is the satisfaction of authentic human needs in all the richness of their specific manifestations in the given historical conditions.

3. The goal of political praxis is not the domination of

one social group over the rest of society, but an activity which has *universal* character and concerns each human individual.

4. Political praxis is not isolated from other modes of praxis. Contrary to alienated political activity it is based on a philosophical vision of human nature and history, it need not violate moral norms, its choices presuppose a scientific knowledge of all real possibilities in the given historical situation. At last it also contains elements of a noble struggle, of a game, of an art. To act politically in a human way implies, among other things, "to create according to the laws of beauty."

5. The people would regard such an activity without subjugation, tutelage, and fear as extremely attractive. By participating in such an activity the individual develops an important dimension of his social being and acquires an ample opportunity to express many of his potential capacities and possibly to affirm himself as a gifted, strong, and creative personality.

This conception of political praxis is far from being an invention of pure imagination or a stanza of philosophical poetry.

All those who have participated in a really revolutionary movement have experienced what politics could be, for at least a limited period of time, when it is not a monopoly of a privileged elite. The questions arise, however: Is not every such attempt at the democratization and humanization of politics limited in time and eventually doomed to failure? Does not a moment come when the principle of freedom has to be replaced by the principle of order, when a new social organization begins to function, or when the revolutionary *avant-garde* becomes the new bureaucracy almost overnight? Is there not always the need for some kind of elite in a complex modern society?

The decisive new historical fact relevant to these questions is that the considerable reduction of compulsory work and production, which will take place on a mass scale in an advanced future society, will liberate enormous human energies and talents for political life. The general education and culture, including political knowledge of these potential political "amateurs," need not be inferior to that of "professionals."[18] By participating in local communal life and in various voluntary organizations, many of them have acquired a satisfactory experience in public relations and the art of management. It should also not be overlooked that due to the penetration of modern mass media of communication into most of its corners and secrets, politics has been demystified to a large extent, and many of its institutions and personalities are losing the magical charm they had in the past. Thus the distance in competence between the leaders of political organizations and their rank and file, and, in general, between a political elite and the large masses of people, is eroding. For the first time in history it becomes clear that in the social division of work there is no need for a special profession of people who decide and rule in the name of others. Bureaucracy as an independent, alienated, political subject becomes redundant.

That the socialist movement up to the present has not succeeded in developing a consistent and concrete theory about the transcendence of bureaucracy and the political structure of the new society is the consequence of a really paradoxical development during the last two decades.

First, a series of revolutions took place in backward East European and Asian countries guided by a theory of democratic socialism, which was created in the conditions of relatively advanced Western capitalism. Marx would never call "socialism" an essentially bureaucratic society. He knew that in the initial phase of industrialization really communal social control over productive forces is not yet possible. That is why in *Grundrisse der Kritik des Politischen Oekonomie* he stated explicitly that such a possibility will be created in an advanced society in which "the relations of production will become universal, no matter how reified," in which man will no longer be directly governed by people but by "abstract reified social forces." Only then will the freely associated producers be able to put the whole process of social life under their conscious, planned control. But this requires a material basis "which is the product of a long and painful history of development."[19]

It is pointless to argue now to what extent Lenin and the Bolshevik Party were aware of the essential difference between the conditions in their country in the period of 1917–22 and those conditions under which Marx's theory of self-government were applicable. The fact is that Lenin and his collaborators did not believe that socialist revolution in Russia would be successful without a revolution in all Europe. The institution of Soviets, introduced during the first Russian Revolution in 1905, was a specific form of self-government. Unfortunately, by the end of the civil war there were no longer Soviets, no longer a strong, organized working class. In order to survive, in order to defeat the external enemy, the counterrevolutionary forces, white terrorism, and hunger, and to overcome the total economic collapse, the Bolshevik Party had no other alternatives but to surrender or to proceed by military and bureaucratic methods. While this dilemma was a historical necessity, nothing of the sort can be said about Stalin's later crimes or about the purely ideological identification of this new type of postcapitalist bureaucratic society with socialism.

It follows then that the revolutionary movement in Russia, China, and other underdeveloped countries did not give rise to a theory about the supersession of bureaucracy by the system of self-government because historical conditions for such a radical change of the political structure did not yet exist.

Paradoxically enough, such a theory has not yet been developed by the *new left* in much more favorable conditions. Due to the high level of material development, economic integration, education, and also to the considerable democratic achievements in the past, at least in some Western countries, bureaucratization in the post-capitalist development is by no means the only and necessary way. Instead of looking for alternative forms of political organization based on the principle of self-government, a widespread attitude in the student movement and among the *new left* is a distrust of any kind of political institution. This kind of attitude is easy to understand as a violent reaction to the process of obvious degeneration of the revolutionary state in the victorious revolutions in the East. It involves, however, a mistaken generalization from experiences which have a specific regional character. A dialectical denial of the state is much less and at the same time much more than a *contestation totale*. It is much less because some of the functions and institutions of the state will have to survive and be incorporated into the new political structure. It is much more because a *total* negation of the establishment is practically no negation at all. A real negation of the state is the abolition of its essential internal limit — the monopoly of power in the hands of a particular social group, and the use of apparently legitimate violence in order to project and promote interests of this privileged elite. This abolition does not lead to anarchy and the lack of any organized authority, but to an alternative, really democratic system of management, without any external alienated power.

The Experience of Yugoslav Self-management

The experience of Yugoslav self-management may be considered a proof of great historical importance — that material production, as well as many other important social activities such as education, health service, scientific research, and mass culture, may be quite successfully directed by the corresponding bodies of self-management, even in a semi-developed and rather disintegrated country. The main economic and political difficulties are the consequence of inconsistency and a basic duality of the Yugoslav system.

In addition to the network of workers' councils and other institutions of self-management at the micro-level of particular enterprises and local communities, there are still the institutions of classical power at the macro-level of the society as a whole: state, party, professional politics, and bureaucracy. These two types of political structure happen to coexist, but in fact, they are incompatible with each other. A natural extension and integration of various bodies of self-management into a whole would be a practical negation of the state and would put an end to professional politics. That is why these institutions make every effort to manipulate workers' councils and to thwart any further vertical evolution of self-management by shrinking its material basis, by reducing, through numerous bills, the scope of its decision-making, by constantly interfering through the party organization, by putting pressure on the managers, and by resolutely resisting any deprofessionalization and genuine democratization of key political functions at the level of global society.

The fundamental lesson which could be drawn from the Yugoslav experience is that self-management by no means should be identified with decentralization and that a local, atomized, disintegrated system of self-management cannot seriously challenge the power of bureaucracy. That is why the structure of integrated self-government should embrace the following three levels: (*a*) the workers' councils in the factories, services, and all other types of local communities; (*b*) intermediary organs, both horizontal (for the coordination within a whole region) and vertical (for a whole branch of activity); (*c*) institutions of self-government of the global society. Let us examine these three levels in more detail.

The workers' councils are the fundamental cells of direct workers' democracy. Within the limits posed by the existing legislation and accepted general policies, these bodies would have full freedom to decide what to produce, what kind of services to offer, with whom to cooperate, how to organize work, in which direction to develop, and how to distribute income after making whatever contribution is necessary for the needs of the whole society. The following difficulties at this level of self-management can be expected:

1. Workers lack general knowledge and information about all aspects of the production process which takes place in their factory. Therefore, as members of workers' councils they tend to be much more active in the debates about general policies and problems of remuneration than in special technological, economic and commercial issues. This is a seriously limiting factor. Experience shows, however, that prolonged education of workers, including special courses for the members of workers' councils, considerably increases their participation.

2. One of the greatest dangers for self-management is the formation of small oligarchic groups made up of managers, heads of administration, and political functionaries (secretaries of the party organization, trade union, youth organization) which tend to assume full control over the workers' council. The strength of such an elite comes from

several sources. First, it has full support from the political factors outside the enterprise in exchange for its unquestionable loyalty and obedience when needed. Secondly, it has full access to information and therefore the possibility of manipulating the workers' council by the appropriate selection and interpretation of data. Finally, it is well organized and monolitic while the workers are not. On the other hand, workers are in the majority in the councils and have the right not to reelect them, or to replace them on the council, to replace them in their functions, and even to dismiss them from the enterprise altogether. The power of these small informal oligarchic groups certainly decreases insofar as workers get political experience and become aware of the new forms of class struggle. It also progressively loses ground in the course of technological revolution and gradual disappearance of the difference between "white collar" and "blue collar" workers.

3. A decisively limiting factor of self-management is a political organization controlled by political bureaucracy. The bureaucracy tends to make a deal with the manager and the technocrats in the enterprise by offering protection in return for loyalty. A poorly educated and incompetent manager needs a lot of political protection; that is why the bureaucracy prefers its own men to opponents with better qualifications. The bureaucracy tends also to manipulate workers directly through their political organization. When the workers' council refuses to make certain decisions which have previously been "cooked up" in some political committee, the party uses the following procedure: the proposed line will, first, be endorsed by the narrow bodies of experts and political "activists," then it will be pushed through the mass meeting of the whole collective, where the opportunity for real discussion will hardly be offered; eventually the whole matter will come to the workers' coun-

cil, which, by that time, finds itself under hard psychological pressure from several sides. There is no doubt that the disappearance of political parties at a high stage of post-capitalist development would be an enormous step forward in the evolution of self-management.

4. Under the conditions of commodity production, self-management does not yet have *universal* human character. While producing for the market, competing, and trying to maximize their income, workers necessarily come into conflict with other workers and sometimes even assume the role of exploiters. They do so by abusing the favorable position of their enterprise or the whole economic branch of the market, by selling goods for prices above their value, or using the investments of the whole working class in order to draw extra incomes. Under such conditions, if the market were the only regulator of production, group property would replace genuine social ownership of the means of production, and the workers would assume the role of a collective capitalist.[20] This shows the need for higher-level bodies of self-management whose function would be to coordinate, direct, and correct the undesirable consequences of commodity relations while they still exist. To be sure, under the conditions of abundance, production for human needs will gradually tend to replace production for profit.

The intermediary organs of self-management embrace two kinds of networks. One is based on the principle of territorial unity, such as a municipality, the other on the principle of a definite type of activity. For a local or regional government to be an institution of self-management at least two conditions should be fulfilled: (*a*) it must have a considerable degree of autonomy from the central authorities and (*b*) it must have a truly democratic election of the members. Item (*a*) presupposes a certain degree of decentralization, or to put it more precisely, a model in which an optimal balance between the principles of democratic centralism and decentralization has been achieved. Item (*b*) implies the absence of any alienated political power, any privileged social elite, any particular social group which has enough economic power to influence the outcome of an apparently free and formally democratic election. The best that can be achieved in the absence of these conditions is a certain political pluralism, a struggle for power between various opposing forces and interests which does not yet allow the ordinary citizen to fully express and affirm his will, but at least it awakens him from lethargy, and allows some room for political initiative.

During the last few years Yugoslav society has recognized an urgent need for intermediary functional organs of self-management and nowadays offers some interesting new forms. In the field of economics these are voluntary associations of enterprises which supply one another with capital investments, new materials, cadres, and information, and join their efforts in planning for the future. There are also communities for education, science, and culture, which are independent from the state administration and run by the elected representatives of schools and universities, of scientific institutes and academies of science, theaters, publishing houses, museums, and galleries. Each of these communities has both local councils and regional and republican assemblies which make final decisions on all matters of educational, scientific, and cultural policy, and also take full responsibility for distribution of available funds. These funds are constituted independently from the state budget and are automatically allocated according to a fixed percentage of the total fund accumulated each year to cover general social needs. It is clear that consistent realization of this form would entirely eliminate the control of bureaucracy over these fields.

In order to prevent this, the bureaucracy made the percentage of income fixed by law so low that it must subsequently intervene to allocate extra funds. This causes frustration and precipitates a feeling that, after all, nothing has really been gained by introducing self-management. This example shows both how these new forms *could* operate under more favorable conditions, and also how incomplete and defective self-management must be if it has not been brought into being at all levels of social organization.

The key problem of self-management is its setting up at *the level of whole society,* in the Federation and in each of its six republics. There has never been any society in which the central political authority took the form of self-government. The only possible exception was the Paris Commune, but this was only a town and existed for a limited period of time. Even Athenian democracy would not qualify since slaves and resident aliens were denied any political rights.

In the Yugoslav system, central political institutions still have the character of the state. Some elements of self-government were introduced into the National Assembly several years ago in the form of councils for economy, for social welfare and health, and for culture and education. Unlike other members of the National Assembly, most members of these bodies were not professional politicians and were regularly rotated. This important step was not followed by subsequent ones. These three councils still have less power than the other ones (for example, the economic council only considers the budget, it does not actually decide on it). The election of members of these councils is still fully controlled by the political organizations without showing any tendency of further progressive democratization.[21]

Before ascribing the character of self-government to a central political structure (Parliament, National or Federal Assembly, Congress of workers' councils) the following conditions must be met:

1. Such a body would be, in practice (and not only in the Constitution and in political declarations), the supreme sovereign authority. It would assume full responsibility for the determination of the long-range goals, and for immediate general policy in economy, culture, and all other spheres of social life. It would also be responsible for all legislation. It would keep under control the implementation of all plans and programs and have the right to appoint, or at any time to replace, any professional official.[22]

2. All other political or semipolitical institutions which are necessary for rational decision-making and efficient realization of accepted projects must be strictly subordinated to the central organ of self-government. This does not hold only for executives, but also for those experts who are engaged in policy-making. Their job will be to explore possible alternatives within prescribed limits and to examine possible consequences of accepted solutions. But the limits will be prescribed and the choices among alternatives made by the self-governing body. One of the most delicate tasks of the latter would be to curb those institutions which are responsible for public order and defense, and are, therefore in immediate possession of material force. It goes without saying that a developed system of self-government is incompatible with spying on its own citizens and keeping a large militia and army mainly for internal needs. To the extent to which wars are impossible and mankind develops a true spirit of international collaboration and solidarity,

the existence of armies and similar organizations can gradually lose any *raison d'être.*

3. It is essential for self-government's central institutions to remain independent of any political party. In post-capitalist societies the party is an even more important center of alienated political power than the state. The basic decisions are being made and the major changes in the general policy accepted in the political bureaus or the corresponding bodies of the party. The radical supersession of bureaucratism involves, therefore, not only the transformation of the organs of the state into the organs of self-government, but also emancipation from the tutelege of the party. At first the party should reduce its functions to purely educational and theoretical ones. At a later stage it should "wither away" completely. Once socialist goals and new socialist morality would be generally accepted, the party would be replaced by a pluralism of less formal political groups and loose political organizations without party apparatuses, hierarchy, and unquestioned loyalty to the leadership instead of to the people.

4. The election of people's representatives must be more democratic than ever before in history. This will be made possible due to the fact that there will be no alienated economic or political power, no big money or party bosses to give preference to some candidates over others. There will be competition, there might be some demagogy, there will be clashing of particular interests. On the other hand, success in the election will offer neither privileges, nor lasting power, nor promising political careers. It will bring nothing but responsibilities and honor. Doubtless this circumstance would profoundly change the motivation and the character profile of the candidates. It should also be taken into account that the candidates would face a new

kind of electorate. Voters would be much more educated, cultured, and politically conscious than ever before in history. Such voters would know how to appreciate the competence, general culture, political skill, and moral integrity of various candidates.

5. Once elected, replaceable by their voters at any time, the representatives of the people would have to govern by the people's consent, remaining in constant contact with lower-level institutions of self-government. Thus for example, the preliminary draft of any important bill, any general project of future policies, any economic plan would be exposed to general discussion and criticism. In its final form it could and should have the characteristics of Hegel's *concrete universal,* that is, a general conception which embraces all the wealth of the specific and individual cases. Of course there is a danger that the final result of too many influences would be an eclectic, incoherent blue-print, never to be realized in practice.

But such are the implicit dangers of any democracy. Democracy does not always secure the most rational and human solutions; even less does it guarantee human happiness. It is solely a form of social organization which offers optimal *possibilities.* Whether these possibilities will be realized depends upon the creativity, imagination, strength of will, intellectual and moral power of personalities who happen to assume supreme political responsibilities at a certain moment, and also upon the mobilization of the best forces of the whole society.

In difficult moments of frustration and defeat, there will always be attempts to regress from self-government to some more authoritarian political structure. Therefore, it is of essential importance to undertake every measure possible to preclude alienation of that limited power which is concentrated in the hands of central bodies of self-government. This power must be temporary, implying a necessary rotation of individuals in possession of political authority. It must not bring with it any permanent place in the hierarchy of power and by no means any material privileges, any salary exceeding the incomes of highly qualified and creative workers and scientists.

In order to hinder possible deformation of its political institutions, the society should undertake certain measures in advance to protect itself from demogogery, lust for power, and potentially charismatic leaders. Surely the best protection is appropriate political education, development of a critical spirit, and the building up of a free and independent public opinion. This will be the most efficient way to identify these retrogressive political tendencies promptly and to ensure resistence to them.

The traditional collective psychic disposition to glorify, to adore, to be always ready for a new myth and a new "cult of personality" should be replaced by an attitude of criticism and resistence to any potential *Machtmensch,* to any authoritarian way of behavior. In a future society this will be much easier to achieve than today, not only due to new accumulated historical experience and greatly improved education, but thanks also to a new feeling of legal and economic security which is for most individuals an indispensable psychological condition of public critical engagement.

Ruling people as if they were things is the fundamental social evil produced by previous history. The evil is twofold because it degrades both the one who rules and the one who is ruled. The radical supersession of this evil is historically possible in any developed society. But this possible future will become reality only if some essential preliminary steps toward it are taken now.

Notes

Introduction

1. A considerable part of research in analytical methodology has been financed by state and military sources. On the other hand, those philosophers in East European countries who developed a positivist version of Marxism, taking an uncritical "scientific" attitude toward the society in which they live, openly declare that they work for the ruling party and its "scientific" ideology.

2. A critical social philosophy has to choose between two possible methods of its foundation. One assumes a definite *objective* pattern of history which is *independent* of human will and the conscious aims of individuals and groups. This pattern may be called "logos," or "dialectical process," or "human realization." This method is deterministic in a strong, traditional sense and leads to an *eschatological* conception of history. The other method, which I prefer, lays more emphasis on human creation of possibilities and relative human freedom in choosing among possible alternatives. Ideal is taken as the optimal real possibility of an essentially open historical process.

3. Marx, "Theses on Feuerbach," *Writings of the Young Marx on Philosophy and Society*, ed. and trans. by L. D. Easton and K. H. Guddat (New York: Doubleday Anchor, 1967), p. 402.

4. Note Marx's remarks, written in 1843, about the nature of German philosophy of his time: "As the ancient countries lived their prehistory in imagination, in *mythology*, so we Germans have lived our posthistory in thought, in philosophy. . . . In politics the Ger-

mans have *thought* what other nations have *done*." But in Marx's opinion philosophy which "expresses the needs of people," which is a "relentless criticism of all existing conditions" can become "the head of human emancipation," "grip the masses," and then turn into a "material force." See Marx, *Writings of the Young Marx,* pp. 255, 259, 212, 264, 257.

5. Soviet philosophers of science have been very suspicious with regard to the theory of relativity. M. A. Leonov in his *Ocherk dialekticheskogo materialisma* [Treatise on dialectical materialism] (Moscow, 1948) says that the appearance of the theory of relativity resulted in all kinds of "idealistic speculations" and that theologians and their "loyal servants, God-fearing philosophers of all sorts" construed this theory as the confirmation of their views. Leonov goes on: "The form in which these theories were expounded is idealistic and Mach-like, because their authors, A. Einstein, N. Bohr, W. Heisenberg, and others were not able to escape the pernicious influence of Mach's philosophy." But he concedes that there is a rational kernel in both the theory of relativity and quantum mechanics, which should be interpreted in a materialistic way. "Being 'subjectively' a follower of Mach, Einstein was not able to grasp that motion is both absolute and relative; he denied the absolute character of motion. Due to their materialistic position the Soviet scholars discovered this error of Einstein" (Leonov, *Ocherk,* pp. 453–54). This kind of reasoning has not been prominent in the USSR since the mid-fifties, but it survived among the epigons of Soviet Marxists in other East European countries. It is surprising that one of them was able to publish the following lines even in Yugoslavia, and as late as 1962: "One may dare to say that neither the special nor the general theory of relativity have conquered the masses, therefore they cannot be considered as accepted in spite of the enormous efforts of the greatest authorities in the fields of physics, philosophy, and the popularization of science. . . . On the basis of its experience, mankind has developed some conceptions about nature and particular natural phenomena which are an adequate picture of objectively existing reality. It is completely groundless to disrupt all this for certain mathematical reasons" (D. Ivanovich, *O teoriji relativnosti* [On the theory of relativity] [Belgrade, 1962], p. 468).

6. In order to support this view three questions should be answered:

First, is it historically possible to organize the economy of a country without competition on the market and profit motivation of the producer? In a large part of the world economic models are in existence which have eliminated production for profit and introduced administrative state planning of production. In this model, individuals can not decide themselves about the priorities in the satisfaction of their needs. This kind of decision is entirely in the hands of political bureaucracy. It follows then, that the profit motivation is dispensable but its abolition need not necessarily lead to the realization of the principle of the satisfaction of human needs.

Second, is there any tendency in developed industrial societies of the West to supersede the principle of production for profit? The answer is affirmative. The state plays an increasingly important role at the market and it buys even greater amounts of goods and services for common needs, not for profitable resale. It is deplorable that again the bureaucratic conception of common needs is entirely biased and overemphasizes expenditures for "defense" and "security." However, the fact that in the United States in 1967 public expenditures amounted to 140 billions of dollars, that is, $682 *per capita,* shows that there is already a large nonmarket sector of economy which will probably continue to develop and gain in significance.

Third, taking into account the present-day conditions of scarcity, is not the very idea of the satisfaction of human needs utopian (even if we disregard the fact that the satisfaction of some needs gives rise to the growth of new ones)? To be sure, the idea of satisfaction of human needs makes sense only as a historical category and with respect to highly developed industrial societies. But technological progress is very fast indeed and the present-day scarcity is quickly giving way to considerable welfare. The general tendency of development of production seems to be, roughly speaking, to double the gross national product each ten or twelve years. The concrete figures for the period 1964–69 are the following: gross national product for the whole world has been 1,903 billions of current dollars in 1964, 2,930 in 1969 (*est.*); out of these in the developed world 1,602 in 1964, 2,450 in 1969 (*est.*). The percentage of growth in both cases has been 50 percent — very high indeed even when we take into account inflationary tendencies. Gross national product per capita in the United States is well over $4,000 ($3,985 in 1967). At this level of national development the problem is no longer scarcity but rational organization and just distribution of goods.

7. Georg Lukács, *Geschichte und Klassen-Bewusstsein* (Berlin: Der Malik Verlag, 1923).

8. Note Marx's criticism of the situation in Germany in 1843: "War on German conditions! By all means! They are below the level of history, beneath all criticism, but they are still an object of criticism just as the criminal below the level of humanity is still the object of the executioner. . ." (Marx, "Toward the Critique of Hegel's Philosophy of Law: Introduction," *Writings of the Young Marx*, p. 252).

9. Instead of speaking about *actuality* and *potentiality* one can distinguish between *existence* and *essence*. See Herbert Marcuse, *Reason and Revolution* (New York: Oxford University Press, 1941), p. 146. Essence is a stronger and less intelligible concept: it means *true* potentiality and the real problem is which among many potential human faculties may be considered *true*. Instead of sliding over this problem it is better and more suitable for a critical theory to state it explicitly and try to find an answer.

10. Overcoming material misery, removal of those social institutions which produce enormous social differences, the replacement of an authoritarian by a democratic social organization, an increase of opportunities for education, and so forth, have many times in history been followed by periods of prosperity which displayed a very high level of creativity on the part of very large numbers of individuals.

11. Marx speaks about the *humanization* of senses: "The supersession of private property is therefore the complete *emancipation* of all the human qualities and senses. This is emancipation because these qualities and senses have become *human* from the subjective, as well as the objective point of view. The eye has become a *human* eye just as its object has become a social *human* object, created by man and destined for him. The senses have therefore become directly theoreticians in practice. . ." (Marx, in *Marx's Concept of Man*, ed. E. Fromm [New York: Ungar, 1961], p. 132).

12. "It is evident that the human eye appreciates things in a different way from the crude, nonhuman eye, the human ear differently from the crude ear. . . . The senses of a social man are different from those of an unsocial man. It is only through the objectively deployed wealth of the human being that the wealth of subjective

— *human* sensibility (a musical ear, an eye which is sensitive to the beauty of form, in short, senses which are capable of human satisfaction and which conform themselves as human faculties) is cultivated or created. For it is not only the five senses, but also the so-called spiritual senses, the practical senses (desiring, loving, etc.), in brief, human sensibility and the human character of the senses, which can only come into being through the existence of *its* object, through humanized nature. The cultivation of the five senses is the work of all previous history. Sense which is subservient to crude needs has only a restricted meaning. For a starving man the human form of food does not exist but only its abstract character as food. It could just as well exist in the most crude form and it is impossible to say in what way this feeding activity would differ from that of animals. The needy man, burdened with cares, has no appreciation of the most beautiful spectacle" (Marx, *ibid.*, pp. 133–34).

13. According to Marx the distinguishing feature of human work in comparison to animal activity is precisely the role of imagination: "A spider conducts operations that resemble those of a weaver, and a bee puts to shame many an architect in the construction of her cells. But what distinguishes the worst architect from the best of bees is this, that the architect raises his structure in imagination before he erects it in reality. At the end of every labor process, we get a result that already existed in the imagination of the laborer at its commencement. He not only effects a change of form in the material on which he works, but he also realizes a purpose of his own that gives the law to his *modus operandi,* and to which he must subordinate his will" (Marx, *Capital* [Chicago: Charles Kerr & Co., 1906] 1: 197–98).

14. Children who survived among animals in the wilderness and were later returned to civilized life were never able to learn any language. A capacity of using signs may be entirely lost if it has not been developed at a proper time. See Susan Langer, *Philosophy in a New Key*. Analogously, persons who have not been exposed to communication with persons of different backgrounds, creeds, life styles, and scales of values, develop a rigid, parochial, self-complacent, dogmatic *Weltanchaung* and finally lose the ability to communicate with any human beings outside the boundaries of their narrow world.

15. In Fromm's opinion, Spinoza, Goethe, Hegel, and Marx have contributed more than anybody else to the idea of productivity

as the essential characteristic of human beings. In his *Man for Himself* (New York: Rinehart & Co., 1947), Fromm has analyzed the productive character orientation in detail.

16. "Consciousness can never be anything else than conscious existence, and the existence of men is their actual life process. If in all ideology men and their circumstances appear upside down as in a *camera obscura,* this phenomenon arises from their historical life process just as the inversion of objects on the retina does from their physical life process" (Marx, *German Ideology, Marx-Engels Gesamtausgabe* [hereafter cited as *MEGA*] vol. 1, 5, pp. 15–17).

17. Marx, *Marx's Concept of Man,* p. 139; also in *Writings of the Young Marx,* p. 314.

18. Marx, *Marx's Concept of Man,* p. 137; also in *Writings of the Young Marx,* p. 312.

19. Marx, *Marx's Concept of Man,* p. 176.

Chapter 1

1. In his article on Hegel's "Philosophy of Law," written in Paris in 1843, Marx refers to the proletariat as "a sphere of society having a universal character because of its universal suffering and claiming no *particular* right because no *particular wrong* but *wrong in general* is done to it." This sphere "cannot emancipate itself without emancipating itself from all the other spheres of society, without therefore emancipating all those other spheres" (Marx, "Zur Kritik des Hegelschen Rechtsphilosophie. Einleitung," *MEGA,* vol. 1, p. 620). It is important to note that Marx did not speak in this way about the *actually existing* proletariat. He asked the question: "Where is there a *real* possibility of emancipation in Germany?" His reply starts with: "A class *must be formed* which has radical chains. . . ." giving then the characterization of the proletariat.

2. In Marx's early writings the concept "ideology" coincides with the idea of "false consciousness." It is the consciousness of individuals who are alienated, that is, in a condition of discrepancy between their existence and their essense (or their *generic* being). In *German Ideology* he criticizes the ideological method of Max Stirner in the following way: "The ideas and thoughts of men were naturally ideas and thoughts about the conditions in which they produced their material life and about real conditions among indi-

viduals in society." But in Stirner and other Young Hegelians these conditions had to take the form of "ideal conditions and necessary relations, i.e., to find expression in consciousness as conditions rising out of the concept of man. . . . What men and their social relations actually were — appeared in consciousness as representations of man as such, of his modes of being, or of his exact determinations." In this way "the ideologists" substituted the history of mind, of "ideas" for "real history." (Marx, *MEGA,* vol. 1, p. 165). The best known of Marx's critical comments on ideology is a passage at the beginning of *German Ideology* where he says: "Men are the producers of their conceptions, ideas, etc. real active men, as they are conditioned by a determinate development of their productive forces, and of the intercourse which corresponds to these, up to its most extensive forms. Consciousness can never be anything else than conscious existence, and the existence of men is their actual life process. If in all ideology men and their circumstances appear upside down as in a *camera obscura,* this phenomenon arises from their historical life process just as the inversion of objects on the retina does from their physical life process" (Marx, in *MEGA,* vol. 1, 5, pp. 15–16; also in *German Ideology* [New York: International Publishers, 1939], pp. 13–14).

3. Speaking about the backwardness of Germany *circa* 1843, Marx expressed the view that "German philosophy is the *ideal extension* of German history" that "Germans have lived their post-history in thought, in *philosophy,*" as "the ancient countries lived their prehistory in imagination, in *mythology.*" Therefore not only "present conditions," but also their "abstract conditions" must be criticized. Philosophy should be transcended *(aufgehoben)* but this can not be done "without actualizing it." Germany should reach a practice *à la hauteur des principes,* that is a revolution. Philosophy should be turned into revolutionary action, action should be enlightened by philosophical revolutionary theory. See Marx, *Writings of the Young Marx,* pp. 255, 257, 263.

4. I have tried to demonstrate this point in the article "Entfremdung und Selbstverwaltung" [Alienation and self-management] in *Folgen einer Theorie* (Frankfurt am Main: Suhrkamp Verlag, 1967), pp. 178–205. A considerable part of that article has been incorporated into chapter 7.

5. In September 1843, Marx wrote a very important letter to

Arnold Ruge about the direction in which "really thinking and independent minds" should work. He said, "We don't anticipate the world dogmatically but rather wish to find the new world through criticism of the old. Until now the philosophers had the solution to all riddles in their desks, and the stupid outside world simply had to open its mouth so that the roasted pigeons of absolute science might fly into it. . . . Even though the construction of the future and its completion for all times is not our task, what we have to accomplish at this time is all the more clear: *relentless criticism of all existing conditions*, relentless in the sense that the criticism is not afraid of its findings and just as little afraid of the conflict with the powers that be."

6. In his criticism of Hegel's *Phenomenology of Mind* Marx summarizes the main defects of this philosophy in the following way: *Phenomenology of Mind* is "nothing but the *expanded essence* of the philosophical mind, its self-objectification. And the philosophical mind is only the alienated world-mind thinking within its self-alienation, that is comprehending itself abstractly.

"Hegel makes a double mistake.

"Firstly, he construes forms of alienation which take place in real life as 'alienation of pure (i.e., abstract, philosophical) thought.' . . . The philosopher, himself an abstract form of alienated man, sets himself up as the measure of the alienated world.

"Secondly, the abolition of alienation occurs in consciousness, in pure thought, i.e., in abstraction. The *human character* of nature, of historically produced nature, of man's products is shown by their being *products* of abstract mind, and thus phases of mind, entities of thought." This solution of the problem of alienation Marx calls "unclear and mystifying." Marx, in *Marx's Concept of Man*, pp. 173–76.

7. "It is impossible to grasp fully Marx's *Capital* and especially its first chapter without studying and understanding Hegel's *Logic* in its entirety. Consequently, none of the Marxists understood Marx during the last half of the century." These lines were written by Lenin in Bern in 1914, while he was studying Hegel's *Science of Logic*. Lenin, *Philosophskiye tetradi* (Moscow: Ogiz, 1947), p. 154.

8. In his letter to Ruge of September 1843, Marx criticizes the idea of communism as developed by Cabet, Dezamy, Weitling, and others. "This communism is itself only a separate phenomenon of

the humanistic principle." He considers such a conception of communism "a dogmatic abstraction." One should not "face the world in doctrinaire fashion with a new principle declaring 'Here is the truth, kneel here.' " Instead of imposing on people absolutely true, just, or reasonable solutions one should "reform the consciousness of people" and bring to consciousness already existing needs and aspirations. "The reform of consciousness exists merely in the fact that one makes the world aware of its consciousness, that one awakes the world out of its own dream, that one *explains* to the world its own acts. . . . It will be evident then, that the world has long dreamed of something of which it only has to become conscious in order to possess it in actuality" (Marx, in *Writings of the Young Marx,* pp. 212–14).

9. Marx was convinced that by studying isolated, particular phenomena one remains at the surface of things and ends with lifeless abstractions. Particular facts can be fully grasped (their "inner essence" will be understood), only if they are taken as elements of a whole social system, and as moments of the whole historical development. The process of inquiry proceeds toward *concrete totality* which is a unity of many variable elements. The knowledge of a social situation as a "concrete whole" is a necessary condition for a conception of its radical change. The knowledge of abstract particulars leads to a superficial criticism.

10. In the opinion of Lukács totality is the central category of Marxist methodology. Social phenomenon can be understood only in its relation toward the whole. Furthermore, only if it has been taken as a moment of historical process can it be grasped as a historically given relationship among people. Isolated phenomena appear as ahistorical, natural forms of reality, analogous to things (i.e., *reified*). Consequently, a holistic approach is of essential importance for a critical social thought which tends to demystify certain relations among men and social groups, and to show that, far from being natural, inevitable, and eternal, they have their origin in specific historical conditions, and in some other conditions they are bound to disappear. See Lukács, *Geschichte und Klassen-Bewusstsein,* chap. 1, sec. 3.

11. See the excellent analysis of the concept of totality in K. Kosik, "Dialectic of the concrete totality," *Dialektika konkretniho* [Dialectic of the concrete] (Praha, 1965), chap. 1.

12. See the section on method in Marx's *Contribution to the critique of political economy.* This is one of Marx's best explications of his method.

13. See Marx, *Economic and Philosophical Manuscripts.* "Labor does not only create goods; it also produces itself and the worker as a commodity. . . . This fact simply implies that the object produced by labor, its product, now stands opposed to it as an *alien being,* as a *power independent* of the producer. . . . The more the worker exerts himself, the more powerful becomes the world of objects which he creates in face of himself, the poorer he becomes in his inner life, and the less he belongs to himself. It is just the same as in religion. The more of himself man attributes to god, the less he has left in himself. The worker puts his life into the object and his life belongs then no longer to himself but to the object. . ." (Marx, in *Marx's Concept of Man,* pp. 95–96; also in *Writings of the Young Marx,* pp. 289–90).

14. In *Wage-Labour and Capital* (1849), Marx attacked the view of the political economists according to which capital consisted simply of raw materials, instruments of labor, and means of subsistance of all kinds. Capital is "a social relation of production, a relation of production of bourgeois society." It is a sum of commodities, of exchange values which becomes capital when there is "a class in society which possesses nothing but the ability to work" (Marx, *MEGA,* vol. 1, 6, pp. 484–85). Or in other words: "For the conversion of his money into capital, therefore, the owner of money must find in the commodity market a free laborer. Free in the double sense, that as a free man he can dispose of his labor-power as his own commodity, and that on the other hand he has no other commodity for sale, and lacks everything necessary for the realization of his labor-power" (Marx, *Capital* [Volksausgabe] 1: 176–78).

Capital "consists in the fact that living labor serves accumulated labor as the means of preserving and multiplying its exchange value" (Marx, *Wage-Labour and Capital, MEGA,* vol. 1, 6, p. 485).

The explanation in the *Manifesto of the Communist Party* is quite simple: Capital is "that kind of property which exploits wage labor and which cannot increase except upon condition of begetting a new supply of wage labor for fresh exploitation" (Marx, in *MEGA,* vol. 1, 6, p. 539).

15. See Marx, "On the Jewish question" (1843): "The state is

the mediator between man and the freedom of man. As Christ is the mediator on whom man unburdens all his own divinity and all his *religious ties,* so is the state the mediator to which man transfers all his unholiness and all his *human freedom.* . . .

"Political emancipation is also the *dissolution* of the old society on which rests the sovereign power, the character of the state as alienated from the people" (Marx, in *Writings of the Young Marx,* pp. 224, 238).

In *German Ideology* (1845–46) there is already a strong emphasis on the class character of the state: "Since the state is the form in which the individuals of a ruling class assert their common interests, and in which the whole civil society of an epoch epitomized, it follows that the state acts as an intermediary for all community institutions, and that these institutions receive a political form" (Marx, in *MEGA,* vol. 1, 5, p. 52).

The *Manifesto of the Communist Party* offers the following telegraphic characterization of the political power: "Political power, properly so-called, is merely the organized power of one class for oppressing another." *Selected Works* (New York: International Publishers, 1968), p. 53.

16. Marx, *Marx's Concept of Man,* pp. 126–27; also in *Writings of the Young Marx,* p. 303.

17. Marx, "On the Jewish Question," in *Writings of the Young Marx,* p. 241.

18. "There is a material result at each historical stage, a sum of productive forces, a historically created relation of individuals to nature and to one another which is handed down to each generation from its predecessor — a mass of productive forces, capital funds, and conditions which, on the one hand, is modified by the new generation, but on the other hand, also prescribes its conditions of life, giving it a definite development and a special character. It shows, therefore, that circumstances make men just as men make circumstances" (Marx and Engels, "On the Production of Consciousness," *German Ideology,* pt. 1; also in *Writings of the Young Marx,* p. 432.

19. See Marx, *Marx's Concept of Man,* pp. 98–103; also in *Writings of the Young Marx,* pp. 289–94.

20. "Under the presupposition of private property my individuality is alienated to the point where I hate this activity and where it is a *torment* for me. Rather it is then only the *semblance* of

an activity, only a *forced* activity, imposed upon me only by external and accidental necessity and not by an *internal* and *determined* necessity. . . . My labor, therefore, is manifested as the objective, sensuous, perceptible, and indubitable expression of my *self loss* and my *powerlessness*" (Marx, "Excerpt-notes of 1844," in *Writings of the Young Marx*, pp. 281–82).

21. "Work is a process between man and nature, a process in which man exchanges matter with nature and starts, regulates, and controls this exchange by his own activity. The process of work . . . is an invariable natural condition for the life of people, therefore, it is independent of any particular form of that life, and equally appropriate to all forms of human society" (Marx, in *Capital*, vol. 1, chap. 5, p. 197).

22. In his very first notes on economic problems, written in the spring and early summer of 1844 (immediately preceding *Economic and Philosophical Manuscripts*), Marx characterized "free human production" (i.e., *praxis* in the field of production) in the following way: "Suppose we had produced things as human beings: in his production each of us would have *twice affirmed* himself and the other. (1) In my production I would have objectified my *individuality* and its *particularity*, and in the course of the activity I would have enjoyed an individual *life;* in viewing the object I would have experienced the individual joy of knowing my personality as an *objective, sensuously perceptible* and *indubitable* power. . . . Labor would be *true, active* property . . ." (Marx, "Excerpt-notes of 1844," in *Writings of the Young Marx*, p. 281).

23. The second dimension of man's self-affirmation in the process of free human production consists in the following: "(2) In your satisfaction and your use of my product I would have had the *direct* and conscious satisfaction that my work satisfied a *human* need, that it objectified *human* nature, and that it created an object *appropriate* to the need of another human being" (Marx, *ibid.*).

24. Speaking about the characteristics of "free human production" Marx continued: "(3) I would have been the *mediator* between you and the species and you would have experienced me as a reintegration of your own nature and a necessary part of yourself; I would have been affirmed in your thought as well as your love. (4) In my individual life I would have directly created your life; in my individual activity I would have immediately confirmed and realized my *true human* and *social nature*" (Marx, *ibid.*).

25. "The universality of man appears in practice in the universality which makes the whole of nature his *inorganic* body: (1) as a direct means of life, and (2) as the matter, object and instrument of his life activity" (Marx, *ibid.*, p. 293).

26. "We presuppose work in a form which stamps it as exclusively human. . . . Besides the exertion of the bodily organs the process demands that, during the whole operation, the workman's will be steadily in consonance with his purpose" (Marx, in *Capital*, vol. 1, chap. 5, p. 198).

27. Marx explains the distinction between "free human production" and "labor" in the following way: "My labor would be a free *manifestation of life* and an *enjoyment of life*. Under the presuppositions of private property it is an *alienation of life* because I work *in order to live* and provide for myself the *means* of living. Working is *not* living" (Marx, "Excerpt-notes of 1844," in *Writings of the Young Marx*, p. 281).

True independence is possible only when one is "his own master, and he is only his own master when he owes his existence to himself." Man is independent only "if he affirms his individuality as a total man in each of his relations to the world, seeing, hearing, smelling, tasting, feeling, thinking, willing, looking — in short, if he affirms and expresses all organs of his individuality" (Marx in *Marx's Concept of Man*, p. 138). The same idea of freedom as both independence and self-realization, unfolding of individual powers, has been expressed in many passages of *Capital*, especially clearly in vol. 3, when Marx makes a distinction between material production as a "realm of necessity" and "the true realm of freedom" which consists in "that development of human power which is its own end" (Marx, *Capital*, 3: 945–46).

28. In an important passage in the *Theories About Surplus Value* Marx explains the difference between *free time* and *time of work*. Time spent in the process of work is a condition of wealth (it provides "substance of wealth") but it is always determined "by the pressure of an external purpose." It could be "reduced to a normal measure. With the abolition of the social conflicts among masters and servants it may become a really social work." Being the basis of free time it would get a different, freer character. "Working time of a man, who at the same time is a man with free time, must have a much higher quality than the working time of a working animal (*arbeits-tier*). In spite of all this, free time is fundamentally different:

it is a *wealth itself* and it is an *end in itself*" (Marx, in *Theorien über den Mehrvert,* ed. Kautsky, 4th ed. [Stuttgart, 1921] 3: 305 f.).

Chapter 2

1. Marx, "Toward the Critique of Hegel's Philosophy of Law, Introduction," in *Writings of the Young Marx,* p. 257.

Chapter 3

1. Joseph S. Berliner, "Innovation and Economic Structure in Soviet Industry" (A paper presented at the joint session of the American Economic Association and the Association for Comparative Economics, New York, December 30, 1969).

2. See John Kenneth Galbraith, *The New Industrial State* (New York: NAL, 1968).

3. Charles A. Crosland, *The Corporation in Modern Society* (Cambridge: Harvard University Press, 1959), p. 268.

4. See David Granick, *The Red Executive* (New York: Doubleday, 1960), pp. 162 ff.

5. See Joseph S. Berliner, *Factory and Manager in the USSR* (Cambridge: Harvard University Press, 1957).

6. Galbraith, *The New Industrial State,* p. 186.

7. *Ibid.*

8. In the period from 1945 to 1965 a number of factories have been built not only to raise the standard of living, but also for political reasons. These have been called "political factories."

9. In 1969 Yugoslav imports exceeded exports by 620 million dollars. In 1970 the trade deficit increased to 1.2 billion dollars.

Chapter 4

1. Traditional morality seems to be as much a favorable factor for industrialization in Japan as is the ideology of workers' liberation in socialist countries. *Per se,* patriarchical loyalty and loyalty to the proletarian state are very different. But in this particular context their role is analogous.

2. "Die Entäußerung des Arbeiters in seinem Product hat die Bedeutung nicht nur daß seine Arbeit zu einem Gegenstand, zu

seiner äuBeren Existenz wird sondern da
frei von ihm existiert und eine selbststandi
wird" Marx, in *MEGA*, vol. 1, 3, p. 83.

3. "Durch die wechselseitige EntäuBerun
des Privateigentums, ist das Privateigentum sel
mung des EntäuBerten Privateigentums geraten" (
vol. 1, 3, p. 538).

4. *Ibid.*, p. 150.

5. "Marx's *Capital* cannot be completely grasped, espe
first chapter, without considering and understanding all of
Logic. Therefore, no Marxist for the past fifty years has unders
Marx" (Lenin, *Philosophskiye tetradi* [Moscow, 1947], p. 154).

6. See *MEGA*, vol. 1, 3, p. 546.

7. Marx, *Das Kapital*, vol. 1, chap. 1, p. 4.

8. *Ibid.*, vol. 1, chap. 23, p. 4.

9. See Marx, "Alienated Labor" in *Marx's Concept of Man*, pp. 93–103; also in *Writings of the Young Marx*, pp. 287–96.

10. Marx, *Das Kapital.*

11. *Ibid.*, vol. 3, chap. 14, p. 1.

12. Marx, *Marx's Concept of Man*, p. 125.

13. *Ibid.*, p. 126.

14. See Marx, *MEGA*, vol. 1, 3, p. 93.

15. See *Marx-Engels-Archiv* (Moscow, 1933), p. 68.

16. Marx-Engels, *Werke* (Berlin, 1955), 1:384.

17. In his "Critique of Hegel's Philosophy of the State and of Law," Marx pointed out that in bureaucracy the identity of state interests and particular economic goals is posed in such a way that state interest becomes a separate private goal competing with other private goals. Marx-Engels, *Werke* (Berlin, 1961), vol. 1, p. 297.

18. *Ibid.*, p. 250.

19. *Ibid.*, p. 248.

20. *Ibid.*, p. 250.

21. Marx-Engels, *Werke*, 1:379.

22. See Marx, *Das Kapital*, p. 379.

23. "Kritik des Gothaer Programms" in Marx-Engels, *Werke*, 19:27.

24. Marx, *MEGA*, vol. 1, 6, p. 227.

25. *The Communist Manifesto* in *The Marx-Engels Reader*, ed. R. C. Tucker (New York: W. W. Norton & Co., 1972), p. 353.

26. "Address to the General Council of International Workers ion concerning the Civil War in France" in Marx-Engels, *Werke,* :339.

27. Marx, *Das Kapital,* vol. 1, chap. 1, sec. 4.

28. *Ibid.,* vol. 3, chap. 48, sec. 2.

Chapter 5

1. It is true that in societies with strong democratic traditions, occasionally it is possible for particular candidates to be elected even against the will of the party bosses. This happens in a national crisis when there is a widespread need for social change, and when a strong nonestablishment personality offers a program to meet the crisis. But these are exceptional cases.

Chapter 6

1. Marx-Engels, "Die Heilige Familie" (Holy family), in *MEGA,* vol. 1, 3, pp. 205–6.

2. *Ibid.*

3. *Ibid.*

4. "Zur Judenfrage" first published in *Deutsch-Französische Jahrbucher,* February, 1844, in *MEGA,* vol. 1, 1, p. 596.

5. *Ibid.*

6. *Ibid.,* p. 597.

7. *Ibid.,* pp. 597–98.

8. *Ibid.,* p. 599.

9. "Kritiche Randglossen zu dem Artikel: 'Der König von Preussen und die Sozialreform. Von einam Preussen,'" in *Vorwärts,* August 10, 1844, in *MEGA,* vol. 1, 3, p. 22.

10. *Ibid.,* p. 21.

11. *Ibid.,* p. 20.

12. *Ibid.*

13. *Ibid.,* p. 22.

14. *Ibid.,* pp. 22–23.

15. Marx, *Misère de la philosophie* (Paris, 1847), in *MEGA,* vol. 1, 6, pp. 227–28.

16. "Battle or Death; bloody struggle or extinction. It is thus that the question is irresistibly put" (Marx, *Selected Writings in Sociology and Social Philosophy,* eds. Bottomore and Rubel [New York: McGraw-Hill, 1964], p. 240).

17. *Manifesto of the Communist Party,* in Marx-Engels, *Selected Works* (New York: International Publishers, 1968), p. 45.

18. The *Manifesto* ends with these words: "The Communists disdain to conceal their views and aims. They openly declare that their ends can be attained only by forcible overthrow of all existing social conditions." *Ibid.*, p. 63.

19. *Ibid.*, p. 46.

20. *Ibid.*, pp. 48–52.

21. *Ibid.*, p. 52.

22. *Ibid.*, p. 53.

23. Marx, *The Civil War in France.* Address to the General Council of the International Working Men's Association, in *Selected Works,* p. 291.

Engels in his introduction to a new edition of the two *Addresses to the General Council of the International* (1891) sees the danger of postrevolutionary bureaucratization quite clearly. He praises the Commune: "Against this transformation of the state and the organs of the state from servants of society into masters of society — an inevitable transformation in all previous states — the Commune made use of two infallible means. In the first place, it filled all posts — administrative, judicial, and educational — by election on the basis of universal suffrage of all concerned, subject to the right of recall at any time by the same electors. And, in the second place, all officials high or low, were paid only the wages received by other workers. The highest salary paid by the Commune to anyone was 6000 francs. In this way an effective barrier to place-hunting and careerism was set up, even from the binding mandates to delegates to representative bodies which were added besides" (Engels, in *Selected Works,* p. 261).

24. In his preface to the English edition of *Capital* in 1886, Engels noted that Marx allowed the possibility that in England "the inevitable social revolution might be effected entirely by peaceful and legal means."

Marx himself said in an interview to *The World* on July 3, 1871 that in England "a rebellion would be a stupidity since the goal could be attained more quickly and more surely by peaceful agitation." In his speech at the London Congress of the International on September 21, 1871, Marx said that workers would rise against governments peacefully whenever possible, or with arms-in-hand should that become necessary. Then, in his speech after the Hague Congress of the

International on September 15, 1872, Marx pointed out that the paths to a new organization of labor are not the same everywhere. The institutions, manners, and traditions in various countries should be taken into consideration. There are countries such as America, England, and perhaps the Netherlands, in which the members can attain their goals peacefully. See M. Steklov, *History of the First International* (New York: International Publishers, 1928), p. 240; Engels, "Introduction to Marx's *Class Struggles in France*" in Marx-Engels, *Selected Works*, pp. 109–27; Engels, *Critique of the Social Democratic Draft Program* (1891) sec. 2.

25. Engels, in his foreword to Marx's *Class Struggles in France*, written in 1895 speaks of political revolution in terms of street fighting and the erection of barricades. Further, he opposes propaganda work and parliamentary activity to *revolutionary* [!] forms of struggle. "We revolutionaries," he said, referring to the conditions in Germany in the last decade of the nineteenth century, "can advance far more quickly by legal means than by illegal and revolutionary tactics."

26. Rosa Luxemburg, *Die Akummulation des Kapitals, in Gesammelte Werke* (Berlin, 1923), 6:379.

27. *The Program of the Communist International*, in *International Press Correspondence*, 8, no. 92 (December, 1928), pp. 1749–68.

28. *Ibid.*, p. 1756.

29. *XIII Siezd Vsesoyuznoi Kommunističeskoi Partiyi*, pp. 166, 245.

30. "Men do not build themselves a new world out of the fruits of the earth as vulgar superstition believes, but out of the historical accomplishments of their declining civilization" (Marx, "Die Moralisierende Kritik und die Kritisierende Moral," in *MEGA*, vol. 1, 6, p. 306.

Chapter 7

1. See K. Mannheim, *Ideology and Utopia* (New York: Harvest Books, n.d.); also see Arnhelm Neususs, *Utopisches Bewusstsein und Freischwebende Intelligenz* (Meisenheim: Anton Hain, 1968).

2. Antonio Gramshi was the only Marxist thinker who did not

hide the fact that for most people revolutionary ideas, no matter how scientifically developed, become a faith which can hardly be challenged by rational argument. He pointed out that among the masses philosophy can only exist as a faith. Gramshi's attitude toward the problem of ideology was very honest, especially with respect to those "Marxists" who seek to give the aura of science to every *ad hoc* pragmatic rationalization.

3. Thus, (*a*) while human work becomes increasingly disintegrated and partialized, there is also a growing need to build up big technological, economic, commercial, and communications systems which require conscious direction and planning; (*b*) the tendency to produce for the market is still dominant even in socialist countries. All human products and capacities have been turned into commodities, including specialized knowledge, pieces of art, protest songs, and sex. However, in the advanced countries an opposite tendency is gaining ground. Because of abundance, or for humanitarian reasons, an increasing quantity of goods and services are no longer treated as mere commodities. Such is the case with free education and health service, free food for the poor, etc. In a postindustrial society this tendency will probably be strengthened; (*c*) one of the consequences of the growing division of labor is that management has become a profession unto itself, with enormous economic and political power. However, a highly articulate division of work has reduced working hours, increased the standard of living, and enabled each citizen to take part in the process of decision-making, hence a growing tendency toward participation and self-government; (*d*) in many countries there is both the revival of nationalistic movements and ideologies (even in socialism) and the creation of supranational communities followed by the rise of the ideology of world state and world government. This is by no means an exhaustive list of the conflicting tendencies in contemporary society.

4. Ernst Bloch criticizes social utopians for paying too little attention to the analysis of objective tendencies in existing society. On the other hand, he points out that a mechanical overemphasis of these tendencies may lead to a weakening of the will for praxis. "An objectivist idolatry of the objectively possible waits, then, blinking until economic conditions for socialism become completely ripe. But they are never completely ripe or so perfect that they would not need any will to action and any anticipatory dream in the subjective factor

of the will" (Bloch, *Das Princip Hoffnung* [Berlin: Aufbau Verlag, 1955], 2:148.

5. This kind of analysis of capitalist society was provided by Marx in *Das Kapital.* His law of the decreasing profit rate is a typical example of a negative objective tendency!

6. John Locke, *Treatise on Government,* vol. 2, chap, 2, p. 5.

7. See Rousseau, *Social Contract,* vol. 1, chap. 1.

8. Condorcet, *Progrès de l'Esprit Humain,* "Introduction to Epoque 1."

9. Marx, *Economic and Philosophical Manuscripts,* in Fromm, ed., *Marx's Concept of Man,* p. 125.

10. Marx, "Theses on Feurerbach," in *Writings of the Young Marx,* p. 402.

11. Marx, "Die Heilige Familie," in *MEGA,* vol. 1, 3, p. 359.

12. Marx, *Capital,* 1:668.

13. Marx, *Marx's Concept of Man,* p. 127.

14. *Ibid.,* p. 140.

15. *Ibid.,* p. 127.

16. "Human emancipation will only be complete when the real, individual man has absorbed in himself the abstract citizen, when as an individual man, in his everyday life, in his work, and in his relationships, he has become a *social being,* and when he has recognized and organized his own powers as *social* powers, and consequently no longer separates this social power from himself as political power." Marx, "Zur Judenfrage" (1843), in *MEGA,* vol. 1, 1, p. 1.

17. Max Weber, *Politik als Beruf* (1919), translated into English as *Politics as a Vocation* (Philadelphia: Fortress, 1965).

18. A gifted Yugoslav sociologist, Stipe Šuvar, was quoted in *Borba,* January 25, 1971 as saying: "Our bureaucrats are not much better educated than the workers. They are also of peasant origin. And much more than the workers they try to promote their own social interests instead of general ones. Anyway, there are more than a million and a half skilled workers who have knowledge and education for performing any political function in our society."

19. Marx, *Das Kapital,* vol. 1, chap. 1.

20. Speaking of "crude," "primitive," "non-reflective" communism, Marx said that in this kind of society the community is a "universal capitalist."

21. The revision of the Yugoslav Constitution in 1971 has considerably weakened the Federal Assembly. Some of its functions

were transmitted to the Republics, some to a new, supreme political body, "The Presidium."

22. Such a high level of democratic socialist integration is no longer feasible in Yugoslavia because of increasingly sharp conflicts and a rapid rise of nationalism in all six republics. But this trend was not necessary and it is far from being inevitable in other countries in the process of a socialist transformation.